ANNE BYRN
SAVES
the
DAY!
COOKBOOK

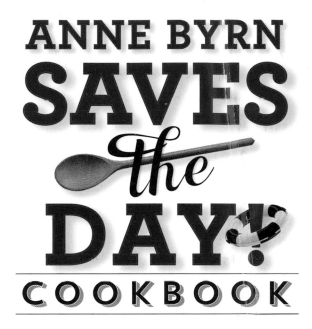

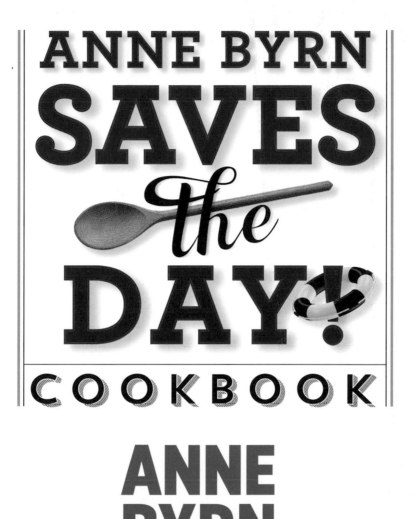

ANNE BYRN SAVES *the* DAY! COOKBOOK

ANNE BYRN

PHOTOGRAPHS BY LUCY SCHAEFFER

WORKMAN PUBLISHING • NEW YORK

Library of Congress Cataloging-in-Publication Data
Byrn, Anne.
  Anne Byrn saves the day! cookbook : 125 guaranteed-to-please, go-to recipes to rescue any occasion / by Anne Byrn ; photographs by Lucy Schaeffer.
    pages cm
  Includes index.
  ISBN 978-0-7611-7610-7 (alk. paper)
1. Cooking. I. Title.
  TX714.B9726 2014
  641.5—dc23   2014030782

Design by Lisa Hollander
Author cover photographs by Ashley Hylbert
Food photography by Lucy Schaeffer
Food styling by Chris Lanier
Prop styling by Sara Abalan
Spot illustration by Steven Guarnaccia

Workman books are available at special discounts when purchased in bulk for premiums and sales promotions as well as for fund-raising or educational use. Special editions or book excerpts also can be created to specification. For details, contact the Special Sales Director at the address below, or send an email to specialmarkets@workman.com.

Workman Publishing Company, Inc.
225 Varick Street
New York, NY 10014-4381
workman.com

WORKMAN is a registered trademark of Workman Publishing Co., Inc.

THE CAKE MIX DOCTOR and THE DINNER DOCTOR are registered trademarks of Anne Byrn.

Printed in the United States of America
First printing October 2014

10 9 8 7 6 5 4 3 2 1

For Flowerree and Janet, who save our day with humor, wisdom, and a steady stream of good food.

WITHDRAWN

acknowledgments

I'd like to mention the little things that save my day: my family, who is always there; my friends who keep me young; and my dog Cooper, who fetches the morning paper so I can read it alongside a cup of Earl Grey tea. Also Tamra, Lisa, Martha, Sherrie, and everyone who works with me testing recipes and getting the cookbooks, website, newsletters, and blog posts ready. Plus Nancy Crossman, who helped me develop this concept and understood why the world needs this book. All the great cooks coast to coast who shared their stories and favorite recipes. And as always, my Workman friends—Suzanne, Jenny, Katie, Lisa, Anne, Pat, Selina, and many more who turned my narrative and recipes into something beautiful. Thank you, everyone.

RELAX, YOUR DAY IS ABOUT TO BE SAVED

RELAX, YOUR DAY IS ABOUT TO BE SAVED

The inspiration for this book came to me a few years ago after swapping recipe ideas with friends at the end of a late-afternoon game of tennis. The four of us were in dire need of last-minute, great-tasting recipes that work every time. You would think with all of the cookbooks on our shelves and the recipes passed down from one generation of a family to the next, not to mention the 24/7 TV food channels and endless online recipe sources, that we would have more recipes than we could ever care to use. But the problem is we didn't have enough of the *right* recipes for when times are crazy—

Get Out of the Rut

No matter where you live or how many years you have been cooking, it's hard not to get into a recipe rut. To prevent this you need to be open to new ideas and recipes. It helps to have a well-stocked pantry in place and switch items in the pantry from time to time to try out new oils, seasonings, chocolate, and grains. Here are some other cures for falling into a rut.

• Shop at a farmers' market to see what's fresh and local in your area.

• Take a cooking class.

• Join a supper club.

• Ask a friend to share a favorite family recipe.

What got my friend Sally out of a cooking rut was that her teenage son had an adventuresome palate and told her he wanted new and different food for dinner. Instead of getting her feelings hurt, Sally selected recipes that might be fun to try and shopped for the groceries over the weekend. Come Monday they were ready to try something new. Says Sally, wisely, "When the groceries are in the house you are more likely to cook something new."

a new take on boneless chicken breasts, something fresh to do with the pork tenderloin in the freezer, a way to cook salmon or soups with a twist, salads perfect for entertaining, sides that please everyone,

and desserts that don't take a week to assemble.

I've always wanted to write a book with go-to recipes. The tried-and-true ones that everyone begs you to make. These are the recipes swapped among close friends, exchanged between mother and daughter in a short, late-night phone call, scribbled on a cocktail napkin at a birthday party, or just committed to memory. What if I could assemble in one book all the great recipes I have learned from so many people? The book might make life easier, and it might save someone's day. That's this book.

Let's face it. With jam-packed family lives, mad-dash weeknight dinners are often the norm. With no time to think, you—like me—probably find yourself serving the same old, same old. But it's not just our dinner menus that are stuck in a rut. There are all those other mealtime pressures. For example, the times that company stops by unexpectedly. And how about when it's your turn to host the Thanksgiving feast? Or this month's book club meeting? Or the company potluck? Not to mention when you've invited the in-laws over for next Saturday night. Or your boss.

You need a collection of delicious all-purpose recipes that save the day. And that's what I've offered in this cookbook. Recipes that are easy to prepare and that will come to your rescue, no matter what your dilemma. Although the chapters are organized in typical cookbook fashion—appetizers, soups, main dishes, salads, sides, and desserts—I've put together a special section that lists a number of possible reasons your stock of recipes may need help. For each category there's a list of recipes to answer that need, along with the page numbers so you can quickly access those recipes to save your day. As you page through the book you'll also find each recipe tells you right at the start what predicaments it helps solve.

Collecting the Recipes

Heading down a Texas freeway to a morning television show in Dallas with my media escort and friend Kathleen Livingston, we talk food, as usual. I ask Kathleen what favorite dish she served her grown children when they were in town over the summer. She said it was the chicken and dressing she makes by slow baking bone-in chicken breasts with onions and celery on top of long slices of French bread. "Haven't I given you that recipe?" Kathleen asked in her slow Texas drawl. "It's so easy. The chicken juices cook down into the bread, and with the celery and onion, it tastes just like dressing does at Thanksgiving. My kids beg me to make it."

Kathleen's kids are grown and have children of their own. The fact that they beg their mother to cook a specific recipe says a lot about the recipe, doesn't it? Kathleen doesn't have to worry about what to serve while her company is in town. She knows the perfect recipe and with this peace of mind, she has more time to spend with her family. Before we reached the TV station, I had found pen and paper in my purse and was making notes about Kathleen's recipe.

I had that same feeling of discovery when other close friends and new friends I've met when touring for my books shared their go-to recipes. Think braised pork tenderloin fragrant with apricots and onions. Tuna steaks that marinate briefly in lemon and dill, then are perfectly grilled. An orzo salad with roasted vegetables that uses up just about every veggie in the fridge and partners with anything from salmon to steak. Or a creamy potato casserole that sits proudly by broiled lamb chops. Missy told me about her make ahead mashed potatoes, Shellie described her spaghetti carbonara with peas, Joy brought a salad of kale and brussels sprouts to a December party, and my friend Ann recalled the only pie recipe you ever really need because it's made from ingredients you probably already have on your shelf—Ole Miss Fudge Pie. Any one of these recipes will banish the regular dinnertime blahs, whether for family, company, or a romantic date.

On the following pages are just a few of the recipes I have gathered to share. They come from people like you all over the country. They've been cooked up and tweaked by me and during the course of writing this book have saved my day plenty of times! My hope is that they will get you out of a bind and surely bring you peace of mind. Perhaps one will even become your signature recipe. Everyone needs a signature recipe—a culinary extension of yourself.

So after you have moved into a new house or apartment and most of your kitchenware is still packed in boxes but you want to cook dinner for good friends; or on some hectic weekday afternoon when you need a fast dinner idea; or before a tailgate, the bake sale, or the book club meeting, when you crave something new and creative to make and share, here are the recipes. When you need to impress at your anniversary dinner or the office potluck, or when an important business client is coming to your house, here are the recipes. Or maybe you want to get organized and freeze meals for a busy time ahead. From my kitchen, and the kitchens of the generous people who have shared with me, to your kitchen, here are recipes and ideas to save your day.

Seven Save-the-Day Strategies

These strategies will not only help you cook faster, they will make you cook better. So, less stressing out, more time spent with family and friends.

1. Identify the foods your family and friends love and make these the backbone of your menus.

2. Create a system for meal planning and food shopping so you don't shop at the last minute, then come home too tired to cook. If shopping on the weekend cuts too much into your free time, do it on a night that you've already got dinner waiting in the slow cooker or prepared and waiting in the fridge.

3. Keep the pantry, fridge, and freezer well stocked.

4. Select the right equipment for save the day cooking. Invest in a slow cooker, a food processor, and an immersion blender (for pureeing soups right in the pot), for example, and keep them close at hand.

5. Reinvent leftovers. Turn yesterday's roast into a stew, the remains of a grilled steak into a salad, and so on. Jazz up those leftovers on day two.

6. Refresh yourself. Get ideas from your favorite local restaurants, shop at a new market—be open-minded to change.

7. Open your kitchen to your children or grandchildren so that they cook with you and create family food memories.

A Save-the-Day Pantry

The first thing that might need rescuing is your pantry. A well-stocked pantry will save many a day. Here are the items I love to have on hand. The keepers. You don't have to replicate my list; adapt it to your own liking, but do make sure your cupboards and fridge are well supplied with the basics. Then, all you need to do on your weekly shopping trip is pick up the things to round out meals, like fresh produce—tomatoes, bell peppers, or berries.

IN THE PANTRY

Chicken broth: Buy quart (32-ounce) cans as well as 14-ounce cans. For additional homemade flavor buy organic reduced-sodium broth.

Beef bouillon and chicken bouillon cubes: Pop them into simmering soups to easily strengthen the flavor and season the pot.

Canned tomatoes: All sizes—pay a little extra and buy some seasoned with chiles or herbs.

Canned beans: Red, kidney, black, white, garbanzo (chickpeas), black-eyed peas—take your pick.

Good tuna, packed in water: I like Costco's Kirkland Signature brand albacore tuna.

Artichoke hearts: Canned, not marinated.

Pasta, dried: Stock your favorite kinds. Mine are thin spaghetti, linguine, orecchiette (ears), orzo, and oven-ready lasagna noodles.

Pasta sauce: Find a favorite. Some people like one of the Rao's brand. Mine is Trader Joe's arrabiata.

French green lentils

Vinegars: Stock an assortment—red or white wine vinegar, balsamic vinegar, sherry vinegar, apple cider vinegar, and distilled white vinegar.

Olive oil and vegetable oil, such as peanut oil or canola oil.

Vegetable oil spray

Soy sauce (store it in the fridge after opening)

Worcestershire sauce

Hot sauces, such as Tabasco sauce, Frank's RedHot, Cholula, and Sriracha (store it in the fridge after opening).

Spices and seasonings, such as ground cinnamon and nutmeg, bay leaves, dried oregano, black peppercorns (to be freshly ground), dried thyme, cayenne pepper, sea salt, Creole seasoning, and garam masala or your favorite curry powder.

Capers: Drain them and toss them into pasta sauces. Add capers to chicken and tuna salads. Sprinkle them over a fast sauté of chicken. (Store capers in the fridge after opening.)

Oatmeal: Old-fashioned or quick-cooking oats, not instant.

All-purpose flour

Your choice of cake mixes, including yellow
cake, angel food, and devil's food.

Baking powder

Baking soda

Cream of tartar

Sugar: light and dark brown sugar, granulated
sugar, and confectioners' sugar.

Pure vanilla and almond extracts

Evaporated milk

Honey

Peanut butter

Chocolate: semisweet or bittersweet chocolate
chips as well as unsweetened cocoa powder.

Onions and garlic

Potatoes

Dried fruit, including raisins, cranberries,
cherries, and apricots.

Assorted crackers and chips

IN THE FRIDGE

Orange juice

*Milk, heavy (whipping) cream, sour cream, and
plain yogurt*

Butter

Cream cheese

Cheeses: Parmesan or pecorino romano, as well
as feta, mild cheddar, and blue cheese.

Large eggs

Lemons: Small and thin-skinned ones have the
most juice.

Tortillas

Bacon (freezes well, too).

Maple syrup

Condiments, such as mayonnaise (I prefer
Hellmann's), ketchup, and mustard.

Olives: both green and black, not packed in
water.

Fresh herbs, such as flat-leaf parsley and thyme.

IN THE FREEZER

Boneless chicken breasts

Ground turkey

Pork tenderloin (buy it on sale).

Shrimp

Frozen vegetables, such as green beans,
chopped spinach, and peas.

Nuts, such as almonds, pecans, pine nuts, and
walnuts.

Frozen pie crusts

Bread crumbs

Your choice of ice cream (be sure to include
vanilla).

Save-the-Day to the Rescue

All the recipes in this book were chosen because they each can save the day in so many ways, whether you need rescuing from the normal dinnertime rut or something as daunting as the big holiday feast. I knew the key to using the book effectively would be to give you a decision-making shortcut. So, as I tested the recipes, I created a list of situations that most of us have needed help with at some time. I think you'll be able to relate to a good many of them . . .

if not all. Each dilemma lists the recipes that I think best solve it in the order they appear in the book. Each recipe is accompanied by the page number it falls on so you can get to it quickly. You'll see that most of the recipes fall into more than one category. That's why they were chosen—besides the fact that they all make delicious dishes, they multitask. Of course, the lists aren't set in stone, but they should certainly help to get you started.

Help Is on the Way

Here are the situations that I feel cause home cooks the most trouble when it comes to choosing just the right recipes. For example, whether Company's Coming means your boss, your in-laws, your best friends, or your neighbor the three-star restaurant chef, you're sure to find great recipes that save the day within the category listing. Jana's Cheese Olivettes. Beth's Autumn Salad with Maple Vinaigrette. Braised Pork Tenderloin with Apricots and Onions. Dave's Ooh-La-La Potatoes. Ole Miss Fudge Pie. And so many more choices. Relax. I've got you covered.

COMPANY'S COMING	SUPER BOWL PARTY
STOCK THE FRIDGE	SOMETHING FROM NOTHING
FREEZE IT	SERVE TO YOUR BOOK CLUB
GIFT IT	TAILGATE TRADITIONS
SNOW DAYS	TOO HOT TO COOK
LAST-MINUTE BIRTHDAY PARTY	APPETIZERS ASAP
POTLUCK PERFECTION	HOLIDAY IDEAS
WEEKNIGHT DINNER	PRETTY IMPRESSIVE
RESCUING BRUNCH	VERY VEGETARIAN
ROMANTIC DINNER	BAKE SALE SUCCESS!

COMPANY'S COMING

STOCK THE FRIDGE

ROMANTIC DINNER

SUPER BOWL PARTY

SOMETHING FROM NOTHING

SERVE TO YOUR BOOK CLUB (Bridge, Bunko, Poker, etc.)

CARA'S COCKTAIL
SHRIMP

JULIE'S
BLOODY
MARY BAR

QUICK STUFFED
MUSHROOMS

PAT'S ARTICHOKE DIP

SLOW-COOKED
CARAMELIZED
ONION
PIZZA

CHAPTER 2

APPETIZERS

True confession—I am more than a little obsessed with appetizers. A grazer at heart, I am always on the prowl for some new nibble to begin the meal, to bring to a party, or just to serve with a green salad for a light supper. I find new ideas on restaurant menus, at book club evenings, or at holiday party buffets. Then I make a beeline to the cook and beg for the recipe in hopes of updating my menus in the way a new scarf adds freshness to a familiar black dress.

Little nibbles, bites, appetizers, hors d'oeuvres—whatever you call them—are fun and they can save your day. Many are based on ingredients that are likely to already be in your fridge—for example, Pat's Artichoke Dip, Kathy's New Year's Caviar, Bacon and Cheddar Torte with Pepper Jelly, and Jana's Cheese Olivettes. Some can be tossed together at the last minute, like Sally's Cranberry Spread, Texas Cottage Cheese Dip, and Stuffed Jalapeño Peppers Witowski. And others are good for getting the conversation rolling—Laurie's Goat Cheese, Pesto, and Fig Cheesecake and Cara's Cocktail Shrimp.

To accompany these nibbles or just to serve on their own, stir together a signature drink and let people sip while you put the finishing touches on the meal. For summer parties choose Bridesmaid Bellini Punch and in the autumn serve Spiced Fall Sangria.

You can't miss. Everything included here will come to your rescue. Deliciously, too.

SERVE TO YOUR BOOK CLUB · TAILGATE TRADITIONS · TOO HOT TO COOK

Texas Cottage Cheese Dip

SERVES: 8 (ABOUT 3 CUPS)
PREP: 10 TO 15 MINUTES

Dayna Turney and her sister Melissa Smith grew up in Houston, Texas, the home of some mighty fine cooking. These ladies know how to entertain friends, and they are always sharing an interesting new appetizer. But they lead busy lives, balancing careers and family. One of their favorite recipes is as easy as one, two, three. They begin with cottage cheese and add spicy seasonings, then serve the impromptu dip with corn chips. "Very refreshing and summery," says Dayna. "Always a big hit." I agree!

1 container (16 ounces; 2 cups) small curd cottage cheese

⅓ cup mayonnaise

2 tablespoons fresh lemon juice

5 scallions, both white and green parts, trimmed and chopped

¼ cup pickled jalapeño pepper juice (from an 8 ounce jar of pickled jalapeños)

2 tablespoons chopped pickled jalapeño peppers

Fritos or your favorite corn chips and/or celery sticks, for dipping

① Place the cottage cheese, mayonnaise, lemon juice, scallions, jalapeño juice, and chopped jalapeño peppers in a large bowl and stir to combine well. Cover the bowl with plastic wrap and refrigerate until time to serve.

② To serve, spoon the dip into a pretty serving bowl. Place the bowl on a large plate and surround the bowl with corn chips and/or celery sticks.

Do Ahead You can make the cottage cheese dip up to 2 days in advance. Cover and refrigerate.

★ RAZZLE-DAZZLE ★ ★ ★

For warm weather gatherings, create a refreshing tablescape centered around this dip. Line a metal tray that is at least 2 inches deep with aluminum foil and fill it with ice. Fill a medium-size glass serving bowl with the cottage cheese dip and nestle the bowl down into the center of the ice to keep it cool. Fill smaller glass bowls each with celery sticks, cucumber sticks, radish quarters, and carrot sticks, as well as corn chips, and nestle these into the ice around the bowl of dip.

Pat's Artichoke Dip

SERVES: 12 (ABOUT 5 CUPS)
PREP: 10 MINUTES
BAKE: 20 TO 25 MINUTES

Let's face it, artichoke dips have been around for a long time. But when you need that hearty big, gooey, rich dip for wintertime potlucks or football parties, campaign fund-raisers, or teenage birthday parties, the artichoke dip always comes to the rescue. This recipe was one of my mother's favorites. It comes from her friend Ella, who got it from her friend Pat. What makes this dip different from others is that it contains crumbled feta cheese and garlic. Yum!

2 cans (about 14 ounces each) plain artichoke hearts, drained and chopped

2 cups (8 ounces) crumbled feta cheese

1 cup mayonnaise, or ½ cup mayonnaise and ½ cup sour cream

½ cup (2 ounces) grated Parmesan cheese

1 jar (2 ounces) diced pimientos, drained (¼ cup)

1 clove garlic, minced

Tortilla chips, for serving

1. Place a rack in the center of the oven and preheat the oven to 375°F.

2. Place the artichoke hearts, feta cheese, mayonnaise, Parmesan cheese, pimientos, and garlic in a large bowl and stir to combine well. Transfer the dip to a 2-quart baking dish and place the dish in the oven.

3. Bake the dip until it is bubbly and lightly browned, 20 to 25 minutes. Serve the dip warm with tortilla chips.

Do Ahead You can assemble the dip, place it in the baking dish, and cover it with plastic wrap to chill the night before baking. Straight from the refrigerator to the preheated oven, it will take 4 to 5 minutes longer to cook through.

RAZZLE-DAZZLE
You can add 1 cup of thawed and drained chopped frozen spinach to this recipe if you like.

Do Ahead While the "caviar" is best made a day in advance, you can certainly prepare it the morning of the party, or even 30 minutes before.

Kathy's New Year's Caviar

SERVES: 12 TO 16 (6 TO 7 CUPS)
PREP: 15 TO 20 MINUTES
CHILL: OVERNIGHT (optional)

Through the years a lot of cooks have taken license with the word *caviar* and created a bean salad/appetizer that looks like caviar in appearance but tastes nothing like sturgeon roe. Kathy Simcoe of Atlanta makes her "caviar" with black-eyed peas, crunchy add-ins like onion, bell peppers, and capers, and a balsamic vinaigrette to moisten and pull it together. This is just the appetizer to bring to New Year's Eve parties because it is festive and dead easy. Plus superstition tells us we should have a spoonful of black-eyed peas after midnight for good luck, and who wants to be cooking up a pot of black-eyed peas at midnight? Make this a day ahead instead. Serve it with tortilla chips or as a side dish for barbecue, steaks, fried chicken—you name it—which makes it perfect for potlucks and tailgates the whole year long.

3 cans (about 16 ounces each) black-eyed peas, drained and rinsed

1 large Vidalia or other sweet onion, finely chopped (2 cups)

½ cup chopped green or yellow bell pepper (half a large pepper)

½ cup chopped red bell pepper (half a large pepper)

1 jar (3 ounces) capers, drained

1 to 2 cloves garlic, minced

¼ teaspoon hot sauce, or more to taste, such as Frank's RedHot or Cholula

Freshly ground black pepper

1 to 2 cups store-bought balsamic vinaigrette

3 to 4 dashes of liquid smoke (optional)

Tortilla chips or pita chips, for serving

1. Place the black-eyed peas, onion, bell peppers, capers, garlic, and hot sauce in an attractive large bowl. Taste for seasoning, adding more hot sauce as necessary and black pepper to taste.

2. Pour 1 cup of the vinaigrette over the black-eyed pea mixture and stir to coat well. Add more vinaigrette if the mixture is too dry. Add a few dashes of liquid smoke, if desired. Cover the bowl with plastic wrap and refrigerate overnight. Stir the "caviar" occasionally while it chills.

3. To serve, place the bowl on a tray and surround it with tortilla chips or pita chips.

SAVE THE DAY NOTE As I said in the headnote, I'd serve the "caviar" with anything, even scrambled eggs.

MONEY SAVER: Rather than black-eyed peas, vary the beans you use depending on what is on sale that week—black beans, white beans, or pinto beans, for example.

★ ★ ★
★ **RAZZLE-DAZZLE**

Place the "caviar" in the center of a pretty tray and surround it with fried chicken wings, Buffalo chicken wings, and skewers of grilled pork tenderloin.

Think Outside the Cracker
for New Ways to Dip and Spread

Whether you're planning a spread for a cocktail party or prepping a dip for a book club get-together, consider offering lettuce leaves as wrappers and raw veggies as dippers in lieu of crackers and chips. You may be surprised at how many folks opt for something green over the same old cracker. Your guests may be eating gluten-free—or simply ready for a change of taste. Crunchy, fresh, vitamin-packed vegetables are just the creative vehicle to liven up that dip or spread. And the beauty of veggies on the party platter is that leftovers can reappear in tomorrow's salad, whereas stale crackers wind up in the trash.

Here are some possibilities:

• Lettuce leaves: Endive, radicchio, iceberg, romaine, and Bibb are just a few of the lettuces that can hold or wrap around one of your favorite dips and spreads. Taking a cue from Asian lettuce wraps, serve your spread surrounded by fresh leaves, or take a little extra time and spoon Kathy's New Year's Caviar (page 21) or Cara's Cocktail Shrimp (page 42) into endive or buttery Bibb lettuce leaves.

• Carrot and cucumber slices: Choose the long European cucumbers that have an edible, soft peel. Slice them diagonally about ¼ inch thick. Slice peeled carrots on the diagonal as well. Serve either with Texas Cottage Cheese Dip (page 16) or The Berry Blue Cheese Spread (page 24).

• Sweet peppers: Warm and gooey spreads like Pat's Artichoke Dip (page 18) can be spooned up with thick slices of red, green, and yellow bell peppers.

• Apple and pear slices: The sweet flavor of fruit marries well with anything cheese. So when serving the Bacon and Cheddar Torte with Pepper Jelly (page 30), arrange thick slices of crisp apples and pears along with crackers on a tray.

The Berry
Blue Cheese Spread

SERVES: 12 (ABOUT 2 CUPS)
PREP: 20 MINUTES

Isn't it funny how one quirky recipe gets everyone's attention and makes the rounds at parties? Katie Maloy of Nashville brought this appetizer to a beach vacation in Destin, Florida, a few years ago, and since then it has been popping up at parties from Florida on north. She says she originally got the recipe online from *Better Homes and Gardens*, and it calls for dried blueberries, which are found on the same aisle as raisins and other dried fruit. It is the sweetness of those berries that contrasts beautifully with the saltiness of the blue cheese. Be careful to fold in the blueberries with a spoon—no electric mixer or the dip will turn blue. And Katie says it is best served the next day when the blueberry flavor is more pronounced.

½ cup dried blueberries

1 cup boiling water

1 package (8 ounces) cream cheese, at room temperature

6 ounces blue cheese, crumbled (1 generous cup)

2 scallions, both white and green parts, trimmed and chopped (¾ cup)

1 clove garlic, minced

½ cup chopped toasted pecans (see Note)

Whole wheat crackers and celery sticks, for serving

1. Place the dried blueberries in a small bowl and pour the boiling water over them. Let the blueberries stand for about 1 minute, then drain them and set them aside.

2. Place the cream cheese and blue cheese in a large bowl and, using an electric mixer, blend them on low speed until nearly smooth, 1 to 2 minutes. Scrape the cream cheese mixture off of the beaters and into the bowl. Using a rubber spatula, fold the scallions and garlic into the cream cheese mixture. Carefully fold in the drained blueberries until just combined; don't overmix.

3. Transfer the cheese spread to a pretty serving bowl and top it with the pecans. Serve the spread with whole wheat crackers and celery sticks.

SAVE THE DAY NOTE To toast the pecans, spread them out on a rimmed baking sheet and bake them in a preheated 350°F oven for 3 to 4 minutes.

Do Ahead You can make the blue cheese spread 2 days in advance. Refrigerate it, covered. Let it come to room temperature before serving.

★ ★ ★ ★ RAZZLE-DAZZLE

Make the cheese spread the centerpiece of a festive cheese tray. Surround the serving bowl with sliced apple, grapes, and fig halves. Add a soft cheese such as a Brie and a firm and nutty pecorino or Manchego on the side.

Sally's Cranberry Spread

SERVES: 6 TO 8 (1½ CUPS)
PREP: 10 TO 15 MINUTES

Sally Goodrich of Nashville first made this recipe for a Christmas holiday for her tennis team. An avid tennis player, she has learned that interesting new appetizers are always a hit, so to speak, at tennis parties. And this spread seems to have it all—a few ingredients, most of which are already in the house, and holiday flavors and color. It's quick to prepare and easy to tote.

1 package (8 ounces) cream cheese, at room temperature

2 tablespoons orange juice concentrate

1 tablespoon sugar

⅛ teaspoon ground cinnamon

1 teaspoon freshly grated orange zest (from 1 medium-size orange)

¼ cup finely chopped pecans

¼ cup finely chopped dried cranberries

French bread toasts or favorite crackers, for serving

1. Place the cream cheese, orange juice concentrate, sugar, and cinnamon in a large bowl and blend with an electric mixer on low speed until the ingredients come together, about 30 seconds. Using a rubber spatula, scrape down the side of the bowl.

2. Add the orange zest, pecans, and dried cranberries to the cream cheese mixture, folding them in with the spatula.

3. Transfer the spread to a serving bowl or onto a wooden cheese board. Serve with toasted slices of French bread.

Do Ahead The cranberry spread can be made 2 days in advance and refrigerated, covered. Let it return to room temperature before serving. If you like more crunch from the pecans, rather than adding them to the spread lightly toast them in a 350°F oven for 3 to 4 minutes. Then sprinkle the toasted pecans on top of the spread just before serving.

Crunchy Almond and Bacon Spread

MAKES: 4 CUPS
PREP: 10 MINUTES

When my sister asked her friend, Veronica Young, who lives in Greenville, South Carolina, what recipe she couldn't live without, she said this is the man-pleasing appetizer she serves most often. She first tasted it when her friend Anita brought it to a tennis match years ago. Their team ended up winning the hospitality award, which means they always served the best food at matches. Veronica says recently a friend made this recipe, and her husband hid it from the rest of the family so no one else would eat it. Sign of a good recipe, for sure. I have adapted Veronica's recipe by adding a little sour cream, which I thought made it more spreadable, and I added hot sauce as a seasoning.

1 can (8 ounces) water chestnuts, drained, rinsed, and chopped

1 jar (3 ounces) real bacon bits, such as Hormel

2 cups (8 ounces) shredded sharp cheddar cheese

1 bunch (about 6) scallions, trimmed, green parts chopped to yield ¼ cup

4 ounces (about 1¼ cups) sliced almonds

½ cup mayonnaise (I like Hellmann's for this recipe)

¼ cup sour cream

Dash of freshly ground black pepper

Hot sauce, such as Frank's RedHot, Texas Pete, or Cholula (optional)

Wheat Thins crackers, for serving

1. Place the water chestnuts, bacon bits, cheddar cheese, scallions, almonds, mayonnaise, and sour cream in a large bowl and stir to combine. Season with pepper and hot sauce, if desired, to taste. You can serve the spread right away or refrigerate it, covered, until ready to serve. Let it come to room temperature before serving.

2. To serve, place the spread in a serving bowl or onto a serving tray and surround it with Wheat Thins crackers.

★
 ★ ★
★ RAZZLE-DAZZLE

If you have leftovers, spread them on slices of rye bread and heat them under the broiler until bubbling. Serve with big, fat slices of tomato.

Bacon and Cheddar Torte with Pepper Jelly

SERVES: 8 (3 CUPS)
PREP: 10 TO 15 MINUTES
BAKE: 12 TO 15 MINUTES

My friend Beth can whip up the most amazing dinner party at the last minute, and with her attention to detail it looks like she has been working on it 24/7. Zinnias falling willy-nilly from antique glass vases set on burlap runners in the center of the table, wine poured, good friends and conversation, roast pork sizzling in the oven, and this amazing "torte" on the kitchen counter for nibbling. It's not really a torte, but it looks like one, and it is a last-minute favorite of Beth's, especially when her husband, Bill, has made pepper jelly from his home-grown peppers. Martha Stewart has nothing on Beth and Bill, I can assure you, but even without homemade jelly in the cupboard, supermarket pepper jelly works just fine.

1 package (8 ounces) cream cheese, at room temperature

1 cup finely shredded sharp cheddar cheese

½ cup mayonnaise

3 scallions, both white and green parts, trimmed and chopped

6 buttery round crackers, such as Ritz, crumbled

6 slices bacon

2 tablespoons pepper jelly

Wheat Thins, or other favorite crackers, for serving

① Place a rack in the center of the oven and preheat the oven to 400°F.

② Place the cream cheese, cheddar cheese, and mayonnaise in a large bowl and blend with an electric mixer on low speed until just combined, about 1 minute. Using a rubber spatula, fold in the scallions. Transfer the cream cheese mixture to a 9-inch glass or ceramic pie pan, top with the crumbled crackers, and place the pie pan in the oven to bake until bubbly, 12 to 15 minutes.

3. Meanwhile, cook the bacon in a large skillet over medium-high heat until crisp, 5 to 6 minutes. Drain the bacon on paper towels, then crumble it.

4. Remove the pie pan from the oven, crumble the bacon evenly over the top of the cheese mixture, and dot it with little spoonfuls of pepper jelly. Place the pie pan on a heat-resistant tray or on a trivet and serve with little knives to spread the cheese mixture onto crackers.

Do Ahead Prepare the torte ahead of time as described in Step 2 but do not bake it. Cover the pie pan with plastic wrap and refrigerate it for up to a day in advance. From the fridge to the oven, the torte will take about 5 minutes longer to bake until bubbly. Then top it with the bacon and pepper jelly.

Mix and Match the Glassware

My friend Beth has a knack for mixing and matching patterns in her clothing and on the table. Go to her house for dinner and you are likely to find some antique treasure from a yard or estate sale alongside the good silver. Flowers are likely cut from the garden. And the glassware? It's all mixed and matched and keeps things fun. She blends old-fashioned glasses with Mason jars, stemmed wineglasses with stemless. And when she serves a signature drink she always thinks of the glasses in which it will be served. So dig out your treasures from the attic. Place a few on a serving tray and mingle them with new, inexpensive simple glasses that are about the same size. For hot drinks, try glass punch cups and demitasse cups. For cold soups, opt for shot glasses. And remember Beth's motto—it doesn't have to match.

★
★ ★
★RAZZLE-DAZZLE

Pepper jelly is either red or green, perfect for serving together— or just choose one—during the Christmas holidays.

Laurie's Goat Cheese, Pesto, and Fig Cheesecake

SERVES: 8
PREP: 15 MINUTES
CHILL: 1 HOUR, OR OVERNIGHT

Laurie Bullington of Birmingham, Alabama, has an appetizer that she says "always gets devoured." It is sort of a torte, has been called a terrine, and has the consistency of cheesecake so Laurie has settled on naming it cheesecake. It is especially welcome at Christmas, when life gets hectic, because Laurie can make it ahead of time and have it ready to go in the fridge. Laurie varies the recipe by the season and what she has on hand. For example, instead of the fig preserves she has used peach preserves or mango chutney. To keep things interesting she scours craft fairs and farmers' markets for homemade preserves, and for special occasions she often tops the cheesecake with toasted spicy pecans.

If you want just a sweet cheesecake, don't include the pesto. If you want a savory one, don't include the fig preserves. But if you want something really special, definitely include both.

Vegetable oil spray,
for misting the loaf pan

4 ounces goat cheese,
at room temperature

4 ounces cream cheese,
at room temperature

½ cup basil pesto (see Note)

½ cup fig preserves

Sweet and Spicy Pecans
(optional; recipe follows),
chopped

Plain unsalted crackers,
such as Carr's water crackers,
for serving

1. Lightly mist a 5½-by-3-inch (mini) loaf pan with vegetable oil spray, line it with waxed or parchment paper, and set it aside.

2. Place the goat cheese and cream cheese in a medium-size bowl and blend with an electric mixer on low speed until creamy, about 30 seconds. Using a rubber spatula, lightly press the cheese mixture into the prepared loaf pan. Spoon the pesto over the cheese mixture, spreading it out evenly. Cover the pan with plastic wrap and refrigerate the cheesecake until serving time, at least 1 hour.

3. Just before serving, remove the cheesecake from the fridge. Remove the plastic wrap and invert the cheesecake onto a serving plate. Spoon the preserves over the top. Top the cheesecake with the Sweet and Spicy Pecans, if desired, and serve with unsalted crackers.

SAVE THE DAY NOTE Use a 3½-ounce jar of prepared pesto found in the supermarket or, better yet, make your own. See the recipe for My Easy Pesto on the facing page.

Do Ahead After you top the cheesecake with pesto, you can refrigerate it for 3 days before unmolding and topping it with the preserves. If you are garnishing the cheesecake with the pecans, you can prepare these 3 days ahead and keep them in a sealed plastic bag until it's time to garnish.

★ RAZZLE-DAZZLE

Laurie likes to serve this with chutney for really festive, fun occasions. If she doesn't have mango or peach chutney, she'll stir hot sauce into store-bought peach preserves to kick it up a bit. And, if you really want to run with the salty-sweet-spicy flavor combo, crumble 6 slices of crisp, cooked bacon on top instead of topping the cheesecake with pecans.

Sweet and Spicy Pecans

Spicy pecans are an indispensable ingredient in the busy kitchen. Made ahead, they are at the ready for tossing onto green salads, or dressing up easy appetizers such as the "cheesecake." Adjust the pecan flavorings to your liking, adding the amount of sugar and heat that suits you.

1 tablespoon salted butter

2 tablespoons light brown sugar

1 teaspoon hot sauce, such as Tabasco

1 cup pecan halves

1. Place a large cast-iron skillet over medium heat. Add the butter, brown sugar, and hot sauce and cook, stirring, until the butter melts. Remove the skillet from the heat. Add the pecan halves and stir to coat the pecans with the butter mixture.

2. Place the skillet over low heat and cook the pecans, stirring, until they are lightly toasted, about 1 minute (be careful not to let the sugar burn).

3. Remove the skillet from the heat and let the pecans cool completely, about 20 minutes, before using or storing.

My Easy Pesto

To keep pesto green, mix fresh basil and fresh parsley. The basil gives the pesto flavor and the parsley keeps it green.

1 clove garlic, peeled

½ cup packed fresh flat-leaf parsley leaves

½ cup packed fresh basil leaves

2 tablespoons pine nuts

¼ cup grated Parmesan cheese

Freshly ground black pepper

½ cup olive oil

1. With the food processor motor running, drop the garlic clove down the feed tube and process until minced, about 5 seconds. Turn off the machine, add the parsley and basil leaves to the processor, and pulse until well chopped, 7 to 8 times. Add the pine nuts and Parmesan cheese and season with pepper to taste. Pulse 5 to 6 times.

2. With the motor running, pour the olive oil into the feed tube and let the pesto process until it thickens and comes together. Turn off the machine, scrape the pesto into a glass bowl with a lid, and store in the refrigerator for up to 3 days.

Jana's Cheese Olivettes

MAKES: 4 DOZEN
PREP: 25 MINUTES
CHILL: 1 HOUR
BAKE: 15 TO 20 MINUTES
COOL: 10 MINUTES

For Atlanta resident Jana Bibat these are the ultimate save the day appetizer. With a little advance preparation, you can serve freshly baked goodies. Jana rolls olives in a quick cheese pastry and freezes them until needed. She got the recipe from her mother, Barbara Murphey, who has been making them for twenty-five years. When just baked and pulled from the oven, they are the perfect companion to a glass of wine or a bowl of tomato soup. Arrange to take them to parties unbaked, and bake them off in batches once you arrive. Pass them warm, and people will follow you for second helpings. And the olivettes make a terrific holiday gift, baked and packed into pretty metal tins.

2 cups (8 ounces) shredded mild cheddar cheese blend (see Note)

8 tablespoons (1 stick) lightly salted butter, at room temperature

1 cup all-purpose flour

½ teaspoon hot pepper sauce, such as Tabasco or Frank's RedHot

1 clove garlic, minced, or a dash of granulated garlic

1 jar (5¾ ounces) pimiento-stuffed green olives (about 48 olives)

① Place the cheese blend and butter in a large bowl and blend with an electric mixer on low speed until just combined. Add the flour, hot pepper sauce, and garlic. Blend on low speed until just combined, about 15 seconds. Increase the speed to medium and blend until smooth, 30 to 45 seconds more. Cover the bowl with plastic wrap and refrigerate the dough until firm, about 1 hour.

② Preheat the oven to 375°F.

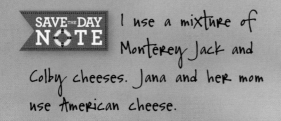

SAVE THE DAY NOTE I use a mixture of Monterey Jack and Colby cheeses. Jana and her mom use American cheese.

③ Break off a 1-inch piece of dough and tuck a stuffed olive into it, then roll the dough between your palms so that it completely covers the olive. Place the olivette on a baking sheet. Repeat with the remaining dough and olives, placing them 1 inch apart on the baking sheet. Place the baking sheet in the oven and bake the olivettes until they are golden brown, 15 to 20 minutes. Transfer the olivettes to a wire rack and let cool for about 10 minutes, then serve.

Do Ahead

Prepare the olivettes, but do not bake them. Flash freeze them uncovered on a baking sheet until firm, about 1 hour. Transfer the frozen olivettes to a plastic bag and seal it. As you need them freshly baked, remove the olivettes from the plastic bag and place them on a baking sheet to thaw, 30 minutes. Bake as directed.

Stuffed Jalapeño Peppers Witowski

MAKES: 36 STUFFED PEPPER HALVES
PREP: 20 MINUTES
BAKE: 10 TO 15 MINUTES

Several years ago I sat next to Bill and Kathy Witowski at a Chicago dinner that featured recipes from my *What Can I Bring? Cookbook*. While chatting, the Witowskis shared one of their favorite appetizers with me, a stuffed jalapeño pepper that their Wisconsin lake house neighbor made for them. I jotted the recipe down on a note card, which disappeared soon after. I wound up searching for it for a couple of years until voilà—I found it! With just four ingredients this recipe could not be easier to make, making it perfect when you don't have a lot of time to pull together an appetizer pronto for the party at the lake or a football party. And it contains two of the favorite food groups of most male football fans: sausage and jalapeños. You can't miss if you serve it at a Super Bowl party.

Vegetable oil spray, for misting the baking sheet

18 fresh jalapeño peppers

1 pound hot pork sausage meat

1 package (8 ounces) cream cheese (see Note), at room temperature

1 cup grated Parmesan cheese

①　Place a rack in the center of the oven and preheat the oven to 425°F. Lightly mist a baking sheet with vegetable oil spray.

②　If you have a pair of powder-free disposable kitchen gloves, put them on to prepare the jalapeño peppers. Slice the jalapeños in half lengthwise and remove the seeds and membranes, leaving the stems intact. Line up the jalapeño halves on the prepared baking sheet.

3. Crumble the sausage into a large skillet over medium heat. Cook, stirring, until the sausage is cooked through and lightly browned, 4 to 5 minutes. Drain the sausage on paper towels.

4. Place the drained sausage in a large bowl and add the cream cheese and Parmesan. Combine with a wooden spoon or, if needed, an electric mixer on low speed. Place a rounded teaspoon of sausage mixture into each jalapeño half.

5. Bake the stuffed peppers until the filling bubbles up and is lightly browned, 10 to 15 minutes.

SAVE THE **DAY** **N❂TE** Instead of cream cheese and Parmesan cheese, you can use 8 ounces of pimento cheese.

Do Ahead Fill the jalapeños, then flash freeze them uncovered on baking sheets in the freezer until firm, 4 to 5 minutes. Place the frozen jalapeños in a plastic bag and store them until needed. To bake, place the frozen jalapeños on a baking sheet and bake until the filling is bubbly, 12 to 15 minutes.

Quick Stuffed Mushrooms from the Hors d'Oeuvre Queen

MAKES: 24 STUFFED MUSHROOMS
PREP: 20 MINUTES
COOK: 30 MINUTES

Jane O'Halloran from Yarmouth, Maine, is known by friends as the "Hors d'Oeuvre Queen" because she is always bringing something fabulous to a party. Jane shared this easy way of stuffing mushrooms. "It disappears within minutes when I make it for a party," Jane says, "and I am constantly asked for the recipe!"

1 pound hot sausage meat

Dash of garlic powder, or granulated garlic

1 package (8 ounces) cream cheese, at room temperature (see Note)

24 medium-size or large mushroom caps

① Preheat the oven to 350°F.

② Crumble the sausage into a large skillet over medium heat and cook until browned, 3 to 4 minutes. Drain the sausage on paper towels, then transfer it to a large bowl. Add garlic powder or granulated garlic to taste.

③ Stir the cream cheese into the sausage. Spoon the sausage mixture into the mushroom caps. Bake the stuffed mushrooms until the stuffing is bubbly, about 30 minutes. (If you are late for the party, says Jane, bake the mushrooms at 375°F for slightly less time.)

SAVE THE DAY NOTE To soften the cream cheese, remove it from the refrigerator about 30 minutes before you plan to stuff the mushrooms or soften it in the microwave by placing it uncovered on a glass plate or in a glass pie pan and microwaving on high for 20 seconds.

Cara's Cocktail Shrimp

SERVES: 8 TO 12
PREP: 15 MINUTES, PLUS OVERNIGHT THAWING OF SHRIMP, IF NEEDED

Hair stylist Cara Duffy in Chattanooga makes this fast appetizer, and no one knows it begins with precooked shrimp. You make the homemade rémoulade sauce a day ahead, and because the shrimp are cooked, the appetizer is pretty much done. My husband's Aunt Janet has toted this to Thanksgiving dinner for the past few years, and it is always well received because it is so fresh and vibrantly colored; it's gobbled up while the turkey is being carved and the gravy stirred on the stove. Leftovers keep in the fridge for another day or two, and again they save the day when guests are in the house because they can be pulled out for a quick lunchtime salad or nibbled before dinner the next day.

1 pound large shrimp, cooked, peeled, and deveined (see Note)

1 cup mayonnaise (see Note)

½ cup chili sauce

½ cup finely chopped celery

2 tablespoons chopped pimiento-stuffed green olives

2 tablespoons chopped fresh flat-leaf parsley

1 tablespoon finely chopped onion

1 tablespoon sweet pickle relish

1 teaspoon fresh lemon juice

Salt and freshly ground black pepper

① If the shrimp are frozen, thaw them in a bowl of cold water, then drain them. Or let them thaw in the refrigerator overnight. Remove the tails from the shrimp, if desired.

② Place the mayonnaise and chili sauce in a medium-size serving bowl and stir

SAVE THE DAY NOTE You can cook the shrimp yourself, but it is a lot easier to keep a pound of already cooked, peeled, and deveined shrimp in the freezer. All you need to do is thaw them and pinch off the tails, if you like. As for mayonnaise, Cara likes to use Hellmann's.

to combine. Fold in the celery, olives, parsley, onion, pickle relish, and lemon juice. Season the sauce with salt and pepper to taste. Cover the bowl with plastic wrap and refrigerate the sauce.

3. Just before serving, fold the shrimp into the sauce. Place the bowl on a tray or large plate. Serve with toothpicks and cocktail napkins.

Do Ahead The sauce can be made a day ahead. Fold the shrimp into the sauce right before serving.

MONEY SAVER: Buy uncooked shrimp and cook them yourself, boiling the shrimp just until they turn pink, about 2 to 3 minutes.

Buying Precooked Shrimp

A superfast way to get an hors d'oeuvre or dinner on the table is to begin with already cooked shrimp. Supermarkets with fish departments that do a lot of business will rotate shrimp through quickly, and this is a sign of freshness. Also, some supermarkets are set up to cook the shrimp for you while you shop. Let them. If you don't have such a fish market available, buy already cooked and peeled frozen shrimp. You will find them at supermarkets and wholesale clubs. Remove the shrimp you need for a recipe, and let them thaw in the fridge overnight or in a bowl of cold water in the kitchen sink. Drain the shrimp well before beginning the recipe. Pull the tails off the shrimp if the recipe says so, but if you are serving them cocktail style for dipping into sauces, leave the tails on so people have something to hold on to.

★
★ ★
★ RAZZLE-DAZZLE

Serve the shrimp for special occasions in a crystal bowl on a silver tray. Garnish them with more chopped parsley.

Slow-Cooked Caramelized Onion Pizza

MAKES: 1 PIZZA (12 INCHES)
PREP: 5 MINUTES
COOK: 10 TO 15 MINUTES
REST: 5 MINUTES

What a relief knowing you have caramelized onions prepared and at-the-ready in the fridge. Caramelized in flavor, they form the basis for a simple and delicious pizza. Add grated Gruyère and Parmesan cheeses, kalamata olives, and sprigs of fresh thyme. Drizzle olive oil on top and bake in a hot oven. Cut the pizza into bite-size squares or thin slices for appetizer servings, or serve more generously as a light supper.

Cornmeal, for prepping the pan

1 pound fresh pizza dough

1 cup Slow-Cooked Caramelized Onions (recipe follows)

1 cup shredded Gruyère or ½ cup grated Parmesan cheese

¼ cup pitted kalamata olives

2 sprigs fresh thyme, roughly chopped or stripped of its leaves

1 tablespoon olive oil

Coarse salt and pepper, to taste

1. Place a rack in the center of the oven, and preheat the oven to 425°F. Sprinkle a dusting of cornmeal over a 12-inch pizza pan and set aside.

2. Mist your hands with olive oil and press the dough out onto the prepared pan so that it stretches into a 12-inch circle or covers the bottom of the pan. Spoon the onions over the top of the dough, scattering them with your fingers so they are distributed evenly. Sprinkle the cheese over the onions. Scatter the olives and thyme over the top of the cheese. Drizzle the olive oil around the edge of the crust

RAZZLE-DAZZLE

Stir the caramelized onions into warm cooked pasta and toss with grated Parmesan cheese. When making grilled cheese sandwiches, spoon the onions into the sandwiches and cook them in a panini press.

and sprinkle the crust with salt and pepper. Place the pan in the oven.

③ Bake until the cheese bubbles and the outside edge of the crust is golden brown, 10 to 15 minutes. Remove the pan and let the pizza rest 5 minutes, then slice and serve.

Slow-Cooked Caramelized Onions

MAKES: ABOUT 4 CUPS
PREP: 10 TO 15 MINUTES
COOK: 12 HOURS

Atlanta artist Nancy Everett came up with her own creative way to caramelize onions—in a slow cooker. The onions cook down to a sweet caramel color and you don't have to watch over them for fear of their burning. The weekend before her kitchen was gutted and remodeled Nancy prepped meals ahead and froze them. She caramelized onions, which she mixes into impromptu fajitas, spoons into steamed green beans, or uses in the simple cream cheese spread recipe you'll find below.

3 pounds Vidalia or other sweet onions, peeled and thinly sliced

8 tablespoons (1 stick) lightly salted butter

① Place the onions in the bottom of a 4-quart slow cooker. Cut the butter into tablespoons and distribute the pieces on top.

② Cover the slow cooker and cook the onions on low power until they are cooked down and a dark rich brown color, about 12 hours.

Do Ahead Make these onions 4 or 5 days ahead and store them, covered, in the refrigerator.

Fleurie's Caramelized Onion Spread

This spread originally ran in my *What Can I Bring? Cookbook*, but it has saved my day so many times, I thought it was worth running it again: Place 1 package (8 ounces) cream cheese, ½ cup mayonnaise, ½ cup sour cream, ¼ teaspoon cayenne pepper, and ¼ teaspoon salt in a food processor and pulse until smooth, 5 to 7 times. Scrape 2½ cups caramelized onions into the processor and pulse until the onions are just distributed, 5 to 10 seconds. Taste for seasoning, adding more cayenne pepper and/or salt as necessary. Serve the spread with bagel crisps or pita chips.

Julie's Bloody Mary Bar

SERVES: 8
PREP: 1 HOUR

Julie Osteen of Georgetown, South Carolina, assembled the classiest Bloody Mary bar for her son Hugh's college graduation brunch. This was really more about the fun array of condiments than the drinks themselves, although Julie says her husband, Graham, used to go to a whole lot of trouble to make Bloody Marys from scratch, but then they tasted the Zing Zang mix. "So I bought the Zing Zang mix and poured it into pitchers and focused on the fixin's." And, wow, were there ever fixin's—pickles, celery, olives, cherry tomatoes, green beans, asparagus—all crammed neatly into Mason jars tied with raffia around the neck of the jar. Julie lined a big straw tray with aluminum foil and filled it with ice, and then she nestled all the condiments in the ice on the tray to keep them cool in the May sun. She also used Mason jars as glasses.

FOR THE BLOODY MARYS

1 quart (32 ounces) Bloody Mary mix (recipe follows) or a store-bought mix, such as Zing Zang, chilled or homemade (page 51)

1 cup vodka, or more as needed

Ice cubes (optional)

FOR THE CONDIMENTS

Celery sticks

Carrot sticks

Large olives stuffed with blue cheese

Large olives stuffed with pimientos

Pickled okra

Pickled asparagus

Pickled green beans

Dill pickle wedges, cut in strips

Cherry tomatoes

Whole pickled jalapeños

Lemon and lime wedges

Old Bay seasoning

Horseradish

Tabasco sauce and Frank's RedHot sauce

Sea salt and freshly ground black pepper

1. Prepare the Bloody Mary ingredients: Pour the Bloody Mary mix into a pitcher.

2. Set aside the vodka for pouring.

3. Assemble the condiments: Fill Mason jars with the celery sticks, carrot sticks, blue cheese–stuffed olives, pimiento-stuffed olives, okra, asparagus, green beans, dill pickle strips, cherry tomatoes, pickled jalapeños, and lemon and lime wedges, placing each condiment in 1 jar. Place the Mason jars with condiments on a tray lined with ice.

4. Place the Old Bay seasoning, horseradish, hot sauces, and salt and black pepper beside the pitcher of Bloody Mary mix and the vodka. Ready to serve.

Do Ahead Everything can be bought weeks ahead and stored in the pantry. Chill the Bloody Mary mix and condiments before serving. The amounts can be doubled or tripled as needed.

Homemade Bloody Mary Mix

SERVES: 8 (1 QUART)

While Julie Osteen loves Zing Zang Bloody Mary mix, you easily can make your own at home. Begin with V8 juice and then add seasonings from your spice rack. You can make this mix a day or two ahead of the party.

1 bottle (32 ounces) V8 juice

6 tablespoons Worcestershire sauce

1 teaspoon cayenne pepper

1 teaspoon garlic powder

½ teaspoon hot sauce, such as Tabasco or Frank's RedHot Sauce, or more to taste

Combine the V8 juice, Worcestershire sauce, cayenne pepper, garlic powder, and hot sauce in a large pitcher and stir well to combine. Taste for seasoning, adding more hot sauce, if necessary. Cover and refrigerate the Bloody Mary mix until serving. It will keep for a week.

★
★ ★
★ RAZZLE-DAZZLE

This drink is razzle-dazzle as is. If you like, add bowls of chilled boiled shrimp for peeling and eating.

Bridesmaid Bellini Punch

SERVES: 24
PREP: 15 MINUTES

My sister Susan was hosting a bridal shower honoring the daughter of a good friend. The theme was "what's your favorite recipe" and everyone brought a favorite recipe written on a note card for the bride, as well as a gadget or small appliance to help cook it. The month was June, the food was light, but what to serve to drink on a Sunday afternoon? Susan decided on a Bellini-like punch made of Prosecco, the Italian sparkling wine, and peach juice. As we were in the Peach State, peach was the perfect partner to Italian Prosecco on this Georgia afternoon.

4 bottles (750 milliliters each) Prosecco or Champagne, chilled

8 cups (2 quarts; 64 ounces) peach juice (see Note), chilled

1 pint fresh raspberries, rinsed and well drained

1 pint fresh blackberries, rinsed and well drained

Ice cubes (optional)

If you are using a large punch bowl, pour all of the Prosecco and peach juice into the bowl and stir to combine. Scatter the berries over the top of the punch. Serve by ladling into chilled punch cups.

If you are serving the punch in Champagne glasses, pour 1 bottle of Prosecco and 2 cups (16 ounces) of peach juice into a pitcher. Place an ice cube in each glass and pour in the punch. Garnish with the raspberries and blackberries. Repeat with the remaining Prosecco and peach juice.

I used Dixie Peach, a juice from Trader Joe's, in this recipe. It comes in 2-quart bottles.

Do Ahead Gently rinse and drain the raspberries and blackberries. Line their plastic containers with paper towels and place the well-drained berries back into the containers. Refrigerate the berries until it is time to serve the punch, but no longer than a day ahead.

How to Make a Berry Ice Mold for a Punch Bowl

My mother and maybe your mother or grandmother used an aluminum ring mold to create gelatin salads. This is a perfect container in which to make a berry ice mold. Simply place raspberries and blackberries decoratively over the bottom and piled up the sides of the mold. Fill the mold with water and cover it with plastic wrap. Place the mold in the freezer until the water freezes, eight hours or overnight. Remove the ring mold from the freezer while you make the punch in the punch bowl. Shake the mold and, if the ice does not loosen, turn the mold over and run warm tap water over it. Shake the mold again and when the ice is loose, invert it, carefully, into the punch bowl.

★
★ ★ ★
★ RAZZLE-DAZZLE

Make a berry ice mold (see above) to place in the punch bowl.

Dayna's Grown-Up Lemonade

SERVES: 4
PREP: 5 MINUTES

My friends Dayna and Beth always have a festive drink planned when we are celebrating a birthday or a weekend getaway. When someone else is hosting the meal or the weekend, and you are asked to bring something, think of toting the makings for a memorable drink. That way the hosts can be busy lighting the fire for grilling, making the salad, or just putting their feet up and relaxing. This lemonade is perfect for the heat of summertime. Serve it in tall glasses garnished with lemon slices and fresh mint from the garden.

24 ounces (3 cups) good lemonade (see Note)

4 jiggers (4 ounces) sweet tea vodka (see Note)

Ice cubes

4 lemon slices

4 fresh mint sprigs

1. Place the lemonade and vodka in a small pitcher and stir to combine.

2. Fill 4 tall glasses with ice cubes and pour in the lemonade mixture. Garnish each glass with a lemon slice and a sprig of mint.

SAVE THE DAY NOTE

Dayna likes Jake's lemonade and buys it at Costco. She has also used sparkling lemonade from Trader Joe's.

Firefly makes a sweet tea flavored vodka. Or you can use Wild Turkey American Honey bourbon instead of the vodka.

 Do Ahead

You can slice the lemons and rinse and pat dry the mint sprigs. Store the mint in the fridge between paper towels till using.

Spiced Fall Sangria

SERVES: 6 TO 8
PREP: 10 MINUTES
CHILL: AT LEAST 1 HOUR

What to serve when a dear friend is leaving town? An impromptu farewell party needed a signature drink for toasting. The weather was too cool for summery margaritas and Bellinis but not cold enough for hot buttered rum and eggnog. A spiced sangria came to the rescue—a combination of a fruity Spanish white wine, spiced apple cider, touch of triple sec, and orange slices. Mediterranean meets fall harvest. Serve it up at a Halloween gathering or even Thanksgiving. Have fun with different add-ins, like dried cranberries or pomegranate seeds, but be forewarned that dried fruit as well as pears sink to the bottom of the pitcher. Citrus and berries float. Serve the sangria from a pitcher or punch bowl.

1 bottle (750 milliliters) fruity white wine, such as a Catalunya from Spain

1 cup spiced apple cider (see Note)

¼ cup triple sec

1 tablespoon sugar (optional)

1 small orange, rinsed and thinly sliced

Ice cubes (optional)

① Pour the wine, cider, triple sec, and sugar, if using, in a large pitcher and stir until the sugar dissolves. Stir in the orange slices. Cover the pitcher and refrigerate the sangria for at least 1 hour.

② To serve, remove the orange slices and cut them into pieces and place a few in old-fashioned glasses or Champagne flutes. Add ice cubes, if desired. Pour in the sangria.

 If you can't find spiced apple cider, use plain apple cider and add 2 cinnamon sticks and a few whole cloves to the pitcher.

 You can make the spiced sangria through Step 1 up to 3 days in advance. Keep covered in the refrigerator.

CHAPTER 3

SOUPS

Whether it's Chilled Cucumber Soup when it's warm outside or Jan's Lentil Soup when it's cold, good soup not only makes your life easier, but it makes memories, too.

I can't envision a snow day without a hearty soup. Can't think of sick days without chicken soup. The Super Bowl without chili. Or summer picnics on the porch without gazpacho.

Soups can be fast, fresh, and have few ingredients, playing up what you want to highlight—fresh vegetables from your own summer garden or a beautiful find from the farmers' market.

Simmered on a back burner on a lazy weekend afternoon, then frozen for busier days ahead, they become real save-the-day heroes. And when they're comforting enough to become a part of your repertoire, such as my Feel Better Chicken Soup, they become family favorites.

And soups not only whet our appetite, but also satisfy us as the entire main dish—wait till you scoop up a bowl of Missy's White Chili. These recipes will rescue many a lunch or dinner, they will definitely make some memories in the process!

SOMETHING FROM NOTHING • TOO HOT TO COOK • VERY VEGETARIAN

Heirloom Tomato Gazpacho

SERVES: 4
PREP: 15 MINUTES
CHILL: AT LEAST 2 HOURS

Outside the temperature soared above 100 degrees, but inside my cool kitchen the food processor was the workhorse, pureeing tomatoes, herbs, and a pepper from the garden, along with garlic, olive oil, and lemon juice. I stuck a spoon in the bowl and pulled up a first taste—perfection. What to cook when the weather is just too hot? What to do with all the tomatoes pouring in from the summer garden? Gazpacho. Juicy, fat summer heirloom tomatoes have loads of flavor, acidity, and sweetness that make gazpacho memorable. Plus they begin dark green with more chlorophyll and ripen into splotchy red tomatoes that are sweeter, have more flavor, and contain more antioxidants than supermarket tomatoes. Store gazpacho in the fridge, but for best flavor, let it come to room temperature before serving.

1 loosely packed cup fresh herbs, such as parsley, chives, basil, oregano, and/or chervil, coarsely chopped, plus fresh herbs, for garnish

1 clove garlic, peeled

1 yellow or pale green sweet bell pepper or large banana pepper, stemmed and seeded

5 cups quartered peeled heirloom tomatoes, seeded (from 3 to 4 large tomatoes)

2 tablespoons olive oil

1 tablespoon fresh lemon juice

Salt and freshly ground black pepper

¼ cup paper-thin slices Vidalia or other sweet onion

1 cup diced cucumber, plus diced cucumber, for garnish

① Place the 1 cup of chopped herbs and the garlic in the bowl of a food processor. Pulse until the herbs are finely chopped, 4 or 5 times. Scrape down the side of the bowl with a rubber spatula.

② Cut the pepper into 1-inch pieces, add them to the processor, and pulse until pureed, 4 or 5 times. Scrape down the side of the bowl.

③ Add the tomatoes to the bowl and puree until smooth. With the motor running, pour in the olive oil and lemon juice. Turn off the machine and scrape down the side of the bowl. Season with salt and pepper to taste and transfer the gazpacho to a serving bowl.

④ Scatter the onion slices on top of the gazpacho and stir to incorporate. Fold in the 1 cup of diced cucumber. Cover the bowl with plastic wrap and refrigerate the gazpacho for at least 2 hours. Remove the gazpacho from the fridge and let come to room temperature. To serve, ladle the gazpacho into bowls and garnish with more diced cucumber and fresh herbs.

Do Ahead The gazpacho can be made and chilled 2 days in advance. However, don't add the onion and cucumber until just before serving.

★ RAZZLE-DAZZLE

Add chopped avocado and a sprinkling of chopped fresh cilantro along with the cucumber. Or, add lump crabmeat and top the gazpacho with some crunchy panfried croutons.

Chilled Cucumber Soup

SERVES: 8
PREP: 15 MINUTES
COOK: 38 TO 46 MINUTES
CHILL: AT LEAST 2 HOURS

In the summer the cucumbers in my garden grow with abandon. They're not finicky like eggplant and they can withstand drought, rain, bugs—you name it—so they grow like crazy. This soup saved the day when the cukes took over my kitchen counters. Easily made ahead, the soup keeps for several days in the fridge and was ready to pull out when I didn't want to heat up the kitchen cooking dinner in 90-degree heat. Another plus: It is good enough to serve company. Garnished with chopped fresh tomato and dill or basil, it is the quintessential summer soup.

3 tablespoons butter

2 cups chopped Vidalia or other sweet onion

3 tablespoons all-purpose flour

5 cups chopped peeled cucumbers (from 5 medium-size cucumbers)

6 cups vegetable broth

¾ cup heavy (whipping) cream

½ cup sour cream, for serving

¾ cup chopped fresh dill, parsley, or basil, plus ¾ cup dill fronds and basil leaves, for garnish

Salt and freshly ground black pepper

Chopped tomato, for garnish (optional)

1. Melt the butter in a large heavy saucepan over medium-low heat. Add the onion and cook, stirring, until it is translucent, 5 to 7 minutes. Add the flour and cook, stirring, until the mixture is thick, about 1 minute. Add the cucumbers and vegetable broth and stir to mix. Increase the heat to medium-high and let the cucumber mixture come to a boil. Reduce the heat to low and let cook, uncovered, until the mixture is reduced by a third, 30 to 35 minutes.

2. Add the cream and cook, stirring, until the cream is incorporated and the soup thickens, 2 to 3 minutes. Add the chopped dill and season the soup with salt and pepper to taste. Turn off the heat.

3. Working in batches, puree the soup in a blender or food processor. To quickly cool down the soup, pour it into a large container with a lid. Fill the sink with ice water. Place the covered container in the ice water for about 1 hour. Wipe off the container and place it in the refrigerator to chill the soup for at least 1 hour, or until serving time.

4. To serve, taste for seasoning, adding more salt and/or pepper as necessary. Ladle the soup into bowls. Swirl a tablespoon of sour cream into each serving and top with dill fronds, basil leaves, and chopped tomato, if using, as a garnish.

Do Ahead It's absolutely fine to make the cucumber soup a day ahead and keep it chilled. Add the sour cream and garnishes right before serving.

★ RAZZLE-DAZZLE

For dinner parties, ladle the soup into shallow bowls and serve it with peeled, grilled shrimp as a garnish.

Fast Asparagus Soup (Easiest Soup in the World)

SERVES: 6
PREP: 5 MINUTES

I scribbled this recipe in one of the many journals I keep in my purse and pretty much forgot it was there until I was looking for something else and came across it. It was obviously dictated to me by a good cook, so my apologies for not remembering any more details. All I know is that I intended to make this with canned white asparagus but when I couldn't find them opted for green instead. What an incredible recipe—the fastest and most delicious soup on Earth. It only has four plus two optional ingredients. You don't dirty a pan, just a food processor. So it saves the day on so many levels. Enjoy it hot or cold.

1 can (15 to 19 ounces) green asparagus spears, drained

1 can (14½ ounces) reduced-sodium chicken broth

1 teaspoon fresh lemon juice (from ½ lemon)

½ cup heavy (whipping) cream

Pinch of ground nutmeg or cayenne pepper (optional)

Parmesan Toasts (optional; page 68), for serving

① Place the asparagus in the bowl of a food processor and process until the asparagus is pureed, about 15 seconds. With the motor running, pour the chicken broth into the feed tube to blend. Turn off the machine and add the lemon juice.

② Turn the motor back on and pour the cream into the feed tube to blend. Turn off the machine and season the soup with nutmeg or cayenne pepper, if desired. Serve the soup at once or refrigerate it until serving time. Or, if you like, warm the soup gently over low heat, not letting it come to a boil. Serve it with Parmesan Toasts.

Do Ahead Definitely do make the asparagus soup 2 to 3 days ahead and keep it refrigerated, covered.

I'd serve it with . . .
roast chicken, grilled steaks, pork tenderloin.
Or, serve the soup as a first course in demitasse cups.

COMPANY'S COMING • VERY VEGETARIAN

Curried Butternut Squash and Apple Soup

SERVES: 8
PREP: 20 TO 25 MINUTES
BAKE: 35 TO 40 MINUTES
COOK: 30 MINUTES

I'm always looking for a festive soup to serve on Halloween night, and while I love the idea of pumpkin soup, this one is far more practical. I got tired of roasting the little sweet baking pumpkins only to find they didn't have enough flesh to turn into a pot of soup. The butternut squash, on the other hand, has a ton of flesh, and I find its roasted texture creamier than the pumpkin. Plus, this soup can be made a day or two in advance and benefits from the time in the fridge. You can host a neighborhood party knowing the soup is made. Thanks to my investment club friend Eugenie for turning me on to the delightful combination of curry, apple, and squash—much like the Indian mulligatawny.

1 large butternut squash
(2½ pounds)

Vegetable oil spray

2 tablespoons (¼ stick) butter

1 cup chopped onion

1 teaspoon curry powder or garam
masala

1 large apple, peeled, cored, and
chopped (1 to 1¼ cups)

¼ teaspoon dried thyme

Salt

1 quart (32 ounces; 4 cups) chicken
broth

½ cup heavy (whipping) cream

Freshly ground black pepper

Parmesan Toasts (optional, recipe
follows)

① Place a rack in the center of the oven
and preheat the oven to 350°F.

② Cut the squash in half lengthwise.
Using a soupspoon, scoop out the seeds
and discard them. Spray the cut sides
of the squash with vegetable oil spray
and place the squash cut side down on
a baking sheet. Bake the squash until it
is just tender when pierced with a sharp
knife, 35 to 40 minutes.

③ Meanwhile, place the butter in a large
soup pot over medium-low heat. Add the
onion and cook, stirring, until the onion
is soft and translucent, 8 to 10 minutes.
Stir in the curry powder, reduce the heat
to low, and cook, stirring, until fragrant,
about 1 minute. Add the apple, thyme,
and ½ teaspoon of salt, stir to mix, and
turn off the heat.

④ When the squash has cooked, scoop
out the cooked squash and place it in
the soup pot. Add the chicken broth.
Let come to a boil over high heat, then
reduce the heat to low, cover the pot,
and let simmer until the flavors combine, about 15 minutes.

⑤ If desired, puree the soup using an
immersion blender or a food processor (if you are using a food processor,
return the pureed soup to the pot).
Stir in the cream. Let the soup return
to a boil over medium-high heat, then
reduce the heat to low, and let the soup
simmer until it thickens slightly, 3 to
4 minutes. Taste for seasoning, adding
more salt, if necessary, and pepper to
taste. Serve the soup warm, garnished
with Parmesan Toasts, if desired.

Do Ahead   The squash soup can be
made 2 days in advance,
refrigerated, covered, and reheated
over low heat.

Parmesan Toasts

MAKES: 16 TO 20 SLICES OF TOAST

Parmesan Toasts are the perfect topper for all sorts of soups, adding crunch and a salty tang. They are a lovely companion to the creamy and sweet butternut soup. You can easily make them from a loaf of French bread an hour or so in advance of serving time. No need to refrigerate; just leave them at room temperature.

1 loaf French bread

3 to 4 tablespoons olive oil

½ cup grated Parmesan cheese

① Preheat the broiler.

② Slice the French bread into 16 to 20 slices, ¼ inch thick. Arrange the slices on a baking sheet. Drizzle olive oil over them and sprinkle them with grated Parmesan cheese.

③ Place the baking sheet under the broiler and broil the toasts until they turn brown around the edges and the cheese melts, 1 to 2 minutes. Remove and set aside.

★
★ ★
★ RAZZLE-DAZZLE

Ladle the butternut squash soup into soup bowls and garnish it with pieces of steamed lobster, minced chives, and a Parmesan Toast. For a festive Halloween party buffet, serve this soup in little mugs or demitasse cups.

Jan's Lentil Soup

SERVES: 8
PREP: 30 MINUTES
COOK: 50 TO 60 MINUTES

Atlanta resident Jan Ficarrotta is partial to lentils. She buys them often, so they are ready on the pantry shelf for simmering up a pot of lentil soup to serve her family or friends at book club. Jan's trick is to soak the lentils overnight in cold water, then drain them, even if the directions on the package don't say to do this. She finds the soaking softens the lentils and improves their texture in the soup. Hearty, filling, flavorful—all you need is a great big salad to round out this meal.

8 ounces lentils (see Note)

½ cup olive oil

2 cups finely chopped onions, (from 2 medium-size or 1 large onion)

2 ribs celery, finely chopped

1 large carrot, peeled and chopped

1 clove garlic, minced

1 sprig fresh flat-leaf parsley, plus ¼ cup chopped parsley, for garnish

1 tablespoon salt

2 chicken or beef bouillon cubes

6 cups water

¼ teaspoon freshly ground black pepper

1 tablespoon fresh lemon juice

① Place the lentils in a sieve and rinse them with warm water. Place the lentils in a large pot and add water to cover. Let come to a boil over high heat, then reduce the heat to medium and let simmer until plumped up and partially cooked, about 10 minutes. Drain the lentils and set them aside.

② Place the olive oil, onion, celery, carrot, and garlic in the same pot over medium heat. Cook, stirring, until the vegetables are cooked through and soft, 10 to 12 minutes. Add the drained lentils, parsley sprig, salt, bouillon cubes, and the 6 cups of water. Season with pepper to taste. Increase the heat to high and let come to a boil. Reduce the heat to low, and let simmer, uncovered, until the lentils are soft, 30 to 35 minutes. Turn off the heat and remove the parsley sprig. Stir in the lemon juice, and serve the lentils garnished with the chopped parsley.

Do Ahead The lentil soup can be made 2 to 3 days in advance. It can also be frozen for up to 4 months.

MONEY SAVER: Lentils are the ultimate money saver, costing pennies per serving.

Lentils are a favorite ingredient in Middle Eastern, Indian, and French cooking. There are various types—the brown European or French green lentil as well as red or Egyptian lentil. For this recipe use brown lentils. Lentils take less time to cook than dried beans, and they are adaptable to most any seasoning or add-in.

I'd serve it with . . . crusty bread, a Caesar or green salad, and a plate of warm cookies or brownies for dessert.

Love the Lentils

The next time you reach for rice or pasta as a side dish, think lentils instead. Their nutty, earthy flavor is perfect to go alongside roasted meat and grilled fish. Here are some ways to definitely pick up the flavor of these lovely lentils.

• When you cook the lentils, add onion, garlic, a clove, some chopped carrot, and a bay leaf to the cooking water. Add a beef or chicken bouillon cube if you like.

• For a partner to grilled fish or sausages, toss cooked lentils with a little lemon juice and olive oil and fold in chopped fresh parsley and basil. When the fish and sausages come off the grill, place them on top of the lentils and scatter more fresh herbs on top.

• While roasting a whole chicken, remove it from the oven halfway through cooking and add chopped onion, lentils, and twice as much water as the amount of lentils to the roasting pan. Return the chicken and lentils to the oven to finish cooking.

• For a next-day main dish salad, scatter cooked lentils on a pretty platter. Surround them with tender lettuce leaves. Top the lentils with chopped fresh tomatoes, olives, flaked canned tuna, and a drizzling of oil and vinegar dressing.

• And, when making your favorite vegetable soup, add a half cup of lentils to the pot.

Feel Better Chicken Soup

SERVES: 8
PREP: 25 MINUTES
COOK: 3 TO 3½ HOURS

Many years ago I was researching a story on the restorative powers of chicken soup. Why the name "Jewish penicillin"? My research found that the fat of the chicken cooks down into the broth, and this fatty broth makes you feel better. Plus, a good bit of salt in the soup helps, too, plus the warmth of the soup soothes a sore throat. I am not Jewish, and in fact, my mom didn't make her own chicken soup. She made home-made vegetable soup, but if we wanted chicken soup, we opened a can of Campbell's.

However, that's beside the point.... I wanted to learn how to make great chicken soup. I had three small children, and we were constantly managing the ups and downs of ear infections and colds. Plus, when they got sick, my husband and I got sick. I made soup beginning with a whole chicken, and after much sampling I settled on my favorite kind—an organic bird. It had the most flavor. And I was careful not to skim the fat from the broth because the fat was the healing factor. That soup I finally came up with was pretty darned wonderful. Through the years I have perfected this recipe, preparing it countless times for ailing family and friends. It will save your day if you or someone you love has a cold or the flu. And even if everyone is perfectly healthy.

★★★ RAZZLE-DAZZLE

Turn Mom's get-well soup into an Italian chicken and pasta stew by ladling it into bowls, adding a favorite small pasta—like farfalle (bowties) or ditalini (short tubes)—and garnishing it with grated Parmesan cheese and a spoonful of pesto.

1 whole organic chicken (3½ pounds)

1 tablespoon kosher or sea salt

3 bay leaves

½ small onion, peeled

2 chicken bouillon cubes

4 large carrots, peeled and chopped

1 cup frozen green peas

1 can (about 15 ounces) white beans, drained

½ cup penne pasta (see Note)

Freshly ground black pepper

3 cups (packed) fresh spinach leaves

Soda crackers, for serving

① Remove the giblets and neck, if any, from the chicken and set them aside for another use or discard them. Rinse the chicken under cold running water. Place the chicken in a large soup pot and add cold water to cover. Add the salt, bay leaves, and onion. Place the pot over high heat and let come to a boil. Skim the foam that rises to the top. Reduce the heat to low, add the bouillon cubes, cover the pot, and let the chicken simmer until it is quite tender, 2½ hours. Turn off the heat, uncover the pan, and let the chicken sit in the broth until cool enough to handle, about 25 minutes.

② Set the broth aside in the pot. Remove and discard the chicken skin and bones. Shred the meat with your hands and return it to the pot. Add the carrots, peas, white beans, and pasta. Season with pepper to taste. Let come to a boil over high heat. Reduce the heat to low, cover the pot, and let simmer until the carrots and pasta have cooked through, 35 to 40 minutes. Uncover the pot, add the spinach, and cook, stirring, until the leaves wilt, 2 to 3 minutes.

③ To serve, remove and discard the bay leaves. Ladle the soup into bowls and serve with soda crackers.

SAVE THE DAY NOTE You can use any dried pasta that you have on hand. Break spaghetti noodles into 2-inch pieces.

Do Ahead This soup can be made a day or two in advance. You can make it ahead and freeze it, but it freezes best without the pasta. Thaw the soup, let it come to a boil, add the pasta, and let simmer until the pasta is tender.

Mary Ann's Taco Soup

SERVES: 8 TO 10
PREP: 10 TO 15 MINUTES
COOK: 1 TO 1½ HOURS

Mary Ann Loweth, who lives in Houston, Texas, shared this recipe with me while I was in Houston on a book tour. We were chatting during my book signing, and I asked Mary Ann if she had a signature recipe. Nothing like putting someone on the spot! But Mary Ann immediately replied, "My taco soup. It's a crowd-pleaser." And then without looking at her phone to search the recipe, she effortlessly rattled off the ingredient list. This was obviously a recipe that isn't really a recipe, just a process of combining the right ingredients. What you get is a chunky soup, which some people eat with a spoon and others, like Mary Ann's son, scoop up with tortilla chips. Be flexible when shopping for the canned beans; Mary Ann is accustomed to buying every canned bean under the sun in Houston. In areas of the country where pinto beans with jalapeños are unavailable, substitute plain pinto beans and up the seasoning.

FOR THE TACO SOUP

2 pounds lean ground beef

1 medium-size onion, chopped (1 cup)

1 package (0.4 ounce) dry ranch dressing seasoning

1 package (about 1 ounce) dry taco seasoning

1 can (15¼ ounces) yellow or white corn, undrained

2 cans (10 ounces each) Ro-Tel original diced tomatoes and green chilies

1 can (about 15 ounces) pinto beans, undrained

1 can (about 15 ounces) pinto beans with jalapeño peppers, undrained

1 can (16 ounces) ranch-style beans or plain pintos, undrained

1 can (about 4½ ounces) chopped green chiles, undrained

FOR THE TOPPINGS

Tortilla chips

2 avocados, cubed

¼ cup chopped fresh cilantro leaves (optional)

½ cup chopped scallions, both white and green parts

Sour cream

Shredded mild cheddar cheese or a Mexican cheese blend (optional)

① Crumble the beef into a large heavy saucepan or Dutch oven over medium heat. Add the onion. Cook, stirring, until the beef is cooked through and the onion is translucent, 7 to 8 minutes. Stir in the ranch seasoning, taco seasoning, and corn. Add the tomatoes, then fill both cans with water and add that to the pan. Stir to combine. Add all of the cans of beans and the green chiles. Add 2 more cups of water (see Note). Stir to combine. Increase the heat to medium-high.

② When the soup comes to a boil, reduce the heat to low, and place a lid on the pan so that it is partially covered. Let the soup simmer and cook down until the seasonings have blended, 1 to 1½ hours.

③ To serve, spoon the soup into bowls and serve with tortilla chips, avocado cubes, cilantro, scallions, sour cream, and cheese, if desired.

SAVE THE DAY NOTE The consistency of this soup is a personal thing. The soup is intended to be chunky. So, add the cans of water followed by the 2 cups of water. If as the soup cooks down you find it is too thick, add 1 more cup of water. Also, if you wish to drain the liquid off the beans, do so. Add another cup of water if you are using drained beans.

Do Ahead The taco soup can definitely be made a day or two in advance and refrigerated, covered. Reheat it in a covered pot over low heat for 15 to 20 minutes. Stir the soup occasionally as it reheats.

MONEY SAVER: Use dried pinto beans and cook them according to the package directions. Use 2 cups of cooked dried beans and their juices for each can of beans. Add chopped jalapeño peppers to spice things up if you are using dried beans.

I'd serve it with . . . all of the toppings. Then I'd serve a big green or Caesar salad on the side.

Missy's White Chili

SERVES: 8 TO 10
PREP: 20 MINUTES
COOK: 45 MINUTES

Everyone needs a white chili recipe, the type you can pull together in a snap before you head out to a potluck. Or something fast and cheap to serve when you're feeding a crowd. White chili works because young and old love it. And what's not to like? For vegetarians you can simply omit the chicken and substitute vegetable broth instead of chicken broth. Or, just serve chicken on the side, as a topper, and then everyone's happy. This recipe was passed along by my friend Missy Myers, and I vary the seasoning and add-ins every time I put the pot on the stove. If you're feeling decadent, add a splash of heavy cream to the chili for the last few minutes of cooking.

FOR THE CHILI

1 tablespoon olive oil

1 large white onion, chopped (about 2 cups)

6 cloves garlic, minced (about 2 tablespoons)

2 to 3 ribs celery, chopped

1½ pounds boneless cooked chicken, chopped in small pieces (4 cups; see Note)

1 can (about 4½ ounces) chopped green chiles, undrained

2 cans (14½ ounces each) chicken broth

3 cans (about 15 ounces each) white beans, such as great northern or navy beans, undrained

2 teaspoons ground cumin

2 teaspoons dried oregano

¼ teaspoon cayenne pepper

Salt and freshly ground black pepper

FOR THE TOPPINGS

Shredded cheese, such as cheddar, Monterey Jack, or a Mexican blend

Sour cream

Chopped fresh cilantro

Pickled jalapeño pepper slices

Chopped fresh tomatoes

Tortilla chips

Guacamole or chopped avocado

(1) Place the olive oil in a large skillet over medium heat. Add the onion, garlic, and celery and cook, stirring, until they soften, 3 to 4 minutes. Remove the pan from the heat and stir in the chicken and chiles. Set aside.

(2) Place the chicken broth and beans in a large pot over low heat. Stir in the cumin, oregano, and cayenne pepper.

Stir the onion and chicken mixture into the pot with the beans. Increase the heat to medium-high and stir until the mixture comes to a boil. Reduce the heat to low, cover the pot, and let the chili simmer until it thickens, about 30 minutes.

(3) Taste the chili for seasoning, adding salt and pepper to taste. Ladle the chili into bowls and serve it with your favorite chili toppings.

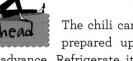

SAVE THE DAY NOTE When you are in a rush, buy a rotisserie chicken (they're usually 3 to 3½ pounds). Remove the skin and chop enough meat to yield 4 cups.

Do Ahead The chili can be completely prepared up to 2 days in advance. Refrigerate it, covered, until time to serve.

I'd serve it with . . .
all the suggested toppings and other favorites of yours.
Make a chili bar!

CHAPTER 4

SIGNATURE SALADS

If your signature is your own unique way of signing your name, then a signature salad should be your own take on greens and other fresh things. Sure, it is easy to just grab a bag of mixed greens and pour on whatever bottled salad dressing is in the refrigerator. But does that make a great salad? Not likely. And is this a salad you want to take to a party or impress someone with? Not likely either. So you need some salads that save your day. And your culinary reputation. And, boy, do I have some great recipes to share.

Salads can nourish people, especially when you're in a hurry and the weather's hot. Think Kitchen Sink Tabbouleh, Investment Club Orzo Salad, and one of my bean salads, either succotash or white bean. And no salad chapter is complete without chicken salad—I've got two great ones to share— as well as a special relish for holiday events. Virginia's Cranberry Relish is cranberry sauce meets fruit bowl, and you will love it.

If you're leaning toward a green salad, you'll like the seasonality of Beth's Autumn Salad and its medley of apple, pecans, and blue cheese, all drizzled with a maple vinaigrette. And you'll enjoy the summer freshness of the Watermelon, Arugula, and Cucumber Salad with a spicy lime vinaigrette. Get a week's worth of greens in with Joy's Kale and Brussels Sprouts Salad, or the Spinach Salad with Apple, Almonds,

and a Tart Cherry Vinaigrette, and feed an army with the Big Fat Greek Salad.

Composed salads are pretty to the eye—salads placed attractively on white platters so the vibrant colors of the salad stand out. In the composed world, I love Libby's Avocado and Pink Grapefruit Salad, and I love it even more during the holidays with a scattering of bright red pomegranate seeds on top. I also love the sliced tomato salad with my friend Ann's roasted garlic dressing. With yellow, red, and green tomatoes of all sizes and names, this is one amazing mosaic of color and flavor.

Salads should be fun and beautiful. People who love to make salads are usually people who love to eat salads. And I am one of those people. With constant experimentation and a roving eye for new ideas, my salads get increasingly better.

Surely, one of these salads will win your heart and become your signature.

St. Paul's Chicken Salad

SERVES: 6 TO 8
PREP: 45 TO 50 MINUTES
COOK: 2 HOURS

My friend Ann Buchanan is the reason I say so many good cooks come from Mississippi. Ann's hometown is Columbus, where some of the finest chicken salad in the South is made. This is the Columbus recipe that originated with the ladies of St. Paul's Episcopal Church. The church is not only famous for this chicken salad; playwright Tennessee Williams's grandfather was a priest here, and Williams was born in the parsonage next door. Anyway, Ann gave me the recipe about seven years ago after I nagged her incessantly for it. It's a little more trouble than your typical chicken salad because you not only cook the chicken, you also make a cooked dressing (best cooked salad dressing ever—think homemade Durkee with its tangy creaminess). But both Ann and I know that this recipe, when served with slices of ripe tomato for brunch or lunch, will save any day.

FOR THE COOKED DRESSING

⅓ cup distilled white vinegar

4 large egg yolks

⅓ cup vegetable oil

2 teaspoons Worcestershire sauce

½ teaspoon dry mustard

2 teaspoons sugar

½ teaspoon salt

Dash of cayenne pepper

⅓ cup milk

FOR THE CHICKEN SALAD

1 whole chicken (4 pounds)

Salt and freshly ground black pepper

2 cups chopped celery

Juice of 1 lemon

Dash each of paprika and cayenne pepper

½ cup mayonnaise

Lettuce leaves or toasted bread, for serving (optional)

★ ★ ★
★ RAZZLE-DAZZLE

Spread the chicken salad onto thin slices of soft, fresh bread.
Trim off the crusts and cut the sandwiches into triangles or three
rectangles. Pour a cup of tea for a friend and enjoy these tea
sandwiches.

(1) Make the cooked dressing: Pour water to a depth of 3 to 4 inches into a 6- to 8-quart pot and bring it to a boil. Reduce the heat so the water simmers.

(2) Place the vinegar in a small saucepan and warm slightly over low heat. Do not boil.

(3) Place the egg yolks in a 2-quart stainless steel bowl that you will place over the simmering water and use as a double boiler. Beat the yolks with a fork until they have lightened to a pale lemon yellow color, 2 to 3 minutes. Whisk in the oil, then add the Worcestershire sauce, dry mustard, sugar, salt, and the dash of cayenne pepper. Place the bowl over the simmering water and whisk in the milk. Whisk the vinegar mixture into the egg yolk mixture.

(4) Cook the dressing, stirring slowly, until it has the consistency of eggnog, 8 to 9 minutes. Because the cooked dressing uses egg yolks, you must take care to cook the dressing through. Let the

dressing cool to room temperature, then refrigerate it until it is time to make the chicken salad.

(5) Make the chicken salad: Remove the giblets and neck, if any, from the chicken and set them aside for another use or discard them. Rinse the chicken under cold running water. Place the chicken in a large soup pot and add cold water to cover. Season with salt and black pepper to taste. Place the pot over high heat and let come to a boil. Reduce the heat to low, cover the pot, and let the chicken simmer until it is cooked through, about 1½ hours.

(6) Remove the pot from the heat and transfer the chicken to a platter to cool. Set the chicken broth aside for making soup. When the chicken is cool enough to handle, after about 20 minutes, remove and discard the skin. Remove the chicken meat from the bones and shred it or chop it into cubes. Let the chicken cool completely, then cover it and refrigerate until ready to use.

7. To assemble the chicken salad, place the celery and lemon juice in a large bowl. Add the shredded chicken and season it with ¼ teaspoon each salt and black pepper, the paprika, and cayenne pepper to taste, tossing the chicken to coat it with the spices. Add the mayonnaise and 1 cup of the cooked dressing. Mix well.

8. Serve the chicken salad at once on lettuce leaves or on toasted bread for sandwiches. Or cover the bowl with plastic wrap and refrigerate the salad for up to 1 day.

SAVE THE DAY NOTE There will be enough dressing left over to use on sandwiches (delicious!) or to spoon over grilled salmon.

Do Ahead The dressing, chicken, and chopped celery can all be prepared ahead of time. And the salad can be made a day in advance; refrigerate it covered.

Susie's Catalina Chicken Salad

SERVES: 6 TO 8
PREP: 15 TO 20 MINUTES
MARINATE: 1 HOUR

Susie Ries received the *Better Homes and Gardens Cooking for Two* cookbook as a gift when she was newly married. One of her favorite recipes is this easy chicken salad adapted from that book. It is a summer staple in her Nashville kitchen, and once she had children she doubled the recipe so they could enjoy it, too. Adding bottled Catalina dressing to sauces, dressings, and marinades is very retro, and people have hung on to those recipes today. Just last weekend, my husband marinated lamb chops in Catalina salad dressing, then grilled them. So retro and fun.

*4 cups diced cooked chicken
(see box, page 153)*

¼ cup Kraft Catalina salad dressing

2 cups seedless red grapes, cut in half lengthwise or quartered lengthwise if the grapes are extra large

1 cup finely chopped celery

⅓ cup toasted sliced almonds or cashews (see Note)

2 teaspoons fresh lemon juice

⅔ cup mayonnaise

① Place the chicken in a large bowl and toss it with the Catalina salad dressing. Cover the bowl with plastic wrap and let the chicken marinate in the refrigerate for about 1 hour.

② Remove the bowl from the fridge and fold the grapes, celery, and nuts into the chicken. Stir the lemon juice into the mayonnaise and fold the mayonnaise into the chicken mixture. Serve at once (or see Do Ahead below).

SAVE THE DAY NOTE To toast the sliced almonds or the cashews, spread them out on a rimmed baking sheet and bake them in a 350°F oven until lightly toasted, 2 to 3 minutes for the almonds, 4 to 5 minutes for the cashews. If you use cashews, you'll need to coarsely chop them.

Do Ahead You can make the chicken salad up to a day ahead. Refrigerate it, covered.

$ MONEY SAVER: Use the rest of the Catalina salad dressing as a marinade for lamb or chicken before grilling.

★ ★ ★ ★ RAZZLE-DAZZLE

You'll love the blushing pink color of this salad. To carry out the seventies California theme, place the chicken salad on a bed of lettuce leaves. Surround the salad with thin slices of avocado and nectarine.

Grilled Tuna Salade Niçoise

SERVES: 6
PREP AND COOKING TIME: 55 MINUTES

When I returned from cooking school in Paris many years ago I brought with me all sorts of recipes for baking croissants and French bread, as well as some clever ways that the French used canned tuna. One such recipe was the *salade niçoise*, and it became a favorite summer salad and it still is except for one thing—I no longer use canned tuna for the salad. Not after grilling tuna one evening and having leftovers for a salad the next night. This grilled tuna *niçoise* is better than the salad I ordered in Nice, and it has the required tomatoes, olives, thin green beans, anchovies, hard-cooked eggs, and potatoes. Feel free to add your improvements as well.

Lemon and Dill Marinated Grilled Tuna (page 185; see also Note on page 88)

2 cups salad greens, such as baby romaine, arugula, Bibb, or mâche, for lining the platter

2 large eggs

1 cup tiny new potatoes

Salt

½ cup French vinaigrette (recipe follows), or your favorite oil and vinegar dressing, or as needed

2 cups thin green beans

2 medium-size ripe tomatoes, peeled and quartered

¼ cup niçoise or kalamata olives, or more, to taste, pitted

4 anchovy fillets (optional)

1 tablespoon capers (optional), drained

I'd serve it with . . . crusty bread and chilled white wine.

① If the grilled tuna has been refrigerated, let it come to room temperature, about 1 hour.

② Line a salad platter with the salad greens and set it aside in a cool place.

③ Place the eggs in a medium-size saucepan and add enough cold water to cover them by at least 1 inch. Let come to a boil over medium-high heat, then cover

the pan and remove it from the heat. Let the eggs sit in the hot water for 20 minutes before removing them to cool.

④ Place the potatoes in a medium-size saucepan. Add cold water to cover and a pinch of salt. Let come to a boil over high heat, then reduce the heat to low and let the potatoes simmer until just tender and easily pierced with a fork, 10 to 12 minutes, depending on the size of the potatoes. Potatoes continue to cook as they cool, so be careful not to overcook them. Using a slotted spoon to drain them, transfer the potatoes to a bowl. Let cool enough to handle easily; slice or halve any big ones. Leave the water in the pan. Toss the potatoes with a little of the vinaigrette and set them aside.

⑤ Place the pan of water over medium-high heat and when the water is boiling, add the green beans. Let the green beans cook until bright green, 3 to 5 minutes, then transfer them to a colander in the sink and run cold water over them. Let the green beans sit in the colander until well drained, then place them in a second bowl and toss them with a little vinaigrette.

⑥ When you are ready to serve, peel and quarter the eggs. Slice the tuna into ½-inch-wide strips. Arrange the potatoes and green beans in the center of the salad greens and place the tuna

How to Make Great Tuna Salad

Tuna salad can save your day as either an impromptu lunch or dinner. Here are a few steps to ensure your tuna salad is great every time.

1. Begin with the best tuna: a high-grade albacore, packed in water.

2. Drain off the water and flake the tuna into a bowl. Squeeze a couple of teaspoons of fresh lemon juice over the tuna to refresh it. Season the tuna with a little salt and pepper.

3. Add crunchy things—a tablespoon of minced sweet onion, a tablespoon or two of minced celery—plus a tablespoon of drained capers, and a healthy tablespoon or two of chopped fresh flat-leaf parsley.

4. Add just enough Hellmann's mayonnaise to moisten the tuna salad. Slice tomatoes and get ready to eat.

Add grilled shrimp—½ pound—in addition to the tuna (will serve 8) or 1 pound tuna and ½ pound shrimp (for 6 servings). Add a showering of chopped fresh herbs—thyme, flat-leaf parsley, and chives—just before serving.

strips on top. Arrange the tomatoes, olives, and egg quarters around the edge of the salad. If desired, place the anchovies and capers on top of the salad. Pour enough vinaigrette over the salad to just moisten it, then serve more vinaigrette on the side.

Leftover grilled tuna can be refrigerated for up to 2 days. Place it on a serving plate and cover it with plastic wrap.

Do Ahead The majority of the ingredients for this salad can be prepared a day ahead. Cook the green beans and potatoes. Grill the tuna. Hard cook the eggs. Keep all of the do-ahead ingredients refrigerated. Assembling the salad will be only a matter of minutes.

How to Make a French Vinaigrette

**MAKES: ABOUT ½ CUP
PREP: 5 MINUTES**

We can get salad greens rinsed and ready at the market, but a decent vinaigrette? Best make it yourself. And it isn't that difficult. In fact it's a blend of science and art. Begin with an acidic ingredient in the bowl—vinegar. Add a little mustard, which pulls everything together. Whisk in olive oil. Add salt and pepper, a shallot, fresh herbs, and whatever else suits your mood and the season. Serve the vinaigrette over salad greens, sliced tomatoes, steamed green beans, or grilled fish.

2 tablespoons white wine vinegar or sherry vinegar

1 tablespoon Dijon mustard

6 tablespoons olive oil

Salt and freshly ground black pepper

1 large shallot, peeled and finely minced

1 tablespoon minced fresh flat-leaf parsley (optional)

Place the vinegar in a small bowl. Stir in the mustard. Whisk in the olive oil in a steady stream. Season the vinaigrette with salt and pepper to taste and stir in the shallot and parsley, if desired. This will keep for several hours at room temperature or covered in the fridge for up to 1 week. If refrigerated, take it out 30 minutes before serving so that it comes to room temperature.

SAVE THE DAY NOTE For a lemony vinaigrette, use lemon juice instead of the vinegar and reduce the mustard to 2 teaspoons, or add ½ teaspoon of grated lemon zest to the regular vinaigrette when you add the shallot and parsley.

For a heartier dressing, use balsamic vinegar. To take the edge off the balsamic vinaigrette and make it less acidic, add a teaspoon of sugar or honey.

Big Fat Greek Salad

SERVES: 8
PREP: 35 TO 40 MINUTES
COOK: 15 TO 20 MINUTES

Jan Ficarrotta grew up in Dunedin, Florida, near the town of Tarpon Springs, renowned for its vibrant Greek community. And anyone who knows Tarpon Springs knows of the legendary Greek salad at the old Louis Pappas restaurant. When the salad arrived at your table it was the size of a small Greek fishing vessel, and underneath the lettuce lay the secret stash of potato salad. You really haven't lived unless you have eaten one of those salads, and that is why Jan has perfected that Greek salad at home—just carrying on the legend. She knows getting the potato salad right is step one. You've got to make it yourself; no supermarket potato salad will do. Then, you need the classic Greek salad toppings like cucumber, olives, feta cheese, bell pepper, and scallions. Lastly, you've got to cover the top of the salad with boiled shrimp, so everyone gets plenty of shrimp with the salad. Jan's salad is a hit at book club in Atlanta, her home for the past twenty-one years.

FOR THE POTATO SALAD

6 medium-size (about 3 pounds) red-skinned or Yukon Gold potatoes

Salt

½ cup chopped scallions, green parts only

¼ cup chopped fresh flat-leaf parsley

½ cup mayonnaise

Freshly ground black pepper

FOR THE GREEK SALAD

2 heads romaine lettuce

2 large ripe tomatoes, cut into 8 wedges each

1 large cucumber, peeled, cut in half crosswise, then sliced into matchsticks

1 large avocado, cut into 12 slices

½ cup (about 4 ounces) crumbled feta cheese

1 green bell pepper, stemmed, seeded, and sliced crosswise into rings

4 to 6 fresh beets, peeled and cooked until tender (or canned beets), and chopped into 1-inch pieces (2 cups pieces)

1 pound jumbo shrimp, cooked and peeled (see Note)

4 anchovy fillets

16 pitted kalamata olives

4 whole scallions, trimmed

¼ cup distilled white vinegar or fresh lemon juice

¼ cup olive oil

¼ cup vegetable oil

1 teaspoon dried oregano

(1) Make the potato salad: Peel the potatoes and cut them in half. Place the potatoes in a medium-size saucepan. Add cold water to cover and a pinch of salt. Let come to a boil over high heat, then reduce the heat to low, cover the pan, and let the potatoes simmer until they are just tender and easily pierced with a fork, 15 to 20 minutes. Potatoes continue to cook as they cool, so be careful not to overcook them. Using a slotted spoon, transfer the potatoes to a plate to cool.

(2) When the potatoes are cool enough to handle cut them into 1-inch pieces and place the pieces in a bowl. Stir in the chopped scallions, parsley, and mayonnaise. Season the potato salad with salt and black pepper to taste and refrigerate it until serving.

(3) Make the Greek salad: Rinse the heads of lettuce well and pat the leaves dry with paper towels. Line a large platter with some of the lettuce leaves. Place the potato salad in a mound in the center.

(4) Tear the remaining lettuce into pieces and cover the potato salad with them. Arrange the tomato wedges, cucumber, and avocado around the edge of the platter. Scatter the feta cheese over the lettuce. Arrange the bell pepper, beets, shrimp, anchovies, olives, and whole scallions in an attractive pattern on top. If you are preparing the salad ahead of time, however, do not add the beets until the last minute as they will stain the rest of the salad.

(5) Just before serving, sprinkle the salad with the vinegar or lemon juice. Drizzle the olive oil and vegetable oil over the top and sprinkle the oregano on the salad.

I'd serve it with . . . toasted French bread.

RAZZLE-DAZZLE

This salad is the original razzle-dazzle. Want to gild the lily? Add lump crabmeat to the top with the shrimp. And add roasted peppers— either the roasted red bell peppers or the pickled green Salonika peppers (also known as peperoncini), both found in jars at the supermarket.

Kitchen Sink Tabbouleh

SERVES: 8
PREP: 30 MINUTES
SOAK: 1 HOUR

I am a big fan of the kitchen-sink concept. I first tried it in cookies, adding everything under the sun—pecans, cranberries, oatmeal—to chocolate chip cookies. And then I delved into gingerbread, including chopped apple, orange rind, and brandy. Now I am moving to tabbouleh. For me, the store-bought tabbouleh mixes are ho-hum. It is just as easy to make your own by pouring boiling water over coarse cracked wheat and then you can clean out the fridge and add anything you like. Chopped tomatoes and cucumbers, currants, toasted pine nuts, garbanzo beans or white beans, roasted eggplant cubes, caramelized onions, feta cheese—you name it. And leftovers are delish tucked into brown bag lunches or paired with strips of grilled chicken and crumbled feta for tomorrow night's dinner.

1½ cups bulgur (coarse cracked wheat)

1½ to 2 cups boiling water

1 cup chopped tomato

1 cup chopped peeled cucumber

½ cup chopped scallions, green parts only, or Vidalia onion

1 clove garlic, minced

¼ cup fresh lemon juice (from 2 medium-size lemons)

¼ cup olive oil

Salt and freshly ground black pepper

1 cup canned chickpeas (garbanzo beans), rinsed and drained

⅓ cup currants or chopped raisins (see Note)

⅓ cup pine nuts, lightly toasted (see Note)

½ cup chopped fresh flat-leaf parsley

¼ cup chopped fresh mint

1. Place the bulgur in a strainer and rinse it under warm running water. Transfer the bulgur to a large heatproof bowl and pour 1½ cups of boiling water over it. Let the bulgur sit for about 30 minutes and if after that time the water has been totally absorbed and the bulgur hasn't softened enough, add another ½ cup of boiling water. Let the bulgur sit for 15 to 30 minutes longer.

2. Stir the bulgur to make sure it has absorbed all of the water; if not, drain off any excess. Add the tomato, cucumber, scallions, and garlic to the bulgur. Stir to combine. Pour the lemon juice and olive oil over the top and stir to combine well. Season with salt and pepper to taste.

3. Fold in the chickpeas, currants, pine nuts, parsley, and mint and serve.

SAVE THE DAY NOTE You can omit the currants or add another dried fruit of your choice for that touch of sweetness. To chop dried fruit, spray a heavy knife with vegetable oil spray so the fruit doesn't stick to the knife when you chop the fruit into small pieces.

To toast the pine nuts, place them in a cast-iron skillet over medium-low heat and cook them just until they take on a little brown color, 3 to 4 minutes.

Do Ahead The tabbouleh salad can be prepared the day before and kept refrigerated. However, if you are making the salad ahead, add the toasted pine nuts and fresh herbs at the last minute.

★★★
★ RAZZLE-DAZZLE

Season this salad as you like, adding a little heat with cayenne pepper or a little exotic seasoning like a pinch of cinnamon. And instead of bulgur, use couscous or orzo.

Investment Club Orzo Salad

SERVES: 8
PREP: 45 MINUTES
BAKING: 30 TO 35 MINUTES

My high school classmate Evelyn first made this salad for our investment club meeting, and the next day people were more interested in getting Evelyn's recipe than hearing what stocks we had purchased. Guess you have to understand the group dynamics—we have known each other a long time, which makes everything at the meeting pretty comfortable and friendly and not too businesslike. Food is a constant at the meetings, and recipe sharing, too. Evelyn said she got the original recipe from a Barefoot Contessa cookbook. But through the years she has tweaked it by reducing the amount of dressing and by using what is growing in her summer garden. I, too, found that this recipe is extremely adaptable to what's in season and what veggies need to be cleaned out of the fridge. You roast the vegetables in the oven first, then cook the orzo and toss it with a little olive oil. After that you make the dressing and assemble the salad. This salad will anchor your dinner party meal, and all you need to add is some grilled chicken or steak, shrimp kebabs or lamb chops. Make it ahead and it is ready when you are.

FOR THE ROASTED VEGETABLES

2 medium-size yellow squash, trimmed and cut into ¾-inch cubes

2 medium-size zucchini, trimmed and cut into ¾-inch cubes

1 small eggplant, peeled and cut into ¾-inch cubes

1 red or yellow bell pepper, stemmed, seeded, and cut into ½-inch dice

1 red onion, cut into ½-inch dice

1 teaspoon salt, or to taste

Freshly ground black pepper

⅓ cup olive oil, or more as needed

FOR THE ORZO AND GARNISH

½ teaspoon salt

8 ounces orzo (about 1⅓ cups)

1 tablespoon olive oil

Tomatoes, cut in quarters, or cherry tomatoes, cut in half (2 cups)

Toasted pine nuts (see Note)

Feta cheese, crumbled

Fresh basil leaves

FOR THE OLIVE DRESSING

3 tablespoons fresh lemon juice

5 tablespoons olive oil

Freshly ground black pepper

1 clove garlic, minced

2 tablespoons chopped pitted kalamata olives

① Place a rack in the center of the oven and preheat the oven to 400°F.

② Roast the vegetables: Place the yellow squash, zucchini, eggplant, bell pepper, and onion in a large mixing bowl and toss to mix. Season the vegetables with the 1 teaspoon of salt (adjust to taste) and black pepper to taste. Add enough olive oil to coat the vegetables generously (start with ⅓ cup). Spread the vegetables out on a rimmed baking sheet. Roast the vegetables until

Save Your Roasted Vegetables for Salad

Roast plenty of butternut squash, beets, carrots, and other fall and winter veggies for dinner on one night, keeping in mind leftovers for salad the next night. That's how it goes at my house. I load up the baking pan with veggies fully planning on there being leftovers.

One of the best salads I have ever eaten was at the Little Owl in New York City. I was with my editor Suzanne Rafer and the late Peter Workman and we were discussing my next book. But it was really hard for me to focus on the business at hand because the salad the waiter placed in front of me was so gorgeous and so delicious. I will never forget it. On a bed of tender Bibb lettuce leaves were cubes of roasted butternut squash and roasted thinly sliced yellow beets. There was a lemony vinaigrette. On top toasted pumpkin seeds and good grated Parmesan cheese. It was a work of art and it pleased my palate: To this day I add roasted veggies to my salads.

they are cooked through and browned around the edges, 30 to 35 minutes, turning them once with a metal spatula. Set the baking sheet with the vegetables aside to cool.

③ Meanwhile, prepare the orzo: Bring a large pot of water to a boil over high heat and add the ½ teaspoon of salt. When the water is boiling stir in the orzo. Once the

How to Make Chopped Salad Like a Steak House Restaurant

It dawned on me while sitting in an overpriced steak house that the secret to charging more money for a salad is to pack it into a small round mold and then unmold it with great flourish on a chilled white plate. The pricey salad I ordered was just chopped lettuce with a creamy dressing—you can use blue cheese, Caesar, you name it—and finely diced add-ins of cucumbers, green olives, mushrooms, crisp bacon, croutons—the kitchen sink, really. You can prepare this for a seated dinner party by packing your salad into custard cups and refrigerating them until serving time. Unmold the salads onto plates just before serving and top them with something crunchy and wonderful like fried onion rings or something beautiful like a tiny basil leaf and quarter of a cherry tomato.

water returns to a boil, cook the orzo until al dente, 7 to 8 minutes. Drain the orzo, toss it with the 1 tablespoon of olive oil, and transfer the orzo to a large serving bowl.

4. Make the olive dressing: Place the lemon juice in a small bowl and whisk in the 5 tablespoons of olive oil until smooth. Season the dressing with black pepper to taste and stir in the garlic and olives.

5. Top the orzo with the roasted vegetables and the tomatoes, toasted pine nuts, feta cheese, and basil leaves. Dress the salad and serve at once or let it sit at room temperature, without the dressing, for up to 3 hours. Add the dressing right before serving.

To toast the pine nuts place them in a cast-iron skillet over medium-low heat and cook them just until they take on a little brown color, 3 to 4 minutes.

You can make the orzo salad up to 2 days ahead. Add the dressing and refrigerate it, covered. You will need a little extra dressing to toss with the salad as it comes back to room temperature before serving.

Joy's Kale and Brussels Sprouts Salad

SERVES: 8
PREP: 30 TO 35 MINUTES

When my husband celebrated a milestone birthday one year, I decided to throw a party on a Tuesday night. His birthday falls a week before Christmas, so it's a hectic but festive time. I relied on friends R.B. and Mindy to cook fillets over a wood fire, and my friend Joy said she would bring her kale salad. I took Joy up on her offer, happy to have the salad checked off my list. I'll admit I was hesitant at first about a kale salad but now this seems ridiculous because kale salads are among my favorites. This salad recipe was a winner with everyone—even my daughter Kathleen, who has adopted it as her own salad to bring to parties. Joy has made some tweaks to that first recipe, as have we. The beauty of this salad is that all of it can be done the morning of a party. You make the dressing and prep the kale and brussels sprouts, but keep all the ingredients separate until serving. Leftovers are fantastic for lunch the next day.

FOR THE DRESSING

2 tablespoons fresh lemon juice

1 tablespoon Dijon mustard

1 tablespoon minced shallot

1 small clove garlic, minced

⅓ cup olive oil

Salt and freshly ground black pepper

FOR THE SALAD

1 bag (12 ounces) kale (Tuscan or curly kale), rinsed and dried

10 to 12 ounces brussels sprouts (see Notes), rinsed and drained

½ cup almonds with skins (see Note), chopped

1 cup grated pecorino romano or Parmigiano-Reggiano cheese

1. Make the dressing: Place the lemon juice and mustard in a medium-size bowl and whisk to combine. Stir in the shallot and garlic. Set aside 1 tablespoon of the olive oil to toast the almonds, then whisk the remaining oil into the lemon mixture until thickened. Season the dressing with salt and pepper to taste and set it aside.

2. Make the salad: Remove and discard the center stems of the kale. Stack the leaves on top of each other and slice them thinly crosswise to create what is called a chiffonade. (If you are pressed for time, remove the center stems but chop the leaves in the food processor, pulsing the machine on and off until the pieces of kale are the size you want.) Place the kale in a large serving bowl.

3. Cut the stem ends off the brussels sprouts and, using a sharp knife, cut them in half lengthwise and then thinly slice the halves crosswise. Place the brussels sprouts in the bowl with the kale and toss to combine.

4. Place the reserved 1 tablespoon of olive oil in a medium-size skillet over medium heat. Add the almonds and cook, stirring, until they begin to take on color, about 2 minutes. Remove the almonds from the heat and let them cool.

5. To serve, toss the kale and brussels sprout mixture with the dressing. Sprinkle the cheese over the top and toss to combine it well. Sprinkle the almonds over the top of the salad and serve.

SAVE THE DAY NOTE I don't make as much dressing as the original recipe called for because there was always dressing left over. If you like a lot of dressing, double the amounts called for here. My friend Kren Teren also makes this salad and looks for already shredded brussels sprouts at Trader Joe's stores to save time. And instead of using almonds, she will often use pine nuts.

Do Ahead Please do make this salad ahead as the kale softens once it has been dressed with the olive oil and lemon juice dressing.

MONEY SAVER: It is cheaper to buy loose kale than to buy the plastic bags of rinsed kale leaves. Choose the smallest loose leaves and rinse them well, then pat them dry with paper towels. Remove the tough stems and proceed with the recipe.

White Bean Salad with Fresh Herb Vinaigrette

SERVES: 4
SOAK: 20 MINUTES
COOK: 1¾ HOURS
COOL: 20 MINUTES

When my children were young they would help me in the garden. At the time I wasn't enough of a tiger mom to plan the long-term positive effects of farming on their SAT scores. It was just to keep them occupied—busy—while I enjoyed a few peaceful moments playing in the dirt myself. We mostly grew herbs because our yard didn't get enough sun for tomatoes. And herbs are forgiving: They grow anywhere, need water infrequently, and can adapt if they get pulled by little hands. And without the fresh thyme and parsley this salad would be just a bowl of beans. Add the quick reduction of lemon juice and white wine that is poured on top and the fast sauté of scallions, red bell pepper, and tomatoes and you have a spectacular salad for a picnic or just weekend burgers at home. Add vegetable broth instead of chicken and you have a spectacular vegetarian recipe. Add grilled shrimp, and you have a feast.

8 ounces dried great northern beans (about 1¾ cups)

Boiling water, for soaking the beans

1 small onion

1 carrot

1 rib celery

1 clove garlic

3 tablespoons olive oil

2 sprigs fresh flat-leaf parsley, plus 1 heaping tablespoon chopped fresh flat-leaf parsley

1 bay leaf

2 cups chicken broth or vegetable broth

4 scallions, both white and green parts, trimmed

½ red bell pepper

2 plum tomatoes
(for ½ heaping cup chopped)

2 tablespoons fresh lemon juice
(from 1 lemon)

¼ cup dry white wine

Salt and freshly ground black pepper

2 tablespoons fresh thyme leaves

Thyme and parsley sprigs,
for garnish

1. Place the beans in a large heatproof bowl. Pour boiling water over the beans to cover and let them soak until all the water is absorbed, about 20 minutes.

2. While the beans are soaking, peel and quarter the onion. Chop the carrot and celery and mince the garlic.

3. Heat 2 tablespoons of the olive oil in a large pot over medium heat. Add the onion, carrot, celery, and garlic and cook, stirring, until the onion is soft, 4 to 5 minutes. Add the parsley sprigs, bay leaf, and chicken broth. Drain off any water from the beans and add them to the pot. Add enough fresh water to cover the beans, if necessary. Let come to a boil, reduce the heat to low, cover the pot, and let the beans simmer until tender, 1 to 1½ hours.

4. While the beans are cooking, chop the scallions, bell pepper, and tomatoes.

5. Remove the pot of beans from the heat and remove and discard the parsley sprigs and bay leaf. Drain the beans over a medium-size bowl, then return the cooking liquid to the pot. Let the cooking liquid boil over high heat until it is reduced to about ½ cup, 15 to 20 minutes. Squeeze the juice from the lemon into the pot and add the white wine. Season with salt and black pepper to taste and the thyme leaves. Pour this liquid over the beans, let cool for 20 minutes, then refrigerate the beans.

6. Add the remaining 1 tablespoon of olive oil to the pot used for cooking the beans and heat over medium heat. Add the scallions, bell pepper, and tomatoes. Cook, stirring, until the bell pepper is soft, 3 to 4 minutes. Remove the beans from the refrigerator and fold the scallion mixture into the beans. Season the beans with salt and black pepper to taste and serve garnished with thyme and parsley sprigs.

Do Ahead The bean salad can be made a day in advance and refrigerated, covered, but remove it from the refrigerator an hour before serving so it can return to room temperature.

I'd serve it with . . . anything.

Beth's Autumn Salad with Maple Vinaigrette

SERVES: 8
PREP: 25 MINUTES

Help! My salad is boring! That's what happens when you fall back on bagged salad greens and bottled dressing. Go the extra stride and make a quick dressing, toast your pecans, and chop an apple. This salad from my friend Beth Meador is the answer to what to serve during autumn and into the winter holidays. Tote it to potlucks and parties, and serve it to your family on weeknights if they're nice to you.

FOR THE MAPLE VINAIGRETTE

¼ cup apple cider vinegar

2 tablespoons fresh lemon juice

1 tablespoon pure maple syrup

2 tablespoons minced shallots

¼ teaspoon salt

¼ teaspoon freshly ground black pepper

½ cup vegetable oil

FOR THE SALAD

8 cups packaged spring mix lettuce (6 to 8 ounce package), prewashed

2 medium-size apples

¾ cup Sweet Roasted Orange Pecans (recipe follows)

¾ cup crumbled blue cheese

1. Make the maple vinaigrette: Place the cider vinegar, lemon juice, and maple syrup in a medium-size bowl and whisk to combine. Fold in the shallots, salt, and pepper. Whisk in the vegetable oil in a steady stream until the vinaigrette thickens. Set the vinaigrette aside.

★★ ★ RAZZLE-DAZZLE
★ Use a pear along with an apple. Add roasted cubes of butternut squash. Toast walnuts instead of pecans. Add dried cranberries.

2. Make the salad: Place the lettuce mix in a large serving bowl. Cover it with a damp paper towel and refrigerate it until needed.

3. When you are ready to serve, remove the bowl of lettuce mix from the refrigerator. Core and chop the apples and scatter the pieces on top of the lettuce mix. Add the pecans and the blue cheese. Spoon just enough maple vinaigrette over the top to coat the greens lightly when tossed. (You can always add more vinaigrette, but you cannot take it away, so begin with a light hand.) Serve any extra vinaigrette on the side.

Do Ahead Make the salad up to 3 hours ahead. You can even chop the apples ahead of time, but toss them with a little lemon juice to keep them from darkening. Toss the salad with the vinaigrette just before serving.

I'd serve it with . . .
roasted pork, steaks on
the grill, a fillet of beef,
marinated and grilled chicken—
just about anything.

Sweet Roasted Orange Pecans (or Walnuts)

MAKES: 2 CUPS
PREP: 10 MINUTES
BAKE: 50 TO 55 MINUTES
COOL: 30 MINUTES

I have tried all different combinations of seasonings and sugar in trying to perfect my glazed, toasted nuts used on top of salads, like Beth's Autumn Salad with Maple Vinaigrette, or just enjoyed eating out of hand. This is the easiest and the best method. You can double this recipe to cook a pound of nuts at a time, but you will need to use two baking sheets if you do, as a pound of nuts will be too crowded in one. You want the nuts to have room around them when they roast, so that they get nice and toasty.

3 tablespoons sugar

2 tablespoons (¼ stick) butter

2 tablespoons orange juice or water

¾ teaspoon salt

½ teaspoon cayenne pepper

2 cups (8 ounces) pecan or walnut halves

1. Preheat the oven to 250°F.

2. Place the sugar, butter, orange juice, salt, and cayenne pepper in a medium-

size saucepan over medium heat. Let come to a boil, stirring, until the sugar dissolves and the mixture thickens slightly, 2 to 3 minutes. Stir in the nuts. Spoon the nuts and sugar mixture onto a rimmed baking sheet and spread them out so that they are in a single layer.

③ Bake the nuts until they darken and become crisp, 50 to 55 minutes. Remove the baking sheet from the oven and let the nuts cool on it for about 30 minutes. Using a metal spatula, transfer the nuts to a metal tin or plastic bag for storing (nuts stay crisp longer in a metal tin— up to a week).

POTLUCK PERFECTION • WEEKNIGHT DINNER

Succotash Salad with Cilantro Lime Vinaigrette

SERVES: 6 TO 8
PREP: 20 MINUTES
COOK: 35 TO 40 MINUTES

White corn is the backbone of many summer salads. Sure, we enjoy it fresh, eaten right off the cob, but we also turn it into mind-blowing salads that are not only visually stunning but that capture all the flavors of summer. So what to make for the next potluck when you are completely out of ideas? This easy salad. It has a Southern vibe with the combination of the South's version of succotash—beans, corn, tomato, and bacon—but it's fresher with the lime vinaigrette and cilantro. Plus as this salad is best at room temperature, it can be made and allowed to rest on the counter for an hour or so. Add the bacon garnish just before serving so it stays crisp.

★ RAZZLE-DAZZLE

Add ½ cup rinsed and drained canned black beans to the salad and serve as a fabulous dip with Scoops! or other tortilla chips. Or, add 1 cup of cooked Israeli couscous or quinoa to turn this into a substantial main dish salad.

FOR THE CILANTRO LIME VINAIGRETTE

2 tablespoons fresh lime juice
(from 2 limes)

1 tablespoon honey

1 teaspoon hot sauce, such as Frank's
RedHot or Cholula

1 clove garlic, minced

Salt and freshly ground black pepper

⅓ cup olive oil

¼ cup chopped fresh cilantro

FOR THE SALAD AND GARNISHES

1 cup purple-hull peas, black-eyed peas,
or baby lima beans (fresh or frozen)

Salt

3 ears white corn, shucked

1 tablespoon olive oil

½ cup finely minced onion

1 cup whole cherry or grape tomatoes
cut in half

Freshly ground black pepper

Romaine or Bibb lettuce leaves
(optional), for serving

1 large avocado, cut into ½-inch cubes,
for garnish

4 slices bacon, cooked until crisp and
crumbled, for garnish

2 tablespoons chopped fresh cilantro or
flat-leaf parsley (optional), for garnish

① Make the cilantro lime vinaigrette: Place the lime juice, honey, hot sauce, and garlic in a small bowl. Season with salt and pepper to taste and whisk to combine. Whisk in the ⅓ cup of olive oil in a steady stream until the vinaigrette thickens. Fold in the ¼ cup of cilantro and set the vinaigrette aside.

② Make the salad: Place the peas or beans and a pinch of salt in a small pan and add cold water to cover. Bring to a boil over medium-high heat, then reduce the heat and let simmer until the peas or beans are cooked through, 25 to 30 minutes. Drain the peas or beans and set them aside in a large bowl.

③ While the beans are cooking, hold an ear of corn upright on a cutting board and, using a sharp knife, cut close to the cob to slice off the kernels. Repeat with the remaining ears of corn. You should have about 2 cups of corn. Set the corn aside.

④ Place the 1 tablespoon of olive oil in a large skillet over medium heat. Add the onion and cook, stirring, until it is soft, 2 to 3 minutes. Stir in the corn kernels,

reduce the heat to low, and cook until the corn is just cooked through, 3 to 4 minutes. Spoon the corn and onion mixture into the bowl with the peas. Add the tomatoes and stir gently to mix. Season the salad with salt and pepper to taste and set it aside until ready to serve.

5 When ready to serve, spoon the corn and pea mixture onto a long platter. You can line the platter with romaine or Bibb lettuce leaves if you like. Drizzle the cilantro lime vinaigrette over the salad. Garnish the salad with the avocado and bacon and the 2 tablespoons of cilantro or parsley, if desired.

Do Ahead The cilantro lime vinaigrette can be made a day in advance and refrigerated, covered. If you like hot flavors, use a small fresh hot pepper, such as a jalapeño, instead of the hot sauce. Seed and devein the pepper, then finely mince it and add it to the vinaigrette for a flavor that will grow in intensity.

MONEY SAVER: Keep frozen black-eyed peas and white corn kernels in the freezer to make this salad inexpensively any time of the year.

Spinach Salad with Apple, Almonds, and a Tart Cherry Vinaigrette

SERVES: 6 TO 8
PREP: 45 MINUTES

Book tours up to Michigan introduced me to so many recipes using the local tart cherries. Until then I had put dried cherries in breads and cookies but I had never made a vinaigrette using them. Once I tasted a dressing like this on a spinach salad I knew I had something new to carry to a potluck. This salad is pungent and rich and pronounced and downright bossy. I love it! Serve it in the fall and winter when good apples come into season. Toast the almonds so that they have a rich crunch. Add grilled chicken or salmon to turn this side salad into a feast.

FOR THE CHERRY VINAIGRETTE

½ cup dried cherries

¼ cup balsamic vinegar

1 tablespoon honey

1 teaspoon Dijon mustard

Salt and freshly ground black pepper

¼ cup olive oil

¼ cup light vegetable oil, such as safflower oil

FOR THE SPINACH SALAD

6 to 8 cups baby spinach leaves, rinsed and dried

1 large Granny Smith apple, peeled, cored, and finely chopped

2 to 3 ounces soft goat cheese

¼ cup toasted sliced almonds (see Note)

1. Make the cherry vinaigrette: Place the cherries in a small microwave-safe bowl and pour the balsamic vinegar over them. Toss to coat. Place the bowl in the microwave oven and heat on high power, until the cherries absorb most of the vinegar and plump up, about 1 minute. Remove the bowl and let the cherries sit in the vinegar for about 5 minutes.

2. Place the softened cherries and balsamic vinegar in a food processor fitted with a steel blade. Process the cherries until they are finely chopped, 15 to 20 seconds. Add the honey and mustard, season with salt and pepper to taste, and process until just combined, about 10 seconds. With the motor running, add the olive oil and then the vegetable oil in a slow and steady stream. Set the vinaigrette aside.

3. Make the spinach salad: Place the spinach in a large serving bowl. Scatter the apple pieces over the top. Drop teaspoonfuls of goat cheese on top of the apple. Scatter the toasted almonds over the salad.

4. When ready to serve, taste the cherry vinaigrette, adding more salt and/or pepper if necessary. Spoon a generous couple of tablespoons of vinaigrette on top of the spinach salad and, using salad forks, toss the salad, adding more vinaigrette if needed. The extra vinaigrette can be stored, covered, in the refrigerator. It will keep for a week and goes well with all green salads and salads topped with chicken or salmon.

SAVE THE DAY NOTE To toast the sliced almonds, spread them out on a rimmed baking sheet and bake them in a 350°F oven until lightly toasted, 2 to 3 minutes.

Do Ahead Make the vinaigrette a day ahead and refrigerate it, covered. Let the vinaigrette return to room temperature before tossing it with the salad.

★ RAZZLE-DAZZLE

When fresh cherries are in season in the summertime, stem and pit them, adding a half cup of cherry halves on top of the salad with the apple. Add strips of grilled chicken or chunks of grilled salmon. Or instead of the almonds, break apple chips over the top of the salad for crunch.

Ann's Tomato Salad with Roasted Garlic Dressing

SERVES: 6
PREP: 25 MINUTES
BAKE: 45 MINUTES
COOL: 20 MINUTES; CHILL: 30 MINUTES

When someone brings you dinner in the South you might expect a chicken casserole and fruit salad. But never would you expect a grilled fillet and a green salad with this exceptional creamy, salty, garlicky dressing. My friend Ann went way too far but we appreciated every last bite. I have made this dressing several times since and love how it works for greens as well as sliced ripe tomatoes. The recipe makes enough to dress a salad and have a little left for another day.

FOR THE ROASTED GARLIC DRESSING

1 head garlic

1 tablespoon olive oil

½ cup mayonnaise

¼ cup buttermilk

¼ cup grated Parmesan cheese

1 tablespoon fresh lemon juice (from ½ lemon)

½ teaspoon Worcestershire sauce

¼ teaspoon hot sauce, such as Tabasco or Cholula

Salt and freshly ground black pepper

FOR THE SALAD

6 to 8 Bibb lettuce leaves, rinsed and patted dry

3 to 4 large ripe tomatoes

1 tablespoon chopped fresh flat-leaf parsley (optional)

① Preheat the oven to 400°F.

② Make the roasted garlic dressing: Cut ½ inch off the top of the head of garlic so the garlic cloves are exposed. Place the garlic head on a square of aluminum foil and drizzle the olive oil over the top of the

③ Remove the foil-wrapped garlic from the oven and open up the foil so that the garlic can cool enough to handle, about 20 minutes.

④ Holding the head of garlic upside down over a medium-size bowl, squeeze out the cloves of garlic. Using a fork, mash the garlic until smooth. Add the mayonnaise, buttermilk, Parmesan cheese, lemon juice, Worcestershire sauce, and hot sauce and whisk until smooth. Season the dressing with salt and pepper to taste. Cover the bowl with plastic wrap and refrigerate the dressing for at least 30 minutes, or until serving time.

⑤ Make the salad: Arrange the lettuce leaves on a serving plate. Peel and slice the tomatoes and arrange them attractively on top of the lettuce.

⑥ When ready to serve, lightly drizzle the dressing over the tomatoes. Garnish the salad with the chopped parsley, if desired. Serve more dressing on the side. Any leftover dressing can be refrigerated, covered, for up to 5 days.

garlic. Pull the sides of the foil up around the garlic to encase it. Place the foil-wrapped garlic on the oven rack and bake the garlic until tender, about 45 minutes.

★ ★ ★
★ RAZZLE-DAZZLE

Choose the best tomatoes you can find. The salad is especially beautiful made with red, yellow, and Green Zebra tomatoes, arranged interchangeably. You can also add cherry tomatoes for variety.

Do Ahead Make the dressing up to 5 days in advance and keep it in the refrigerator.

Watermelon, Arugula, and Cucumber Salad with Lime Vinaigrette

SERVES: 6
PREP: 35 MINUTES

We grew watermelon in our garden this past summer for the very first time. It was pretty wonderful watching those baby melons grow from the size of a tennis ball to a soccer ball and larger. I felt sort of maternal about them and had a hard time slicing into them and actually eating them. And while our summer here was unusually rainy and cool—not the perfect melon-growing conditions—the melons were still pretty darned good. And if one wasn't sweet enough to eat out of hand, no worries, as I sliced and served it in a salad. This salad saved my day this summer as it was the perfect vehicle for using excess watermelon, plus it was bright in color and cool and quenching to the hot weather palate.

Lime vinaigrette (see Step 1)

4 cups arugula

2 cups watermelon balls (see Note)

⅓ cup thinly sliced cucumber (see Note)

¼ cup (about 2 ounces) crumbled feta cheese, or more to taste

2 tablespoons toasted pine nuts (see Do Ahead)

① Make the lime vinaigrette found in the Succotash Salad with Cilantro Lime Vinaigrette recipe on page 107, omitting the cilantro, if desired. You can substitute an equal amount of chopped fresh flat-leaf parsley or chives instead.

② Place the arugula on a long serving platter. Scatter the watermelon balls across the top, interspersed with cucumber slices. Shower the top of the salad with feta cheese, adding more than ¼ cup if you like feta.

③ Drizzle ¼ cup of the lime vinaigrette over the top of the salad. Add a couple of tablespoons more if you are feeling generous. Top the salad with the toasted pine nuts and serve.

SAVE THE DAY NOTE To make perfect balls from watermelon and other melons, buy a melon baller tool at a cookware store. The best cucumbers for this salad are freshly grown. If you don't have a tender fresh cucumber, buy a plastic-wrapped European cucumber. Remove the plastic, rinse the cucumber, and slice it very thinly, leaving the skin on. If you can only find a regular supermarket cucumber, peel off the skin.

Do Ahead Make the lime vinaigrette a day ahead. To toast the pine nuts, spread them out on a rimmed baking sheet and toast them in a 350°F oven until they turn golden, 5 to 6 minutes. (To toast pine nuts in a skillet, see page 94.) Let the pine nuts cool to room temperature for a few hours. Place them in a plastic bag if you're keeping them overnight.

★ RAZZLE-DAZZLE

Stack the salad into towers for easy summer entertaining. Slice the watermelon into 3-inch squares. Buy a block of feta instead of crumbled feta and cut it into ¼-inch-thick slices that are about the same size as the watermelon squares. Place a square of watermelon on a plate. Top it with a slice of feta, arugula leaves, cucumber slices, and some of the vinaigrette followed by another slice of feta, some arugula and cucumber slices, some of the vinaigrette, and another slice of watermelon. Top the stack with a little more vinaigrette and the pine nuts. Make as many stacks as there are diners. Delish!

Libby's Avocado and Pink Grapefruit Salad

SERVES: 6 TO 8
PREP: 30 MINUTES

Libby Patterson remembers a jar of her mother's sweet vinaigrette always being in the refrigerator at home in Mobile, Alabama. It was the go-to dressing for all salads, the way her mother was able to transform avocado, grapefruit, and lettuce within minutes into a masterful arrangement of vivid greens and pale pinks, tangy vinegar and sweet fruit. Libby follows in her mom's footsteps, keeping the vinaigrette on hand for impromptu dinner parties. And when my family traveled to Chattanooga for Thanksgiving dinner and I was asked to bring a salad, I took the cue from Libby. I packed a jar of vinaigrette, two ripe avocados, one fat pink grapefruit, a ripe mango, and rinsed lettuce leaves. While everyone else fussed over casseroles in the oven and frantically whisked lumps out of the gravy, I easily assembled this elegant salad on a long white platter. It was bright, fun, and refreshing. Plus, we had plenty of vinaigrette to stash in the refrigerator for future salads—green, fruit, or a combination of both.

FOR THE VINAIGRETTE

½ cup plus 2 teaspoons apple cider vinegar

½ cup sugar

2 teaspoons salt

½ teaspoon freshly ground black pepper

¾ cup vegetable oil

1 clove garlic (optional), peeled and cut in half

FOR THE SALAD

1 medium-size head Boston or Bibb lettuce

1 large pink grapefruit

1 large ripe mango

2 ripe medium-size Hass avocados

1. Make the vinaigrette: Place the cider vinegar, sugar, salt, and pepper in a mixing bowl and whisk to combine. Add the vegetable oil a little at a time, whisking to combine. Add the garlic, if using, to the vinaigrette. Set aside. Discard the garlic before serving.

2. Make the salad: Rinse the lettuce under cold running water and gently pull the leaves from the stem. Place the lettuce leaves on a tea towel lined with paper towels. Cover the rinsed leaves with more paper towels and gently roll up the lettuce to let it dry, placing it in the refrigerator. Or use a salad spinner, rinsing the lettuce leaves and then placing them between layers of paper towels and refrigerating them while you prepare the fruit.

3. Peel the grapefruit and separate it into sections. Remove and discard the membranes from the grapefruit sections, using a small paring knife to cut off the ends of the membranes. You will have 10 to 12 sections per grapefruit. Set these aside.

4. Using a small paring knife, peel the mango. Place the mango on a cutting board. The wide flat pit is in the center of the mango, so cut the flesh off the pit in as large chunks as possible. Place each chunk on the cutting board and slice it into pieces that are about ⅓ inch thick. Set these aside.

5. Peel the avocados and, using a small paring knife, cut them in half and remove the pits. Place each avocado half cut side down on a cutting board and slice it into ¼-inch-thick lengthwise slices. You will have 8 to 12 slices per avocado. Set these aside.

6. To assemble the salad, line a platter with the reserved lettuce leaves. Arrange the avocado slices on one third of the platter, then the grapefruit slices on the second third, and then the mango slices on the remaining third. When ready to serve, discard the garlic, drizzle ¼ to ⅓ cup of the vinaigrette over the fruit and lettuce, and serve the remaining vinaigrette on the side.

★ RAZZLE-DAZZLE

Turn this into a festive holiday salad by omitting the mango and adding a handful of fresh pomegranate seeds to the top of the salad, as shown in the photo on the facing page.

I'd serve it with . . .
grilled steaks, fish, or chicken.
Add a baked potato or basmati rice.

Do Ahead You can make the vinaigrette 2 or 3 days in advance and refrigerate it, covered.

If you are not going to serve the salad at once, drizzle a little of the vinaigrette over the avocados to keep them from darkening and wrap the platter with plastic wrap. The salad can be refrigerated for up to 1 hour.

MONEY SAVER: Making your own salad dressing is less expensive per ounce than buying salad dressing at the store. To save money on the fruit, use what is local and in season. In the winter, choose citrus and pears. In the spring, look for fresh strawberries and specials on avocados coming into the market. In the summer, the sky is the limit, so use ripe peaches and mango, fresh blackberries and blueberries, and melons such as cantaloupe and watermelon.

STOCK THE FRIDGE · HOLIDAY IDEAS

Virginia's Cranberry Relish

MAKES: ABOUT 8 CUPS
PREP: 30 MINUTES
CHILL: OVERNIGHT (optional)

Many years ago Virginia Routon, a sweet lady in Paris, Tennessee, shared a cranberry relish recipe with me. It was her signature cranberry relish to serve at the holidays with turkey and ham. And what made the recipe unique was that it included not only fresh cranberries but also pears, apples, and oranges. The crunchy flavor of this recipe goes perfectly with that turkey or ham, but I love it the day after Thanksgiving, when it is spread onto turkey sandwiches.

1 pound fresh cranberries

1 can (8 ounces) crushed pineapple in juice, undrained

1 cup chopped pecans (optional)

1½ cups sugar (see Note)

2 thin-skinned oranges

2 medium-size apples

2 ripe pears

① Get out a meat grinder or fit a food processor with a steel blade. Grind the cranberries or place them in the food processor and pulse it 9 or 10 times. Place the ground cranberries in a medium-size bowl.

② Dump the pineapple with its liquid on top of the ground cranberries. Add the pecans, if using. Add the sugar to the bowl with the cranberries.

③ Cut the skin off 1 orange. Grate the skin of the second orange into the bowl with the cranberries. Cut both oranges in half. Remove the seeds and the core. Chop the oranges into small pieces and toss them in a separate bowl.

④ Core the apples but leave them unpeeled. Cut the apples into a fine dice and put them in the bowl with the oranges.

⑤ Core the pears but leave them unpeeled. Cut the pears into a fine dice and add them to the bowl with the oranges and apples.

⑥ Stir the cranberry mixture to combine. Fold in the oranges, apples, and pears, and stir gently until most of the sugar has dissolved. Cover the bowl with plastic wrap and refrigerate the relish until serving time.

Do Ahead Make the cranberry relish a day ahead. It tastes better made in advance.

SAVE THE DAY NOTE The original recipe calls for 2¾ cups sugar. I like 1½ cups and think that is plenty of sugar, but taste for yourself. How much sugar you need to sweeten the relish really depends on how sweet the oranges are.

LIFESAVER LASAGNA

ANN'S FRESH TOMATO PIE

BROWN SUGAR & BOURBON SALMON

CLASSIC OSSO BUCO

SHRIMP & CHEESE GRITS

CHAPTER 5

MAIN COURSES

Why do we fuss so much over the main dish? It anchors the meal, sets the tone, provides a focal point, and gives people something to talk about, that's why. Whether it is a roast, steak, chop, chicken, casserole, pasta, or pie, the main is the main for a good reason. And knowing what main dish to serve can really make cooking easier.

How does a main dish save our day? One way is when it's a do-ahead we can assemble it the night before or early in the morning and not bother about it for the rest of the day. Examples in this chapter include Easy Korean Chicken and Lecia's Lamb Chops.

Mains can also cook on their own without needing us to fuss over them. These would be Roasted Sticky Chicken that cooks slowly for five hours, Laurie Nicholson's Party Beef, Ina's Sweet-and-Sour Brisket, and Courtnay's Crock-Pot Ribs.

But when we're not that organized, when we don't have a plan, fast-to-fix mains come to the rescue. Look to Ann's Fresh Tomato Pie, Kathleen's Chicken and Dressing, Lou Ann's Salmon Croquettes, Brown Sugar and Bourbon Salmon, and Shrimp and Cheese Grits.

Mains like Adam's Linguine with Asparagus Pesto and Lifesaver Lasagna appeal to the unexpected, making dinner fun for everyone to enjoy. And main dishes that establish a tradition to be repeated each year bring peace of mind. For many years I cooked fresh lobster on New Year's Eve, just as Barb Ellis cooks her big fat pork chops on Christmas Day and Shirley Hutson roasts a leg of lamb on Easter Sundays.

This chapter is full of ideas that come from what people serve as their save-the-day mains. Try the recipes on your family. I hope they'll come to your rescue.

Gimme 5 Ideas, or How to Cook . . .

EGGS: Make omelets, frittatas with leftover veggies, and quiches. Or bake eggs in tomato sauce. And there's always French toast.

GROUND BEEF OR TURKEY: Start with 1 pound and then grill burgers, make meat loaf, brown the meat and season it for tacos, make chili, or simmer it in a spaghetti sauce.

BONELESS CHICKEN BREASTS: Dice the chicken breasts and add them to chicken broth along with sliced carrots and cooked noodles or rice; smash them until flat and sauté them with Italian seasonings in olive oil; or cook them in a slow cooker with taco seasonings for 3 hours and then shred them for burritos. Bake the chicken breasts with mushrooms and rice or marinate them in Indian seasonings and grill them.

SALMON: Steam salmon with lemon slices; bake it in a hot oven with soy sauce and honey; grill it with Cajun seasonings; poach and flake it into pasta; turn any leftover salmon into salmon cakes.

FROZEN SPINACH: Add thawed spinach to white bean soup or beef and pasta casseroles; stir it into a cream sauce with Parmesan cheese; bake spinach in a cream sauce with artichoke hearts; add it to omelets along with sliced sautéed mushrooms.

Ann's Fresh Tomato Pie

SERVES: 6
PREP: 20 MINUTES
BAKE: 30 MINUTES, PLUS 5 MINUTES COOLING TIME

Ann Evers remembers being home with a new baby and how hard it seemed just to get dinner on the table. And then her friend Cindy arrived with this tomato pie, which saved her day. Ann has consistently prepared this pie through the years for her husband, Gary, and herself, their son Clem, and for others. Why? It is easy to prep in the morning and bake when she gets home from work, tastes great even when made with supermarket tomatoes, and makes a nice meal with a salad or vegetable side.

1 pie crust (9 inches), thawed if frozen

3 to 4 ripe tomatoes (for 2 cups sliced)

½ cup mayonnaise

2 tablespoons chopped fresh basil

2 tablespoons chopped fresh chives

1 cup (4 ounces) shredded sharp cheddar cheese

½ cup (2 ounces) grated Parmesan cheese

Salt and freshly ground black pepper

(1) Place a rack in the center of the oven and preheat the oven to 400°F.

(2) Place the pie crust in a 9-inch pie pan, pressing it into the pan, folding over or cutting off any excess crust. Using a fork, prick the bottom of the crust a few times, then bake the crust until very lightly browned, 7 to 8 minutes.

(3) Meanwhile, peel and slice the tomatoes ¼ inch thick. Drain the tomato slices on paper towels and set them aside.

★
★ ★
★ RAZZLE-DAZZLE
For even more basil flavor, drop little dollops of pesto on top of the tart just before baking. You'll find a recipe for pesto on page 35 or use store-bought.

Oven-Roasting Tomatoes

This is a no-brainer for summer months when tomatoes are in peak season. But oven roasting is also handy in the wintertime when you can use hydroponically grown tomatoes.

Slice plum tomatoes in half lengthwise. Remove the cores. Place the tomato halves on a baking sheet cut side up and add a pinch of sugar and a sprinkling of salt and ground black pepper to each half. Drizzle olive oil and balsamic vinegar over the tomatoes. Add a sprinkling of dried herbs such as oregano and basil. Bake the tomatoes at 275°F until they have lost most of their moisture, 2½ to 3 hours. Transfer the tomato halves to a rack to cool.

Use the roasted tomatoes as a topping for homemade pizzas, in sandwiches, and on grilled chicken and fish. Toss the tomatoes with cooked pastas like orzo or fold them in roasted brussels sprouts or sautéed zucchini along with a little fresh (soft) goat cheese. Toss leftover tomatoes with olive oil and store, covered, in the fridge for up to a week. Bring to room temperature before using in recipes.

④ Place the mayonnaise in a bowl and stir in the basil, chives, and cheddar and Parmesan cheeses. Season the mayonnaise mixture with a little salt and pepper.

⑤ Let the browned pie crust cool on a wire rack for about 15 minutes. Leave the oven on. Place the drained tomato slices in the bottom of the pie crust. Spread the cheese and mayonnaise mixture over the top. Place the tomato pie back in the oven to bake until golden, 18 to 22 minutes. Let the pie cool for about 5 minutes, then slice and serve.

Do Ahead The ingredients can be prepped in the morning, covered, and stored in the refrigerator. Assemble and bake the pie when you get home.

I'd serve it with . . . a green salad.

Janet's Church Lady Casserole

SERVES: 8 TO 10
PREP: 10 TO 15 MINUTES
BAKE: 45 TO 55 MINUTES

My husband's Aunt Janet has a holiday ritual of asking our family to her home for brunch the morning after Thanksgiving. She is warm and gracious and sets an arrival time that suits everyone, important when you've got teenagers who want to sleep in. Every year she's got some delicious brunchy casserole she serves along with ham or corned beef, and I am always amazed she call pull this off the day after Thanksgiving. The year she served this casserole—temptingly puffy and golden brown—I begged for the recipe. Janet shrugged modestly at my request. "It's not much," she offered, "just church lady casserole." And the name stuck. "People tell me that church ladies make this casserole all the time."

2 containers (16 ounces each; 4 cups total) cottage cheese

6 large eggs

8 tablespoons (1 stick) unsalted butter, melted

6 tablespoons all-purpose flour

8 ounces Velveeta cheese, cut into 1-inch cubes

About ¼ teaspoon salt

About ¼ teaspoon freshly ground black pepper

I'd serve it with . . .
fresh fruit and a green salad, slices of ham and bacon.

① Place a rack in the center of the oven and preheat the oven to 300°F.

② Place the cottage cheese in a large mixing bowl and add the eggs. Blend using an electric mixer on low speed or with a wooden spoon until the eggs are incorporated. Add the melted butter, flour, and Velveeta cubes, stirring until just combined. Season with salt and pepper to taste. Pour the cottage cheese mixture into a 13-by-9-inch glass baking dish.

③ Bake the casserole until it is golden brown and puffy, 45 to 55 minutes. Spoon it onto plates and serve at once.

Do Ahead You can assemble the casserole the day before, cover it with plastic wrap, and refrigerate it overnight. Bake the casserole directly from the refrigerator, uncovered, for 5 to 10 minutes longer than the time in the recipe.

★
★ ★
★ RAZZLE-DAZZLE

Add 1 cup of diced ham or crumbled cooked sausage to the cottage cheese mixture before baking. Or, try making it with the Mexican-seasoned Velveeta.

Shellie's Spaghetti Carbonara

SERVES: 4
PREP: 15 TO 20 MINUTES
COOK: 15 TO 20 MINUTES

My high school friend Shellie Unger is a fabulous cook. I remember her mother growing fresh herbs and preserving fruit in brandy during those stodgy casserole years of the South when few cooks prepared food that was out of the ordinary. Shellie took her mother's creativity in the kitchen and added her own flourishes along with the practicality that comes from working for years as an executive for a huge mutual fund group, raising two children, and traveling with her family. Shellie says the recipe that her kids request when they come home to Pennsylvania to visit or that she turns to when she needs to impress friends quickly is her spaghetti carbonara. She studied Mario Batali's recipe, then Ruth Reichl's recipe, and then perfected her own. On a trip to London she and her son Trey ordered this as a brunch appetizer and it included baby peas, so now she adds peas. Shellie says this recipe originated in the coal mining region of Italy. She adds with a smile, "What could be better than bacon and eggs with pasta, Italian style?" I agree, wholeheartedly.

2 tablespoons salt

2 tablespoons olive oil or butter, or a combination of the two

6 to 8 ounces pancetta (see Note), chopped

2 cloves garlic, peeled

1 pound spaghetti

4 large eggs, at room temperature

1¼ cups grated good Parmesan cheese (Parmigiano-Reggiano or Grana Padano)

Freshly ground black pepper

½ to ¾ cup frozen baby peas, thawed

I'd serve it with . . .
steamed spinach or
broccolini.

① Bring a large pot of water to a boil over high heat and add the salt.

② Meanwhile, place the olive oil or butter, pancetta, and garlic in a large skillet over medium-high heat and cook until the pancetta renders its fat but is not crisp, 3 to 4 minutes. Remove the skillet from the heat and discard the garlic cloves. Do not drain the fat from the skillet.

③ When the water is boiling, add the spaghetti and stir to separate the pasta strands. Reduce the heat to medium and let the spaghetti cook at a simmer until al dente, 6 to 7 minutes.

④ While the spaghetti cooks, break the eggs into a large shallow serving bowl and whisk until the yolks and whites are just combined. Add 1 cup of the Parmesan cheese, the cooled pancetta and drippings, and a generous grinding of pepper.

⑤ When the spaghetti has cooked, drain it, setting aside ¼ cup of the pasta cooking water, and add the spaghetti to the bowl with the egg mixture. Toss the spaghetti until the egg sauce cooks and the pasta is well coated. Add enough of the reserved pasta water as needed so the strands of spaghetti do not stick together. Fold in the peas.

⑥ Serve the spaghetti at once with the remaining ¼ cup of Parmesan on the side for sprinkling on top.

SAVE THE DAY NOTE Pancetta is Italian bacon, and you can find it at delis that specialize in Italian ingredients.

Do Ahead While this is a last-minute recipe, you can pre-chop the pancetta and place it back in the fridge, peel the garlic cloves, thaw the peas, and grate the Parmesan. If you want to reheat leftovers, save a little extra pasta cooking water to pour over the top.

MONEY SAVER: Omit the pancetta and use thick-sliced bacon.

Adam's Linguine with Asparagus Pesto

SERVES: 4
PREP: 20 TO 25 MINUTES

When it comes to cooking for friends and family, Adam Deixel, who lives in Brooklyn, New York, likes to serve something different. So he makes pesto with fresh springtime asparagus. While the usual add-ins are present—the pine nuts, Parmesan, garlic, and olive oil—Adam forgoes the basil and lets the clean taste of asparagus shine through. This is a lovely pesto, at home on penne as a side dish or tossed with linguine or *bucatini* as a main. And there are many twists and turns you can take to make this your own. For example, Adam often uses toasted walnuts instead of pine nuts. Or you can steam more asparagus tips to toss with the pesto and pasta for a dressier look. The recipe was originally from epicurious.com, but Adam has added his creative touches. At the end of the day, even with the step of steaming the asparagus, the sauce is quick, easy, and unusual. Serve it not only with pasta but with grilled salmon any time of the year.

Salt

Ice cubes

1 pound fresh asparagus (see Note), rinsed

2 cloves garlic, peeled

¼ cup pine nuts or walnuts (optional; see Note)

Freshly ground black pepper

¼ cup grated good Parmesan cheese (Parmigiano-Reggiano) or Grana Padano, plus ¼ to ½ cup grated Parmesan, for serving

⅓ to ½ cup olive oil (see Note), plus olive oil for the pasta

1 pound linguine or the pasta of your choice

1. Fill a large pot about half full with water. Add salt to taste. Let the water come to a boil over high heat.

2. Meanwhile, fill a large bowl half full with water and add a handful of ice cubes. Set it aside. You will use this to refresh the asparagus.

3. Snap the woody stems off the bottoms of the asparagus stalks. Cut the asparagus into 2-inch pieces, setting the tips aside from the stalks. Place a steamer that fits the large pot over the boiling water. Add the stalks and let them steam, covered, until bright green and just tender, about 4 minutes.

Add the asparagus tips to steam for about 1 minute. Immediately plunge the cooked asparagus in the bowl of ice water to stop the cooking and refresh them for about 30 seconds, then transfer the asparagus to paper towels to drain for 3 to 4 minutes. Set the large pot of water aside.

4. Place the garlic in a food processor and pulse 4 or 5 times to mince. Removing the top for each addition, add the pine nuts, if using. Season with a dash each of salt and pepper to taste and pulse 3 times. Add the asparagus pieces and pulse 7 or 8 times until coarsely chopped. Add the ¼ cup of Parmesan cheese and pulse 2 or 3 times. With the motor running (and the top on), pour ⅓ cup of the olive oil into the feed tube and process until the pesto is smooth. If you want a smoother pesto, add more olive oil. Set the asparagus pesto aside.

5. Bring the pot of water back to a boil, add the linguine to the pot, and stir to separate the pasta strands. Cook the linguine until al dente, 8 to 9 minutes, or following the suggested cooking time on the package. Drain the linguine, setting aside ½ cup of the pasta cooking water, and toss the linguine with a little olive oil.

⑥ When ready to serve, you can either top the linguine with the asparagus pesto and some Parmesan cheese or you can toss the cooked pasta with the pesto and add a little of the reserved pasta cooking water to smooth out the sauce. Sprinkle the linguine with Parmesan cheese and season it with salt and pepper to taste.

SAVE THE DAY NOTE
Do not begin with less than a pound of asparagus. Snapping off the woody ends loses 2 to 3 ounces of asparagus. If you want to include asparagus tips as an add-in, buy another quarter pound of asparagus just for the tips and cook as described in Step 3 or the box on the facing page. Add the tips to the linguine before sprinkling with cheese.

For a fuller flavor from the pine nuts or walnuts, toast them. Spread them out on a rimmed baking sheet and bake them in a 350°F oven until golden brown, for 4 to 5 minutes. If you want a pristine green color, omit the nuts. You can add as much or as little oil to this pesto as you desire.

Do Ahead
Steam the asparagus ahead of time, let dry, and set aside in the kitchen for a couple of hours. The pesto will keep for 3 days, covered, in the refrigerator.

★
 ★ ★
★ **RAZZLE-DAZZLE**

Make asparagus pesto primavera: Buy an extra 4 ounces of asparagus and steam the tips separately from the stems until bright green, about 1 minute. Refresh in ice water for 1 minute, then drain and set aside. Cook ½ cup fresh or frozen peas until just done. Make the pesto. Cook a pound of your favorite pasta. Toss the drained and warm pasta with the pesto, peas, and asparagus tips. Season with salt and pepper. Sprinkle with grated Parmesan cheese.

Nonna's Mostaccioli

SERVES: 10 TO 12
PREP: 1 HOUR, 15 MINUTES
BAKE: 50 TO 55 MINUTES

Italian cooks are blessed with recipes handed from generation to generation. They seldom hesitate as to what to serve for a family get-together because they serve what their mother served. Such is the case with Leslie Powers Degalan of Grand Rapids, Michigan, whose go-to recipe is the rich and cheesy Nonna's Mostaccioli. Nonna is her mother, Bice, who was born in the small Italian mountain town of Rignano Garganico in Puglia. Bice was skiing in Italy in the early 1950s and met and fell in love with an American accountant with the U.S. foreign service. She married him and moved to Grosse Pointe Woods, where she raised three daughters on the dishes—such as this one—of her native Italy. After her mother died, Leslie assumed the tradition of making mostaccioli, but she makes it for special occasions when she needs that one great dish. The recipe is named for the shape of the pasta. Called mostaccioli, it is a penne with slant-cut edges and either a smooth or ridged surface. The latter version is perfect for holding the sauce, which is important. If you cannot find it at your supermarket or an Italian market, you can use penne.

FOR THE PASTA SAUCE

3 cans (28 ounces each) crushed Italian plum tomatoes

8 tablespoons (1 stick) butter

2 beef bouillon cubes

1 tablespoon sugar

1 to 2 tablespoons olive oil, to taste

1 cup finely chopped onion

2 cups fresh basil leaves

FOR THE MOSTACCIOLI

1 pound mostaccioli or penne pasta

½ cup (2 ounces) grated Parmesan cheese, plus grated Parmesan cheese, for serving

4 ounces prosciutto, chopped
(about ⅔ cup)

4 to 6 eggs, hard cooked and sliced
¼ to ½ inch thick

1 pound fresh mozzarella cheese,
cut into 1-inch cubes

1. Make the pasta sauce: Place the tomatoes, butter, bouillon cubes, sugar, olive oil, and onion in a large pot over medium-low heat. Cook, stirring every 5 minutes, until the onion is soft. Add a few basil leaves to the sauce every time you stir. The sauce will be ready in 30 to 35 minutes. Set the sauce aside; you will have more sauce than you need for the mostaccioli.

2. Prepare the mostaccioli: Cook the pasta until al dente, about 10 minutes, or following the suggested cooking time on the package. Drain the pasta and toss it with about 3 cups of the pasta sauce until it is well coated.

3. Place a rack in the center of the oven and preheat the oven to 350°F.

4. Ladle ½ cup of the pasta sauce into a 13-by-9-inch glass baking dish to just thinly coat the bottom. Add half of the pasta mixture and sprinkle ¼ cup of the Parmesan cheese over it. Sprinkle the prosciutto and hard-cooked eggs on top. Ladle 1 cup of the sauce over the eggs and top with the mozzarella cubes, the remaining pasta, and 1 more cup of sauce. Sprinkle the remaining ¼ cup of Parmesan cheese over all.

5. Bake the mostaccioli until the cheese is bubbly and melted and the pasta has cooked through, 50 to 55 minutes. Serve the mostaccioli at once with more grated Parmesan and more sauce, if needed.

Do Ahead Make the pasta sauce the day ahead and refrigerate it. It will keep for up to 4 days. Frozen, it will keep for 4 weeks. Once the dish is assembled, you'll have about 2½ cups to serve on the side. If any is left over, it is delicious tossed with any of your favorite pastas. Boil the eggs a day ahead and refrigerate them. Peel and slice the hard-cooked eggs when you are ready to cook the mostaccioli.

I'd serve it with . . . a green salad.
But when served in the Italian fashion, this is the *primo piatto*, or first course, followed by meat, vegetables, and a green salad.

Easy Baked Ravioli Casserole

SERVES: 12 TO 16
PREP: 15 TO 20 MINUTES
BAKE: 55 MINUTES, PLUS 20 MINUTES RESTING TIME

Cooking for soup kitchens requires special recipes. They should be filling, flavorful, and contain ingredients eaten by all. That is why this casserole recipe is such a good one, plus it is a snap to prepare. So when you've offered to bring a big casserole to feed the soup kitchen or the football team, give this one a try. It is based on a recipe from St. Philip's Episcopal Church in Durham, North Carolina.

1 to 1½ pounds ground beef or turkey

1 package (10 ounces) frozen chopped spinach, thawed

Salt and freshly ground black pepper

Pinch of nutmeg (optional)

2 jars (26 ounces each) marinara sauce

¼ cup grated Parmesan cheese

1 package (20 ounces) refrigerated cheese-filled ravioli

2 cups shredded mozzarella cheese

① Place a rack in the center of the oven and preheat the oven to 350°F.

② Crumble the beef or turkey into a non-stick skillet and cook over medium heat until cooked through, 4 to 5 minutes. Drain off the excess fat. Squeeze the water out of the spinach and scatter the spinach over the meat, stirring to combine. Season the spinach mixture with salt and pepper to taste and the nutmeg, if using. Spoon half of the spinach mixture into a 13-by-9-inch glass baking dish or aluminum foil pan.

I'd serve it with . . . a green vegetable and crusty bread.

③ Pour 1 jar of pasta sauce over the spinach mixture, spreading it out evenly with a rubber spatula. Sprinkle the Parmesan cheese evenly over the sauce.

④ Transfer the ravioli to a cutting board and slice the pieces in half. Scatter the ravioli halves over the pasta sauce. Spoon the remaining spinach mixture over the ravioli halves. Pour the second jar of pasta sauce on top of the spinach mixture, spreading it out evenly. Cover the baking dish with aluminum foil.

⑤ Place the baking dish in the oven and bake the ravioli casserole until nearly cooked through and bubbly, about 45 minutes. Remove the foil, scatter the mozzarella cheese over the top, and bake until the cheese melts and the casserole has cooked through, about 10 minutes more.

⑥ Remove the ravioli casserole from the oven, let it rest, tented with aluminum foil, for about 20 minutes, then serve.

Do Ahead If you want to bake the ravioli casserole at home and transfer it to a soup kitchen or potluck, cover it with aluminum foil, wrap the entire baking dish in a clean towel, and place the casserole in a cooler, with no ice, to keep it warm in transit. You can also assemble the casserole without adding the mozzarella cheese, then cover and freeze it for up to a month. Thaw the casserole before baking it.

★
★ ★
★ RAZZLE-DAZZLE

Use Italian sausage instead of the ground beef or turkey.

★★★
★ RAZZLE-DAZZLE

You can dab spoonfuls of pesto, either homemade
(page 35) or store-bought, onto the béchamel sauce
before it goes into the oven.

Lifesaver Lasagna

SERVES: 4 TO 6
PREP: 20 MINUTES
BAKE: 40 TO 45 MINUTES, PLUS 20 MINUTES RESTING TIME

Many years ago in Nashville a fund-raiser was being held at the home of one of Nashville's best-loved and generous hostesses. It did not matter how many people needed to be fed an Italian buffet that night for in the kitchen was a woman with a wonderful plan. Attractive empty casserole dishes were lined up on the marble counters. Under her direction volunteers dutifully turned a partially thawed frozen lasagna into each dish, ladled a generous helping of warm béchamel sauce over it, covered the top with grated Parmesan cheese, then popped these lasagnas into the oven to bake. "Genius," I thought to myself. Begin with a good frozen lasagna, give it that authentic rustic flavor by covering it in homemade béchamel—the classic white sauce of butter, flour, and milk—then bake it until browned and bubbling. The lasagna did not disappoint; everyone wanted the recipe. The trick here is to make your own béchamel sauce. And for best results, use good Parmesan cheese, Parmigiano-Reggiano or Grana Padano, for topping.

1 package (38 ounces) frozen lasagna (see Note)

2 cups milk

4 tablespoons (½ stick) butter

3 tablespoons all-purpose flour

Salt and freshly ground black pepper

½ cup grated good Parmesan cheese (Parmigiano-Reggiano or Grana Padano)

I'd serve it with . . .
Joy's Kale and Brussels Sprouts Salad (page 11) and crusty bread.

1. Place the lasagna on the kitchen counter an hour before you plan to bake it or thaw it in the microwave oven following the directions on the package. Set aside a rectangular 2-quart casserole dish.

2. Preheat the oven to 350°F.

3. Place the milk in a small saucepan over medium-low heat. Let it come nearly to a boil, 4 to 5 minutes; a ring of bubbles will form around the side of the pan.

4. Meanwhile, melt the butter in a heavy medium-size saucepan over low heat. Add the flour, stirring with a wooden spoon or whisk. Cook, stirring, until the flour is well mixed but does not begin to color, about 2 minutes. Remove the pan from the heat.

5. Pour the hot milk into the flour and butter mixture, a few tablespoons at a time, stirring constantly. Repeat this until you have added about ½ cup, then pour in the rest of the milk, stirring constantly until the sauce is smooth. Place the pan back over low heat, season the béchamel sauce with salt and pepper to taste, and stir just until the sauce is thickened, 30 to 60 seconds. Remove the pan from the heat.

6. Place the thawed lasagna in the casserole dish. Pour the béchamel sauce over the lasagna. Sprinkle the Parmesan cheese over the top. Place the dish in the oven and bake the lasagna until it has cooked through and the sauce is lightly golden and bubbly, 40 to 45 minutes. Remove the dish from the oven, let the lasagna rest for about 20 minutes, then slice and serve it in wedges.

SAVE THE DAY NOTE I like to use Stouffer's family-size frozen lasagna—both the meat and meatless varieties—for this recipe. Because frozen lasagnas can be salty to some palates and because the cheese has salt in it, I tend to underseason the béchamel sauce.

Do Ahead You'll find it handy to keep frozen lasagnas at the ready. Buy them when they are on sale and store them in your freezer for up to 6 months.

Indian Silken Chicken

SERVES: 4
PREP: 15 TO 20 MINUTES
MARINATE: 10 TO 15 MINUTES
BAKE: 15 TO 20 MINUTES

My hat goes off to cookbook author Madhur Jaffrey for completely saving my day by showing me how to quickly marinate boneless chicken breasts. You know the scenerio: Coming in the door at six, with hungry children staring you in the eye, you're determined to put a fresh from-scratch meal on the table and not cave in to takeout. You've got a package of boneless chicken breasts in the fridge. My solutions: I'm either smashing those chicken breasts down to a quarter-inch thickness with a rolling pin, or quickly marinating them in lemon juice and salt and then roasting them with a fast Indian sauce. Even if you are not a fan of Indian flavors, you will love how well just lemon juice and salt can turn ordinary chicken breasts into silken perfection.

FOR THE CHICKEN

4 skinless, boneless chicken breast halves (1 to 1½ pounds total)

½ teaspoon kosher salt

2 tablespoons fresh lemon juice

FOR THE SAUCE

¼ cup heavy (whipping) cream

1 teaspoon good curry powder or garam masala

½ teaspoon ground cumin

1 large clove garlic, minced

1 teaspoon grated peeled fresh ginger (optional)

Salt and freshly ground black pepper

1 tablespoon light brown sugar

Cooked rice, for serving

1. Place a rack in the top third of the oven and preheat the oven to 450°F.

2. Prepare the chicken: Using a sharp paring knife, cut 1-inch slits all over the chicken, being careful not to cut all the way through the breasts. Place the chicken on a plate and rub the kosher salt on both sides. Sprinkle the lemon juice over the chicken and massage it into the slits. Let the chicken sit for about 5 minutes.

3. Make the sauce: Place the cream, curry powder, cumin, garlic, and ginger, if using, in a small bowl and stir to mix.

Pour the sauce mixture over the breast pieces and turn to coat them well. Let the chicken marinate for about 10 minutes.

4. Line a baking pan with aluminum foil and transfer the chicken and the sauce that clings to it to the pan. Season each chicken breast with a little salt and pepper and top it with a little brown sugar. Bake the chicken until it has cooked through, 15 to 20 minutes. Serve the chicken as is or cut it into chunks, accompanied by the rice.

I'd serve it with . . .
basmati rice, mango chutney, and steamed broccoli or peas.

Easy Korean Chicken

SERVES: 4
PREP: 10 MINUTES
MARINATE: 15 MINUTES TO 3 HOURS (optional)
BAKE: 30 TO 35 MINUTES

Boneless chicken breasts are convenient, but if you don't give them a bit of pizzazz they can be downright boring. Many years ago cookbook fan Christine McLaughlin shared this recipe with me, and I have used it ever since to spice up the weekly chicken repertoire. Talk about easy! The marinade is also the cooking sauce and the chicken marinates and bakes in the same dish. Plus, the cooking juices are delicious spooned over cooked rice. And when you're tired of chicken, try the marinade on salmon. The cooking time is shorter for salmon—ten to fifteen minutes—and the oven hotter—400°F.

4 skinless, boneless chicken breast halves (1 to 1½ pounds total)

½ cup low-sodium soy sauce

3 tablespoons Asian (dark) sesame oil

3 tablespoons honey

3 cloves garlic, minced

½ cup chopped scallions, both white and green parts

2 teaspoons grated peeled fresh ginger

① Place a rack in the center of the oven and preheat the oven to 350°F.

② Place the chicken breasts in a shallow glass baking dish. Using a sharp paring knife, cut three or four 1-inch slits in the chicken, being careful not to cut all the way through the breasts.

③ Place the soy sauce, sesame oil, honey, garlic, scallions, and ginger in a small bowl and stir to combine. Pour the marinade over the chicken and turn the breasts with a fork to coat them well. Let the chicken breasts marinate at room temperature for about 15 minutes.

④ After 15 minutes, bake the chicken at once until it is cooked through and lightly glazed to a deep mahogany brown on top, and the juices have cooked down and are bubbly, 30 to 35 minutes. Turn the chicken once as it cooks.

Do Ahead

Prepare the Korean chicken ahead and refrigerate it for up to 3 hours before cooking. Or completely cook the chicken, let it cool, cover it, and refrigerate it for up to 2 days. Reheat it, covered, in a low oven or microwave. It is also delicious cold in wraps and sliced on top of salads.

COMPANY'S COMING • RESCUING BRUNCH • SERVE TO YOUR BOOK CLUB

Chicken Ambassador

SERVES: 6
PREP: 15 MINUTES
COOK: 1 HOUR, 50 MINUTES

My mother didn't entertain ambassadors but she did whip out this recipe to serve special dinner guests. This was the party dish at our house, adapted from Nashville's first Junior League cookbook, *Nashville Seasons*, and still applicable today. In the 1960s, it was popular to baste chicken with beef consommé and sherry while it slowly baked. The only thing better than tasting the sherry-basted chicken was smelling it wafting through the house.

*6 bone-in chicken breasts
(1½ to 2 pounds)*

Seasoned salt (see Note)

Freshly ground black pepper

8 tablespoons (1 stick) butter

1 can (10½ ounces) beef consommé

½ cup medium-dry sherry or amontillado

*1 carton (8 ounces) sliced baby bella or
white mushrooms*

*1 can (about 14 ounces) plain artichoke
hearts, drained*

① Place a rack in the center of the oven and preheat the oven to 325°F.

② Rub the seasoned salt onto the chicken breasts and sprinkle them with pepper. Place the chicken breasts skin side up in a shallow roasting pan and set them aside.

③ Cut the butter into tablespoons and place it in a small saucepan. Add the can of beef consommé and heat over low heat until the butter melts, 3 to 4 minutes. Spoon about ½ cup of this mixture over the chicken.

④ Bake the chicken until it is well glazed, 1 hour, 20 minutes, basting the chicken with the remaining butter and consommé mixture every 20 minutes. Remove the pan from the oven and pour the sherry around the chicken and into the pan juices. Scatter the mushrooms around the chicken. Baste the chicken and mushrooms with the pan juices and return the pan to the oven. Bake the chicken until cooked through, about 30 minutes, basting it once more with the pan juices. After 20 minutes, add the artichoke hearts to the pan.

⑤ To serve, transfer the chicken to a platter or plates and spoon the cooking juices, mushrooms, and artichokes over the chicken.

 Add a dash of your favorite seasoned salt, such as Lawry's or Zatarain's.

I'd serve it with . . .
rice and your favorite green vegetable—asparagus,
brussels sprouts, green beans, or peas.

Kathleen's Chicken and Dressing

SERVES: 4
PREP: 25 MINUTES
BAKE: 90 MINUTES, PLUS 10 MINUTES RESTING TIME

Dallas resident Kathleen Livingston may be busy, but she still makes time to prepare something good to eat when her grown kids and their children come to visit. One of their favorites is this chicken and dressing recipe, and I can see why. The flavors are a complex mixture of garlic, lemon, thyme, and red pepper, and the idea is amusing—your taste buds think you are eating turkey and dressing because all the components of the dressing are there. And the chicken resting on top cooks up moist, crispy, and delicious. Kathleen may be driving authors all over Dallas as a media escort, but she knows this little recipe is in her back pocket to whip up when she gets home.

¼ cup plus 1 tablespoon olive oil

2 cups thinly sliced onions

2 cups thinly sliced celery

2 teaspoons grated lemon zest (from 1 lemon)

1 large clove garlic, minced

Sea salt and freshly ground black pepper

½ teaspoon dried thyme

½ teaspoon red pepper flakes

¼ cup chopped fresh flat-leaf parsley

½ loaf French bread

3 to 4 pounds bone-in, skin-on chicken breasts or thighs or a combination

¼ cup fresh lemon juice

① Place a rack in the center of the oven and preheat the oven to 375°F.

② Heat the ¼ cup of olive oil in a 12-inch ovenproof skillet over medium heat. Add the onions and celery, and cook, stirring, until they are translucent and a little golden brown, 9 to 10 minutes.

Speedy Homemade Chicken and Broth

Need a quick chicken broth to jump start soup? Place 2 bone-in, skin-on chicken breasts in a 2 quart saucepan and add cold water to cover. Add whatever seasonings you have on hand: a grinding of pepper, a bay leaf, a sprig of parsley, some onion slices, and so on, as well as a half teaspoon of salt. Let the mixture come to a boil, reduce the heat, cover the pan, and let simmer until the chicken is cooked through and tender, about 40 minutes. Uncover the pan, remove the chicken from the broth to cool, then let the broth cool. Once cool, remove and discard the chicken skin and bones. Leave the breasts whole, or cut them into cubes, or shred them using clean hands. Use the chicken in salads, on sandwiches, in casseroles, and in soups. The broth can be refrigerated, covered, for 2 days or frozen for up to 6 months. To thaw, transfer the frozen broth to a saucepan and let heat over low heat.

Stir in the lemon zest, garlic, 1¾ teaspoons of salt, ½ teaspoon of black pepper, and the thyme and red pepper flakes. Reduce the heat to low and cook, stirring, until the garlic softens, 2 to 3 minutes. Turn off the heat and fold in the parsley. Spoon the onion mixture into a small bowl and set it aside.

③ Slice the French bread in half lengthwise. Place the halves of bread, cut side up, side by side in the skillet. Spoon the onion mixture evenly over the bread halves.

④ Rub the chicken with the remaining 1 tablespoon of olive oil and season them with salt and pepper to taste. Place the chicken on top of the onion mixture. Pour the lemon juice over the chicken and place the skillet in the oven.

⑤ Bake the chicken until it is golden brown and crispy, about 1½ hours. When done the juices will run clear when the chicken is pricked with a fork. Remove the skillet from the oven and let the chicken rest for about 10 minutes. Cut the chicken and the bread into serving portions and serve with the onion mixture. Put bowls on the table for the chicken bones.

Do Ahead You can make the onion mixture earlier in the day and keep it covered on the kitchen counter.

I'd serve it with . . .
steamed broccoli or asparagus.

My Baked Chicken and Rice

SERVES: 4
PREP: 10 TO 15 MINUTES
BAKE: 2 HOURS

When simple recipes have simple ingredients, the secret to success is to choose the best. For this easy dinner, start with a small organic chicken and trim away the excess fat before cooking the bird. I use a large Le Creuset pan, but a heavy oval casserole works well, too. A slow cooker would also work but you will not get any browning, although more juices will cook out of the chicken and produce more stock (see Note). Add mushrooms if you like.

1 whole organic chicken (3 to 4 pounds)

2 tablespoons vegetable oil

Sea salt and freshly ground black pepper

1 medium-size onion

2 bay leaves

½ cup dry white wine or water

¾ cup long-grain white rice, such as basmati

Chopped fresh flat-leaf parsley, for garnish

① Place a rack in the center of the oven and preheat the oven to 300°F.

② Remove the giblets and neck, if any, from the chicken and set them aside for another use or discard them. Rinse the chicken under cold running water. Using poultry shears, cut the backbone out of the chicken and set it aside for another use or discard it. Remove the thigh and drumstick portions, keeping the thighs and drumsticks in one piece. Keep the breast halves with the ribs and wings in one piece. Pat the chicken dry with paper towels.

I'd serve it with . . .
sautéed sliced apples, roasted brussels sprouts,
and your favorite cranberry sauce.

3. Heat the vegetable oil in a heavy Dutch oven over medium-high heat. When the oil is hot, add the chicken pieces, skin side down, and let sear until they are golden brown, 2 to 3 minutes. Then, using tongs, turn the chicken pieces and brown them all over. You may need to reduce the heat to medium if the pan gets too hot. Turn off the heat and season the seared chicken with salt and pepper to taste. Discard the extra grease in the pan.

4. Peel the onion and cut it into quarters. Tuck the onion quarters around the chicken. Add the bay leaves. Add the white wine or water to the pan and cover it with the lid or foil. Bake the chicken until it is very tender, about 1½ hours.

5. Remove the Dutch oven from the oven; leave the oven on. Remove the lid or foil and sprinkle the rice around the chicken. Pour 1 cup of water over the rice and stir with a fork to moisten the rice with the pan juices. Place the lid or foil back on the Dutch oven, return it to the oven, and bake until the rice has cooked through, about 20 minutes.

6. To serve, remove and discard the bay leaves. Carefully transfer the chicken to a platter. Spoon the rice and onions alongside and scatter chopped parsley over the top.

 If making this dish in a slow cooker, cook the chicken on low for 3 to 4 hours, adding rice for the last hour.

★
 ★ ★
★ RAZZLE-DAZZLE

Use yellow rice, a wild rice blend, or a brown and white rice blend instead of the white basmati rice. If desired, add an 8-ounce carton of sliced white or brown mushrooms along with the rice.

Roasted Sticky Chicken

SERVES: 4 TO 6
PREP: 5 TO 10 MINUTES
CHILL: OVERNIGHT
BAKE: 4½ TO 5 HOURS

Supermarkets and their plethora of rotisserie chickens have pretty much stopped people roasting chicken at home. But here is a roast chicken recipe that supermarkets could never do because it requires seasoning the birds and letting them chill overnight first. Paul Prudhomme, the New Orleans chef made famous for his blackened redfish and seasoning line, created this recipe from a childhood memory. Prudhomme once said it was the spices rubbed into the chicken skin and the fat melting a little at a time as the chicken cooked that carried the seasoning into the meat and flavored and tenderized it. The result is juicy, tender, sweet, and sticky, and you will never, ever get that from supermarket rotisserie chicken. And it is the perfect leave-alone company main dish, giving you time to get all the sides ready and the table set.

1 whole chicken (3 to 3½ pounds)

2 teaspoons salt

1 teaspoon paprika

¾ teaspoon cayenne pepper

½ teaspoon onion powder

½ teaspoon ground thyme

¼ teaspoon garlic powder or granulated garlic

¼ teaspoon ground white pepper

¼ teaspoon freshly ground black pepper

1 cup finely minced onion

I'd serve it with . . .
cooked rice, sautéed zucchini, and sliced tomatoes.

1. Remove the giblets and neck, if any, from the chicken and set them aside for another use or discard them. Rinse the chicken under cold running water and pat it dry with paper towels. Place the salt, paprika, cayenne pepper, onion powder, thyme, garlic powder, white pepper, and black pepper in a small bowl and stir to combine. Rub the spice mixture inside and outside of the chicken, rubbing the seasoning deep onto the skin of the chicken. Place the chicken in a resealable plastic bag and refrigerate it overnight.

2. Place a rack in the center of the oven and preheat the oven to 250°F.

3. Place the chicken in a shallow roasting pan and place the onion in the cavity of the chicken. Roast the chicken until it is golden brown and the juices have caramelized on the bottom of the pan, 4½ to 5 hours. Slice the chicken and serve.

LAST-MINUTE BIRTHDAY PARTY • WEEKNIGHT DINNER • TAILGATE TRADITIONS

Our Turkey Burgers

SERVES: 8
PREP: 25 TO 30 MINUTES
GRILL: 8 TO 10 MINUTES

I never tire of a great burger, but usually those burgers are not prepared in my own kitchen. The best burgers I turn out are made of turkey, and this is my house recipe. I panfry these in a skillet on rainy and cold weeknights or grill them outside on a warmer weekend. Everyone loves them, even the carnivorous guys who usually insist on beef. Add holiday trimmings in the fall if you like—a cranberry mayonnaise or roasted chopped sweet potatoes on the side. And in the summer months, lighten the burgers up with sliced avocado, sprouts, ripe tomato, and whole wheat buns.

FOR THE BURGERS

2 pounds lean ground turkey, either 7 or 15 percent fat content

½ cup soft bread crumbs

¼ cup finely minced white onion or scallions

¼ cup chopped fresh flat-leaf parsley

1 to 2 cloves garlic, crushed in a garlic press

2 egg whites, or 1 whole large egg

½ teaspoon Lawry's seasoned salt

½ teaspoon salt, or a big dash of Worcestershire sauce

¼ teaspoon freshly ground black pepper

Vegetable oil spray, for misting the grill grate

FOR SERVING

Hamburger buns, toasted for 30 seconds on the grill, if desired

Sliced tomatoes

Lettuce leaves

Pickles

Onion slices

Your favorite condiments

Easy Mediterranean Turkey Burgers

Add 1 package (4 ounces) of tomato and basil-flavored crumbled feta cheese to a pound of ground turkey. Add 1 minced clove of garlic and season with ¼ teaspoon freshly ground black pepper to taste. Mix well and form the turkey mixture into patties. Preheat the grill to medium-high. Mist the grill grate with vegetable oil spray and cook the patties until cooked through, 4 to 5 minutes per side. Serve the burgers in soft pita bread halves with chopped romaine, cucumber, purple onion, and a dollop of store-bought *tzatziki* sauce, if desired.

① Place the turkey in a mixing bowl and add the bread crumbs, onion, parsley, garlic, egg whites or whole egg, seasoned salt, and salt. Season with pepper. Using a wooden spoon or clean hands, combine the ingredients until they are just incorporated. Form the turkey mixture into 8 patties about ⅓ inch thick. Set the turkey patties aside.

② Preheat the grill to medium-high. Mist the grill grate with vegetable oil spray so the burgers won't stick.

③ Place the burgers on the hot grill and cook until cooked through, 4 to 5 minutes per side, turning once. Transfer the turkey burgers to a platter or buns and serve with tomato slices, lettuce leaves, pickles, onion slices, and your choice of condiments on the side.

Do Ahead You can season and shape the turkey patties ahead. Place them on a platter lined with waxed paper. Put a piece of waxed paper between each layer of patties. Cover the patties with plastic wrap and refrigerate them for up to a day in advance of cooking.

How to Roast a Turkey

1. Start with a 16- to 18-pound turkey; this will serve 18 to 24 people. Remove the neck and giblets from the cavity. Discard the giblets and set the neck aside for making broth that you'll use when cooking the turkey. Rinse the turkey in cool running water and pat it dry inside and out with paper towels. Season the cavity of the turkey with salt and pepper. Place the turkey in a large roasting pan that is about 2½ inches deep. Fold the wing tips back underneath the turkey and tie the legs together with kitchen string. Place the turkey in the refrigerator while you make the broth.

2. Place the turkey neck in a medium-size saucepan and add 4 cups of water. Add a bay leaf, a handful of chopped onion, and salt and pepper to taste. Add a rib of celery if you have it. Let the water come to a boil over medium-high heat, then reduce the heat to low and let the broth simmer, covered, until the turkey neck has cooked through and the broth is flavorful, about 30 minutes. Remove the broth from the heat and set it aside, uncovered, to cool. Strain the broth, discarding the solids.

3. Preheat the oven to 325°F.

4. Remove the turkey from the refrigerator and rub the skin with 8 tablespoons of room temperature butter. Season the outside of the turkey with salt and pepper to taste. Loosely tent the turkey in the roasting pan with aluminum foil.

5. Place the roasting pan on an oven rack and before sliding the rack into the oven, pour 2 cups of the turkey broth around the turkey. Roast the turkey, basting it every 30 minutes by spooning the cooking juices over the top of it. Add more broth as needed to the pan. Remove the foil from the turkey after 2 hours and roast the turkey uncovered until the skin is golden and an instant-read thermometer inserted in a thigh, but not touching a bone, reads 180°F, 1½ to 2 hours longer for a total cooking time of 3½ to 4 hours.

6. Let the turkey rest in the roasting pan for about 15 minutes, then transfer it carefully to a platter. Let the turkey rest on the platter for about 30 minutes before carving.

Grilled Steaks with Chimichurri Sauce

SERVES: 4
PREP: 25 TO 30 MINUTES
GRILL: 10 TO 15 MINUTES, PLUS 5 TO 10 MINUTES RESTING TIME

Our friend R.B. is a master of the grill, and he once said that a sirloin steak with a little salt and a good sear becomes Brazilian *churrasco* when you serve it up with *chimichurri* sauce while wearing gaucho pants. Seriously, the key is *chimichurri*—a peppery, herby sauce of cilantro, parsley, onion, garlic, red pepper flakes, vinegar, and olive oil. Not only does *chimichurri* take the average steak to another dimension, it will pick up your weekend scrambled eggs, or you can spoon it over grilled chicken or fish. So, steam some rice, open a can of black beans, and put on your gaucho gear. Don't think for a moment you don't know how to grill an amazing steak.

FOR THE CHIMICHURRI SAUCE

1 large clove garlic, peeled

1 bunch fresh cilantro, rinsed, dried, and stems removed

1 bunch fresh curly or flat-leaf parsley, rinsed, dried, and stems removed

1 small sweet onion, roughly chopped

¼ cup red wine vinegar

⅓ cup olive oil

Salt, freshly ground black pepper, and red pepper flakes

FOR THE STEAKS

2 pounds bone-in sirloin, T-bone, or porterhouse steaks (1 to 1½ inches thick)

1 tablespoon olive oil

Coarse sea salt or your favorite steak seasoning

1. Make the *chimichurri* sauce: Place the garlic in a food processor and process until minced, 15 to 20 seconds. Turn off the machine and add the cilantro and parsley. Pulse the machine until the herbs are coarsely chopped, 8 or 9 times. Add the onion and pulse until the herbs are well chopped, 7 or 8 more times. Transfer the herb mixture to a medium-size bowl and add the red wine vinegar and the ⅓ cup of olive oil. Season with salt, black pepper, and red pepper flakes to taste. Cover the *chimichurri* sauce and set it aside.

2. Grill the steaks: Preheat the grill to medium-high heat. If your grill has a thermometer it should register between 350° and 375°F. Or place your hand over the fire; it should be hot enough that you have to move your hand after 2 to 3 seconds. Clean the grill grate with a grill brush.

3. Rub the steaks with the 1 tablespoon of olive oil and season them on both sides with sea salt or steak seasoning to taste. Place the steaks on the hot grill and let sear, 3 minutes. Turn the steaks over and cook them for 3 minutes longer. Turn the steaks again and cook them for 2 to 3 minutes, or until they are cooked to your desired doneness, 9 to 12 minutes total for medium-rare, 130°F on an instant-read thermometer.

4. Transfer the steaks to a platter to rest for 5 to 10 minutes. Then slice and serve the steaks with the *chimichurri* sauce.

Do Ahead You can make the *chimichurri* sauce a day ahead and store it, covered, in the fridge.

I'd serve it with . . .
black beans and white rice.

Laurie Nicholson's Party Beef

SERVES: 8
PREP: 5 TO 10 MINUTES
BAKE: 2 HOURS

My friend Laurie Nicholson generously offered to bring the main course for our investment club holiday dinner. As she walked confidently into the party carrying a large pot of fragrant beef stew our club members followed the aroma to the kitchen like hungry dogs. Laurie was nonplussed when asked if she had been cooking all day as her secret was inside the pot—a dead-easy recipe with few ingredients that yields a meal of stewed beef, red wine, and mushrooms.

2½ pounds cubed lean beef, such as chuck, round, or sirloin (1-inch cubes)

2 cans (10½ ounces each) beef consommé

2 cups red wine

½ cup fine dry bread crumbs

¼ cup all-purpose flour

2 bay leaves

¼ teaspoon freshly ground black pepper

2 cartons (8 ounces each) sliced baby bella or white mushrooms

Boiled rice or egg noodles, for serving

¼ cup chopped fresh flat-leaf parsley (optional), for garnish

I'd serve it with . . .
garlic bread and a green salad or broccoli
as a nice additional dish.

1. Place a rack in the center of the oven and preheat the oven to 350°F.

2. Place the beef in a large Dutch oven. Place the consommé, red wine, bread crumbs, and flour in a medium-size bowl and whisk to combine well. Pour the consommé mixture over the beef, add the bay leaves, season with pepper, and cover the Dutch oven.

3. Bake the stew for 1 hour, then add the mushrooms. Cover the Dutch oven and cook the stew until the meat is very tender, about 1 hour longer, adding ½ cup of water if needed to keep the meat from sticking.

4. Remove the Dutch oven from the oven and leave the lid on while you cook rice or noodles to accompany the beef.

5. Remove and discard the bay leaves, spoon the beef over rice or noodles, sprinkle with the parsley, if using, and serve.

Do Ahead

The stew can be made 2 days in advance and refrigerated, covered. Reheat it in a 300°F oven, adding a little water if needed.

MONEY SAVER: Check the price of good stew beef. You need to buy about a quarter to a third pound more than needed for the recipe in case there is gristle or fat on the stew meat that needs to be trimmed away. It may be less expensive to buy a chuck or round roast on sale, trim away fat, and cut the roast into cubes for this recipe.

★
 ★ ★
★ RAZZLE-DAZZLE

Add a package of frozen pearl onions to the beef when you add the mushrooms and the stew will resemble beef bourguignon.

Ina's Sweet-and-Sour Brisket

SERVES: 8
PREP: 15 TO 20 MINUTES
BAKE: 3 HOURS, PLUS 30 MINUTES RESTING TIME

A good friend of Ina Stern, who lives in North Carolina, saved her day by helping prepare this brisket. Ina's parents had just passed away, and Passover was approaching. Next to Thanksgiving, Passover was the biggest holiday tradition Ina shared with her parents, and she wasn't able to fathom the holiday without them. So, when she received a call from her friend Nancy in Santa Fe, who said without hesitation, "Hey, I'm coming for Passover," it was very welcome. Nancy is not Jewish but that didn't matter as Nancy knew the importance of Ina making it through her first Passover without her parents. Nancy helped Ina cook two briskets, one like a pot roast with vegetables and a second, this recipe, with a sweet-and-sour sauce. They also made chicken soup, says Ina, "the closest to what my mother would make," matzo balls, and all the other Passover accompaniments. "We made a Passover my parents would be proud of."

18 ounces beer (2½ cups from two 12-ounce bottles; see Note)

1½ cups whole berry cranberry sauce (see Note)

¾ cup ketchup

2 tablespoons olive oil or vegetable oil

1 flat-cut beef brisket (4 to 5 pounds)

1 extra-large onion, thinly sliced

I'd serve it with . . .
sweet potatoes and asparagus or as part
of a traditional Passover menu.

1. Place a rack in the center of the oven and preheat the oven to 350°F.

2. Pour the beer into a large bowl and stir in the cranberry sauce and ketchup. Set the beer and cranberry sauce mixture aside.

3. Heat the olive oil in a large Dutch oven over medium-high heat. When the oil is hot, add the brisket and sear it on both sides until it is nicely browned, 3 to 4 minutes per side. Transfer the brisket to a plate. Add the onion to the Dutch oven, stirring. Reduce the heat to low and cook the onion until soft, 6 to 7 minutes. Place the brisket on top of the onion and pour the beer and cranberry sauce mixture over it. Increase the heat to medium-high and let come to a boil. Cover the Dutch oven and place it in the oven.

4. Bake the brisket until it is very tender, about 3 hours. Remove the Dutch oven from the oven and let the brisket rest in the sauce for about 30 minutes.

5. When ready to serve, slice the brisket diagonally across the grain. Place the Dutch oven over low heat, skim any fat off the sauce, and let come to a boil. Return the brisket slices to the sauce. Or place the sliced brisket on a serving platter and spoon the warm sauce over it, serving extra sauce on the side.

SAVE THE DAY NOTE This recipe was originally adapted from epicurious.com, but Ina has changed the proportions over the years. Beer is grain based, so Ina says if you are serving the brisket for Passover use a kosher-for-Passover beer. If you are not cooking it for Passover then she recommends a darker beer like a Samuel Adams Black Lager. The recipe calls for 18 ounces, which means you can open two bottles of beer and pour half of one into a glass to drink while you cook.

Because whole berry cranberry sauce comes in 14-ounce cans, you can just add the entire can.

Do Ahead The brisket reheats very well, so you should cook it ahead of time. Ina makes it up to 2 days in advance so the flavors deepen in the sauce. Skim off the fat before reheating the brisket and sauce. If you reheat it on top of the stove, it will take 8 to 10 minutes over low heat. In a 325°F oven, it will take 20 to 25 minutes.

Mom's Beef Tenderloin

SERVES: 8 TO 12
PREP: 10 MINUTES
MARINATE: OVERNIGHT
GRILL: 25 TO 30 MINUTES, PLUS 10 MINUTES RESTING TIME

This is how Ann Evers marinates beef tenderloin, a staple of her kitchen, before grilling it. The marinade recipe comes from her mother, and it makes the beef even more tender and gives it good flavor. Perfect for cold buffet suppers or for those times when you want to cook the meal in advance, the beef can be marinated one day, grilled the next and chilled, then sliced and served the third day. Granted this may take a little planning, but it does allow you the freedom of not being in the kitchen the entire time you have company.

1 whole beef tenderloin, trimmed (4 to 6 pounds)

2 tablespoons Worcestershire sauce

½ teaspoon garlic powder or granulated garlic

½ teaspoon Lawry's lemon pepper seasoning

1 bottle (16 ounces; 2 cups) Wish-Bone Italian salad dressing

① Place the beef tenderloin in a 13-by-9-inch glass baking dish and spoon the Worcestershire sauce over it. Using your hands, rub the Worcestershire onto the beef, turning the beef to coat it well. Combine the garlic powder and lemon pepper seasoning in a small bowl and sprinkle the mixture all over the beef, rubbing it on evenly. Pour the Italian dressing over the beef, making sure there is enough dressing to come halfway up the beef. Cover the baking dish with aluminum foil and refrigerate it overnight.

② The next day, remove the foil and turn the beef tenderloin over. Replace the foil and return the baking dish to the refrigerator. Turn the beef every 2 hours. An hour before cooking, place the baking dish on the kitchen counter and let the beef come to room temperature.

③ Preheat the grill to high.

④ Remove the beef tenderloin from the marinade, discarding the marinade. Place the beef on the hot grill. Cook the beef for 15 minutes, then turn it over and cook the second side 10 to 15 minutes longer for medium-rare, 130°F on an instant-read thermometer inserted into the thickest part of the tenderloin. Transfer the beef to a platter to rest for about 10 minutes before serving.

Do Ahead After the beef has cooked and rested, wrap in foil and chill overnight in the fridge. Slice and serve chilled or at room temperature the next day.

I'd serve it with . . .
Ann's Tomato Salad with Roasted Garlic Dressing (page 113)
and Flowerree's Overnight Rolls (page 251).

Classic Osso Buco

SERVES: 4
PREP: 25 MINUTES
COOK: 1 HOUR, 45 MINUTES

People whose business is food—whether it be writing about it, owning a restaurant or a food store, or importing and distributing food—don't always get a lot of dinner invitations from friends. That's because people are a little bit intimidated about entertaining someone who knows more about food than they do. I recall many years ago asking a neighbor and his wife, who owned a well-known restaurant in Atlanta, to come to my house for dinner. "What was I thinking?!," I wondered as I thought about what to prepare. Grilled burgers? No, that was too simple. What about a roasted chicken? Too boring. So I settled on osso buco, which they loved. Let the osso buco simmer slowly and then rest in its sauce while you prepare rice and a green salad.

3 tablespoons all-purpose flour

Salt

4 crosscut veal shank slices (each about 1½ inches thick; 2 to 2½ pounds)

¼ cup olive oil

1 small onion, thinly sliced

1 can (28 ounces) crushed Italian tomatoes

1 can (14½ ounces) diced tomatoes

1 large orange

¾ cup red wine

Freshly ground black pepper

Chopped fresh flat-leaf parsley, for garnish

Cooked rice, for serving

① Place the flour and ¼ teaspoon of salt in a large shallow bowl and stir to mix. Dredge the veal shanks all over in the flour mixture and set aside.

② Heat the olive oil in a large heavy Dutch oven over medium heat. When the oil is hot add 2 veal shanks and gently brown them on each side, 3 to 4 minutes per side. Take care not to poke the marrow in the center of the bone or let it fall out.

I'd serve it with saffron rice, or 22-Minute Microwave Risotto (page 172), and a green salad.

Transfer the browned shanks to a plate. Repeat with the remaining 2 shanks.

③ Add the onion to the Dutch oven. Reduce the heat to medium-low and cook the onion, stirring, until it softens, 4 to 5 minutes. To the onion add the tomatoes, both crushed and diced, with their juices, increase the heat to medium, and let cook at a brisk simmer until the mixture pulls together, 4 to 5 minutes.

④ Meanwhile, grate about 1 teaspoon orange zest. Cut the orange in half and juice it. Add the orange juice and orange zest to the tomatoes. Add the red wine, stir to mix, and cook until the flavors blend, 1 to 2 minutes. Return

the browned veal shanks to the Dutch oven and season with salt and pepper to taste. Reduce the heat to low, cover the Dutch oven, and let the veal simmer until it is very tender, about 1½ hours. Garnish the veal shanks with parsley and serve with rice.

Do Ahead You can cook the osso buco completely ahead of time, let it cool to room temperature, then refrigerate it, covered, for up to a day. An hour before serving reheat the veal shanks in a 300°F oven or gently heat them over a very low heat, stirring occasionally, for 25 to 30 minutes.

22-Minute Microwave Risotto

I didn't believe it until I tried it—you can make pretty nice risotto in a microwave oven. Just be aware that the microwave oven you are using needs to have a wattage of at least 1,000 for this recipe to work right. The risotto serves four.

Place 2 tablespoons of butter and 1 tablespoon of olive oil in a large microwave-safe bowl. Add a handful of minced onion (about ⅓ cup) and microwave it on high power until soft, about 3 minutes. Stir in 1 cup of Arborio rice (short grain Italian rice) and microwave this on high power until the rice glistens and begins to cook, about 2 minutes. Stir in 2¾ cups of chicken broth and ¼ cup of dry white wine or 3 cups of chicken broth and no wine (find a recipe for homemade chicken

broth on page 153). Cover the bowl tightly with plastic wrap and microwave the rice on high power until half the liquid has been absorbed and the rice is almost cooked, about 9 minutes. Shake the bowl, but do not uncover it, then return it to the microwave and cook the rice on high power until all the liquid has been absorbed and the rice is fully cooked, about 8 minutes more. Peel off the plastic wrap very carefully and discard it (the bowl will be hot). Add ¼ cup of grated Parmesan cheese and an additional ¼ cup of hot chicken broth to the rice, stirring until creamy. Add a tablespoon or two more chicken broth if needed to thin the rice out. Season with salt and pepper to taste and serve.

Barb's One-Pound Pork Chops

SERVES: 6
PREP: 15 MINUTES
MARINATE: OVERNIGHT
BAKE: 2 HOURS, 15 MINUTES

Every summer when Barb Ellis was young her family would vacation at her grandparent's cottage on Crooked Lake, just south of Traverse City, Michigan. Part of the trip was a stop at The Embers restaurant in Mount Pleasant. It was out of the way, she recalls, but the family happily detoured for the restaurant's legendary pork chops. Barb's mother was able to talk the owners into giving her the recipe for those pork chops and started a tradition of baking them on Christmas Day. Barb continued the tradition with her family, and she says her husband and two sons would rather have these pork chops than prime rib or a beef fillet any day.

FOR THE PORK CHOPS AND MARINATING SAUCE

6 loin pork chops (each 1 pound and 1 to 1½ inches thick)

2 cups soy sauce

½ cup packed light brown sugar

1 tablespoon molasses

1 teaspoon salt

1 cup water

FOR THE RED DIPPING SAUCE

1 bottle (14 ounces) ketchup

1 bottle (12 ounces) chili sauce

⅓ cup water

½ cup packed light brown sugar

1 teaspoon dry mustard

1. Prepare the pork chops and marinating sauce: Arrange the pork chops in a single layer in a large glass baking dish. Place the soy sauce, ½ cup of brown sugar, molasses, salt, and 1 cup of water in a medium-size saucepan and let come to a boil over medium-high heat, stirring often, 4 to 5 minutes. Remove the sauce from the heat and let it cool to the touch, about 20 minutes. Pour the sauce over the pork chops, lifting the chops up with a fork to let the sauce run underneath. Cover the baking dish with plastic wrap and let the chops marinate in the refrigerator overnight.

2. Place a rack in the center of the oven and preheat the oven to 350°F.

3. Remove the plastic wrap from the baking dish and cover the dish with aluminum foil. Bake the pork chops in the marinade until they are very tender, about 2 hours.

4. While the chops bake, make the red dipping sauce: Place the ketchup, chili sauce, ⅓ cup of water ½ cup of brown sugar, and dry mustard in a medium-size saucepan and stir until the brown sugar dissolves. Let come to a boil over medium-high heat, stirring often, then remove the pan from the heat.

5. When the pork chops have cooked, remove them from the oven. Leave the oven on. Using tongs, dip the chops into the pan of red sauce. Place the chops back in the baking dish. Return the chops to the oven and bake them until they are glazed, about 15 minutes. Serve with the remaining dipping sauce in a bowl on the side.

Do Ahead You can make the marinating sauce and red dipping sauce ahead of time and refrigerate them, covered, for up to 2 days. Reheat the dipping sauce before using it.

★★★ RAZZLE-DAZZLE

If you have the grill fired up, after dipping the baked chops in the red sauce place them on the hot grate and grill them until they are glazed, about 5 minutes per side.

Braised Pork Tenderloin with Apricots and Onions

SERVES: 8
PREP: 15 TO 20 MINUTES
BAKE: 1 HOUR, 40 TO 45 MINUTES, PLUS 20 MINUTES RESTING TIME

I adapted this recipe from one I found scribbled on a blue sticky note in my mother's recipe box. She just called it "pork roast," and it was her method for slow cooking pork loin roast or tenderloins most any time of year. I have changed it a bit, using olive oil instead of butter for browning the meat and adding dried apricots to contribute sweetness, giving the pork a rich flavor perfect for serving in the cooler weather.

2 pork tenderloins (about 3 pounds)

1 tablespoon packaged seasoning rub of your choice, such as a combination of paprika, ground thyme, and ground black pepper, preferably without salt

2 tablespoons olive oil

12 dried apricots

1 cup frozen pearl onions, or 1 cup chopped onion

2 cloves garlic, thinly sliced

1½ cups chicken broth

¾ cup red wine

3 to 4 sprigs fresh thyme

2 bay leaves

1. Place a rack in the middle of the oven and preheat the oven to 350°F.

2. Rub the pork tenderloins all over with the seasoning rub. Heat the olive oil in a heavy Dutch oven over medium-high heat. When the oil is hot, add the pork tenderloins and sear them on both sides until nicely browned, 2 to 3 minutes per side. Turn off the heat and add the apricots, onions, and garlic. Add the chicken broth and red wine and stir to combine. Tuck the thyme sprigs and bay leaves in the liquid. Cover the Dutch oven.

3. Bake the pork tenderloins until they are tender and the liquid has reduced by more than half, 1 hour and 40 to 45 minutes. Remove the Dutch oven from the oven and let the pork rest for about 20 minutes.

4. When ready to serve, transfer the pork tenderloins to a cutting board and slice them on the diagonal. The meat will be very tender and will shred. Transfer the slices to a platter. Remove and discard the thyme sprigs and bay leaves, then ladle the apricots and onions over the meat. Pour the juices into a gravy boat and serve on the side.

★
★ ★
★ RAZZLE-DAZZLE

Add 2 cups of peeled and cubed sweet potatoes or butternut squash to the pork for the last 30 minutes of cooking.

I'd serve it with . . .
mashed or roasted potatoes
and spinach.

I'd serve it with . . . a mixed salad or coleslaw and baked beans. Add roasted potatoes and Elaine's Broccoli Jennifer (page 207) to really stage a feast.

Courtnay's Crock-Pot Ribs

SERVES: 4
PREP: 10 MINUTES
COOK: 6 TO 8 HOURS

My tennis friend Courtnay is always talking recipes. It is either her corn chowder or this hands-off rib recipe she can throw together easily before heading to work or the tennis court. The recipe works with baby back ribs or chicken thighs, and the result is always "fall apart tender," in her words. It's a pretty simple recipe as the only mixing is throwing together the five sauce ingredients in a slow cooker, but even this little bit of work far exceeds the taste of bottled premade barbecue sauce. And you can adjust the seasoning as you like, adding more hot sauce or more balsamic vinegar, tossing in a few garlic cloves or sliced onion. And if you don't have a Crock-Pot, rest assured the recipe works just as well made in a cast-iron Dutch oven like one from Le Creuset. Bake the ribs, covered, at 250°F for four hours, then remove the lid, increase the temperature to 375°F, and bake them for thirty minutes longer.

1 rack baby back ribs (about 2 pounds)

1 bottle (12 ounces) chili sauce

⅓ cup packed dark brown sugar

2 tablespoons balsamic vinegar

1 tablespoon Worcestershire sauce

1 teaspoon hot sauce, such as Frank's RedHot or Texas Pete

① Cut the rack of ribs in half. Place one half rack of ribs in the bottom of a slow cooker.

② Place the chili sauce, brown sugar, balsamic vinegar, Worcestershire sauce, and hot sauce in a small bowl and stir to combine. Spoon half of the sauce over the ribs in the slow cooker. Place the remaining half rack of ribs on top and spoon the remaining sauce over it.

(3) Cover the slow cooker and set the power to low. Cook the ribs until they are very tender, 6 to 8 hours. Remove the ribs from the sauce, cut each half rack in half, and serve with the sauce on the side.

MONEY SAVER: Look for specials on baby back ribs and when their price drops or you see a buy-one, get-one-free deal, load up the freezer. Thaw the ribs overnight in the refrigerator.

★
★ ★
★ RAZZLE-DAZZLE

If you want to crisp the ribs before serving, place them in a single layer on a baking sheet and bake them in a 425°F oven until crispy, 4 to 5 minutes.

COMPANY'S COMING • HOLIDAY IDEAS • PRETTY IMPRESSIVE

Lecia's Lamb Chops

SERVES: 8
PREP: 10 MINUTES
MARINATE: 4 HOURS, OR OVERNIGHT
GRILL: 8 TO 10 MINUTES
REHEAT: 10 TO 15 MINUTES

If ever there was a need for food that's ready to serve, it is when you are entertaining good friends and want to linger with them and enjoy the conversation. Lecia Post of South Pittsburg, Tennessee, first tried this method of preparing lamb chops in a cooking class many years ago. Since then it has been one of her most valuable

I'd serve it with . . .
roasted potatoes, mint jelly,
and a quick green salad.

recipes as the lamb chops are marinated and cooked before the guests come to dinner. She then finishes the cooking in a hot oven right before dinner. Pair this with Missy's Make Ahead Mashed Potatoes (page 229) or roasted potatoes and you are ready to enjoy the dinner party yourself.

16 loin lamb chops (1¼ inches thick; about 4 pounds)

¼ cup olive oil

2 tablespoons soy sauce

1 medium-size lemon

1 small sprig fresh rosemary

2 cloves garlic, crushed in a garlic press or minced

① Pat the lamb chops dry with paper towels and arrange them in a glass baking dish or large plastic resealable bag.

② Place the olive oil and soy sauce in a blender or food processor. Zest the lemon and add the zest to the olive oil mixture along with 1 to 2 tablespoons of lemon juice. Pick the leaves from the rosemary sprig and add them to the mixture; you need about 1 teaspoon. Add the garlic. Blend or process the marinade until it is smooth, 10 to 15 seconds.

③ Pour the marinade over the lamb chops, cover the baking dish or seal the bag, and refrigerate the chops for at least 4 hours, or overnight.

④ Preheat the grill to medium-high.

⑤ Remove the lamb chops from the marinade and place them on the hot grill. Discard the marinade. Cook the chops until they are nicely charred with grill marks on both sides, 4 to 5 minutes per side. Transfer the chops from the grill to a pan to cool for 30 minutes. Cover the pan with aluminum foil and refrigerate the chops for up to 2 days.

⑥ About 2 hours before serving remove the grilled lamb chops from the refrigerator and let them come to room temperature. Preheat the oven to 400°F.

⑦ Arrange the lamb chops 1 inch apart on a baking sheet and place them in the oven until they are heated through, 10 to 15 minutes. The lamb chops should be pink in the center.

Shirley's Roast Lamb

SERVES: 6 TO 8
PREP: 20 MINUTES
MARINATE: OVERNIGHT
BAKE: 2 TO 3⅓ HOURS, DEPENDING ON THE WEIGHT OF THE LAMB
AND THE DONENESS YOU PREFER

If there is one worry on Shirley Hutson's mind during the Easter service at church it's her roast lamb. Or at least that's the way it was for many years before her husband retired as an Episcopal priest. Shirley placed the lamb leg in the oven before church, but often the large crowds at church meant they got out later than usual. She would tell her daughter to go "get that lamb out of the oven," which rescued it from over-cooking. Shirley likes lamb roasted to a medium doneness. She buys a whole leg of lamb and has the butcher cut off the shank, which she freezes to make a soup.

FOR THE LAMB

1 tablespoon dried rosemary

1½ teaspoons dried thyme

1 bone-in leg of lamb (6 to 8 pounds; see Note)

2 to 3 cloves garlic, thinly sliced

2 tablespoons olive oil

½ teaspoon freshly ground black pepper

FOR THE GRAVY (optional)

2 cups water

¼ cup flour

Salt and freshly ground black pepper

Gravy browner, such as Kitchen Bouquet (optional)

I'd serve it with . . .
mashed potatoes, steamed asparagus, and mint jelly.

① Place the rosemary and thyme in a small bowl and season with the pepper.

② Pat the leg of lamb dry with paper towels. Using the point of a sharp paring knife, make small slits ½ to 1 inch deep all over the lamb. Insert a slice of garlic into each slit. Rub the lamb all over with the olive oil. Rub the herb mixture all over the lamb. Cover the leg of lamb with plastic wrap and refrigerate it overnight. Remove the lamb from the fridge 30 to 40 minutes before roasting.

③ When ready to cook, place a rack in the center of the oven and preheat the oven to 325°F.

④ Unwrap the lamb and place it on a rack in a shallow roasting pan. Roast the lamb until done to taste, 18 to 20 minutes per pound for meat that is light pink in the center (an internal temperature of 150°F on an instant-read thermometer), 25 minutes per pound for medium (160°F). Remove the lamb from the oven and place it on a platter to rest for at least 15 minutes before carving.

⑤ If you want to make gravy, pour the roasting pan drippings into a measuring cup to measure ¼ cup and set it aside. Pour the water into the roasting pan and scrape up the brown bits that stick to the bottom of the pan. Pour the ¼ cup drippings into a large skillet and whisk in the flour. Cook, stirring, over medium heat until it begins to brown. Add the water mixture from the roasting pan and let simmer, stirring, until the gravy thickens, 3 to 4 minutes. Season the gravy with salt and pepper to taste. Add a gravy browner to color, if desired.

⑥ Carve the leg of lamb and serve it with the gravy on the side, if desired.

SAVE THE DAY NOTE If the leg of lamb is vacuum-packed, it will have a sell-by date on it, and it will last longer in the fridge than if it is not sealed. Shirley says to always ask the butcher how long the leg of lamb can be refrigerated before roasting.

Lemon and Dill Marinated Grilled Tuna

SERVES: 4
PREP: 15 MINUTES
MARINATE: 1 HOUR
GRILL: 8 TO 10 MINUTES

I am not sure what I love more—freshly grilled tuna steaks or leftovers sliced atop a green salad the next day. This recipe came together by complete accident. I had bought a few beautiful tuna steaks and couldn't decide how to cook them. They were so fresh and vivid pink in color—the color of tomato flesh—so I didn't want to douse them with too heavy a seasoning. I had lemons on hand and olive oil, as well as shallots and a bunch of fresh dill. So I stirred together a fast marinade and plunged those tuna steaks into it for about an hour in the fridge. Wow! Is fresh dill ever the best herb for grilled fish. The tuna was exceptional. I'd like to say it was my cooking, but I think the dill gets all the credit. If you're making the tuna as part of a romantic dinner for two, simply halve the ingredients.

4 fresh tuna steaks (1½ to 2 pounds total; see Note)

⅓ cup fresh lemon juice (from 2 to 3 lemons)

⅔ cup olive oil

¼ cup minced shallots (from 6 shallots)

2 cloves garlic, minced

½ cup chopped fresh dill

Salt and freshly ground black pepper

1. Place the tuna steaks in a glass 13-by-9-inch baking dish. Place the lemon juice in a small bowl. Whisk in the olive oil until well combined. Add the shallots, garlic, and dill. Pour the lemon marinade over the tuna steaks and turn the steaks over to coat them with the marinade. Cover the baking dish with plastic wrap and place it in the refrigerator. Let the tuna marinate for about 1 hour.

2. Preheat the grill to medium-high.

3. When ready to grill, remove the tuna steaks from the marinade, setting aside the marinade. Place the tuna steaks on the hot grill and let them sear until grill marks are well formed, 3 to 4 minutes. Spoon some of the marinade over the tuna steaks and turn them to sear the second side, 3 to 4 minutes. The tuna will be done to medium-rare. If you prefer your tuna done to medium, let it cook 2 minutes more. Season the tuna with salt and pepper to taste and serve.

SAVE THE DAY NOTE If you want to use shrimp instead of tuna, this is enough marinade for 16 to 24 large shrimp, shelled and deveined. After marinating them, thread the shrimp onto skewers and grill them until cooked through, 1 to 2 minutes per side.

I'd serve it with . . .
corn on the cob and potato salad or use the tuna
to make salade niçoise (page 85).

Brown Sugar and Bourbon Salmon

SERVES: 6 TO 8
PREP: 10 MINUTES
MARINATE: UP TO 8 HOURS (optional)
BAKE: 15 MINUTES, PLUS 15 MINUTES RESTING TIME

Bourbon has long been a favorite drink in the South, and I have spiked fruitcakes with it to make them palatable and poured it into eggnog to make holidays festive. Now, bourbon is a legitimate ingredient for main dishes, too. And this recipe offers a new solution for how to cook salmon. One of my favorite fast ways has been to coat it in soy sauce and honey and bake it in a hot oven. This year I added bourbon to the mix, along with brown sugar, the soy sauce, garlic, scallions, and a touch of sesame oil. The results were as delicious as you might expect, and we loved the leftovers the next day.

1 skinless salmon fillet (2 to 3 pounds)

½ cup bourbon

¼ cup packed light brown sugar

2 tablespoons soy sauce

3 cloves garlic, minced

½ cup chopped scallions, green parts only

2 teaspoons Asian (dark) sesame oil

Cooked rice, for serving

① Place a rack in the center of the oven and preheat the oven to 425°F.

② Place the salmon fillet in a 13-by-9-inch glass baking dish. Place the bourbon in a small bowl, add the brown sugar, and stir until the brown sugar dissolves. Add the soy sauce, garlic, scallions, and sesame oil and stir to combine. Pour the bourbon marinade over the salmon. Using a fork, pick up the salmon to let some of the marinade run under it.

③ Bake the salmon until it is well cooked and crisp around the edges but still a little soft in the center, about 15 minutes. Remove the baking dish from the oven and let the salmon rest for about 15 minutes. Serve the salmon with rice.

Do Ahead You can let the salmon marinate in the bourbon mixture in the refrigerator, covered, for as long as 8 hours in advance.

Grilled Salmon in a Snap

If you prefer, you can grill the Brown Sugar and Bourbon Salmon or broil it. First, prepare the salmon fillet as described in Step 2.

To grill the fillet, preheat the grill. Remove the salmon from the marinade and discard the marinade. Cut the salmon into serving pieces to make for easier grilling. Place the pieces on the hot grill and sear them for 3 to 4 minutes on the first side. Using a wide spatula, turn the salmon pieces over and let them sear on the second side, 3 to 4 minutes. To test for doneness insert the tip of a sharp knife in the center of the salmon and gently pull the flesh apart. If the salmon isn't done to your liking, move them to the side of the grill grate or reduce the heat on a gas grill to low and let the salmon cook 3 to 5 minutes longer.

To broil the salmon, preheat the broiler. Place the glass baking dish with the salmon and marinade under the broiler. Cook the salmon until crisp on top, 5 to 7 minutes. Let the salmon rest for about 15 minutes before serving.

Lou Ann's Salmon Croquettes

SERVES: 4 (12 CROQUETTES TOTAL)
PREP: 20 TO 25 MINUTES
COOK: 20 MINUTES

Lou Ann Brown makes incredibly easy salmon croquettes from canned salmon and serves them atop salad greens dressed with a light vinaigrette. And when asked to bring a favorite useful recipe to a bridal shower this is the recipe Lou Ann copied onto an index card and shared with the bride-to-be. Lou Ann ate salmon croquettes while growing up as her grandmother made them for luncheons and ladies' events and served them with a cream sauce. Lou Ann wanted a little fresher rendition, so she created this version. She says the recipe is especially helpful on those nights in Naples, Florida, when she is trying to avoid a trip to the grocery. Most of the ingredients are things she keeps on hand, and the resulting croquettes are favorites of Lou Ann's husband, Gary.

I'd serve it with . . .
Kitchen Sink Tabbouleh (page 13), or
arugula tossed with olive oil, lemon juice, and
salt and pepper to taste.

1 can (about 15 ounces) red salmon, drained and picked over to remove bones and skin

1 teaspoon grated fresh lemon zest

2 tablespoons fresh lemon juice

2 to 3 cups panko (Japanese bread crumbs)

½ cup mayonnaise

2 tablespoons Dijon mustard

A few dashes of hot sauce, such as Frank's RedHot or Cholula

¼ cup finely minced celery

¼ cup finely minced fresh flat-leaf parsley

2 tablespoons finely minced onion

1 large egg, lightly beaten

Salt and freshly ground black pepper

2 cups peanut or canola oil, for frying

4 cups arugula, baby spinach, or small lettuces, for serving

Sweet-and-Sour Vinaigrette (recipe follows)

(1) Preheat the oven to 250°F. Line a baking sheet with paper towels and set aside.

(2) Place the salmon in a large bowl and mash it with a fork to break up the flesh and remaining small bones. Stir in the lemon zest and juice. Stir in 1 cup of the panko and the mayonnaise, mustard, and hot sauce. Then, stir in the celery, parsley, and onion. Add the beaten egg and season the salmon mixture with salt and pepper to taste.

(3) Place 1 cup of the panko in a shallow bowl. Form the salmon mixture into twelve 3-inch croquettes. Dredge the croquettes in the panko to cover them completely, and place them on a platter. Add more panko to the bowl as necessary.

(4) Pour oil to a depth of 1 inch in a deep, wide skillet over medium-high heat. Scatter a few panko crumbs in the oil and when they begin to brown, the oil is hot. Place a few croquettes in the skillet, being careful not to crowd it. Cook the croquettes until they are deeply browned on one side, 1 to 2 minutes, then turn and brown the second side, 1 to 2 minutes longer. Drain the croquettes on paper towels, transfer them to the prepared baking sheet, and place it in the oven to keep the croquettes warm while you cook the rest of them.

(5) Serve the croquettes over arugula, baby spinach, or small lettuces that have been drizzled with the Sweet-and-Sour Vinaigrette.

Do Ahead   The croquettes can be made a day in advance. Place them in a glass baking dish, cover it with plastic wrap, and refrigerate. Reheat the croquettes by warming them in the microwave, then crisping them over medium heat in a nonstick skillet for 1 to 2 minutes.

Sweet-and-Sour Vinaigrette

MAKES: ABOUT 1½ CUPS

This is a perfect vinaigrette to have on hand for salads topped with grilled chicken or fish. To jazz it up, add a handful of fresh herbs if you like or some poppy seeds if you are serving it over fruit salad.

1 small shallot, or 1 to 2 cloves garlic, coarsely chopped

½ cup apple cider vinegar

1 tablespoon Dijon mustard

*1 tablespoon ketchup
(a great use for a fast-food ketchup packet)*

1 teaspoon honey or agave nectar

1 teaspoon freshly ground black pepper

½ teaspoon salt

1 cup vegetable oil such as olive, canola, avocado, or walnut

How to Potato Crust Fresh Salmon

With frozen shredded hash brown potatoes in the freezer, you can always prepare fresh salmon with a potato crust. Cut a skinless salmon fillet into serving-size pieces. Remove the hash browns from the freezer and measure out about a half cup per serving of salmon. Season the potatoes with salt and pepper to taste and let them thaw in a mixing bowl. It should take the potatoes about 15 minutes to thaw. Add a teaspoon of flour per ½ cup of hash browns, then add 1 egg white or enough to pull the mixture together when lightly stirred with a fork.

Brush the salmon with olive oil and Dijon mustard, then pack the potato mixture onto the top of each piece of salmon. Heat a little butter and olive oil in a skillet over medium-high heat and, when sizzling, add the salmon to the skillet potato-crusted side down. Cook until the potato crust is golden brown, 3 to 4 minutes. Turn the salmon over and cook it until it tests done (a sharp knife inserted in the center of the fish reveals a pink center), 2 to 3 minutes longer.

Place the shallot, cider vinegar, mustard, ketchup, honey, pepper, and salt in a blender or food processor and blend until smooth. With the motor running, add the oil a bit at a time and blend until the vinaigrette thickens. Store the vinaigrette in a glass jar in the refrigerator. It will keep for up to 1 week.

Marian's Fish and Potato Pie

SERVES: 4
PREP: 20 MINUTES
BAKE: 55 MINUTES TO 1 HOUR

My friend Marian Petrie of Earls Barton, England, makes the most wonderful fish pie. It is the recipe she is known for, but also a recipe she pulls together effortlessly because the ingredients are always on hand. The fish is usually cod—fresh or frozen. Baking potatoes add substance to this pie, but the real star is the fish seasoned with a little dry mustard, nutmeg, and lemon. When my children were little they begged for this pie. It's one of those ultimate comfort foods, no matter where you live, perfect for busy weeknight dinners with the family or casual suppers with friends.

2 pounds baking potatoes, peeled and sliced (⅓-inch-thick slices)

4 tablespoons (½ stick) butter or margarine, plus 2 teaspoons butter, at room temperature, for buttering the baking dish

½ cup all-purpose flour

⅛ teaspoon dry mustard

⅛ teaspoon ground nutmeg

2 cups milk

2 cloves garlic, minced

½ teaspoon salt

¼ teaspoon freshly ground black pepper

1 pound white fish fillets, such as cod or haddock, fresh or frozen (see Note)

2 tablespoons fresh lemon juice

2 tablespoons minced fresh flat-leaf parsley

1. Preheat the oven to 350°F.

2. Place the potato slices in a medium-size saucepan and add water to cover. Bring the water to a boil over medium-high heat, then cover the pan, and remove it from the heat. Leave the potatoes in the hot water while you prepare the rest of the pie.

3. Melt the 4 tablespoons of butter in another medium-size pan over medium heat. Stir in the flour, mustard, and nutmeg and cook, stirring, until the mixture is well blended, about 1 minute. Stir in the milk and garlic and let come to a boil. Reduce the heat to low, and continue to cook, stirring, until the mixture thickens, 4 to 5 minutes. Season the sauce with salt and pepper to taste and set it aside.

4. Butter a 2-quart baking dish with the 2 teaspoons of butter. Drain the water from the potatoes and place half of the slices in the prepared baking dish. Cut the fish into bite-size pieces and place these on top of the potatoes. Sprinkle the lemon juice over the fish and season it with the salt and pepper. Arrange the remaining potato slices on top and season them with salt and pepper. Pour the sauce over the potatoes, making sure they are completely covered.

5. Bake the fish and potato pie until the potatoes are tender and golden brown, 55 minutes to 1 hour. Remove the pie from the oven and sprinkle the parsley on top before serving.

SAVE THE DAY NOTE To thaw the cod, place it in a zip-top plastic bag in a bowl or sink filled with cool water for 1 hour.

Do Ahead The potato pie can be completely assembled, covered with aluminum foil, and kept in the refrigerator overnight. It will take about 10 minutes longer to bake the pie straight from the fridge.

MONEY SAVER: To cut the cost of the fish, look for weekly specials on fresh or frozen white fish.

I'd serve it with . . . a green salad or peas and a glass of white wine.

To upgrade the pie, use a 1-pound mixture of shrimp, scallops, and cod.

Shrimp and Cheese Grits

SERVES: 6
PREP: 25 TO 30 MINUTES
COOK: 10 TO 15 MINUTES

You may not know this random fact, but there are as many ways to cook shrimp and grits as there are ways to roast a chicken. Which is why I love this recipe so much—you can leave your mark on it, make it your own just by doing something so simple as adding mushrooms, or using scallions, not white onions, or by quickly frying the shrimp first as in this wonderful version. Plus, the grits can simply be seasoned with butter or, as I prefer, with cheddar and garlic. This is the recipe my daughter wanted me to make for her eighteenth birthday party with friends. It is a classic Southern brunch recipe inspired by the first shrimp and grits I ever tasted in Charleston, South Carolina. With a big Caesar salad and birthday cake for dessert, the meal was simple, elegant, friendly, and fun.

1½ pounds large shrimp, peeled and deveined (see Note)

¼ teaspoon salt

¼ teaspoon freshly ground black pepper

2 tablespoons all-purpose flour

¼ cup olive oil or vegetable oil

2 tablespoons (¼ stick) butter

1 cup thinly sliced mushrooms

½ cup sliced red bell pepper

2 to 3 cloves garlic, sliced

⅓ cup chopped scallions, green parts only

1 cup chopped fresh tomato

½ cup chicken broth

1 tablespoon fresh lemon juice

Dash of hot pepper sauce or Worcestershire sauce

Cheese grits (see page 198)

Chopped fresh flat-leaf parsley or scallions, for garnish

How to Make Cheese Grits

Cook ¾ cup grits (not instant) in a combination of 1½ cups milk and 1½ cups water following the directions on the box or bag. Add 1 to 2 cloves of minced garlic to the cooking water, as well as salt and ground black pepper. When the grits have cooked, add a tablespoon of butter and a handful (about 1 cup) of shredded mild cheddar cheese or Manchego cheese. Continue to cook, stirring, until the cheese and butter melt. Taste for seasoning, adding more butter and cheese, if desired.

① Place the shrimp in a small bowl and season them with salt and pepper. Add the flour and toss to mix. Set the shrimp aside.

② Place the oil in a large cast-iron or other skillet and heat over medium-high heat. When hot, add the shrimp a few at a time and cook through, 1 to 2 minutes per batch. Transfer the cooked shrimp to a plate and continue until all of the shrimp are cooked.

③ Melt the butter in the skillet over medium heat. Add the mushrooms, bell pepper, garlic, and scallions. Cook, stirring, until the mushrooms and bell pepper are soft, 5 to 6 minutes. Add the tomato, chicken broth, lemon juice, and hot sauce or Worcestershire sauce. Increase the heat to medium-high and cook, stirring, until the tomato releases some of its juice, 2 to 3 minutes. Stir the shrimp and their accumulated juices into the sauce and heat over low heat, 1 minute. Spoon the shrimp over the grits and garnish them with the chopped parsley or scallions.

 Not quite razzle-dazzle, but for a slightly fancier presentation, leave the tails on the shrimp.

 Cut all your veggies up to 1 day ahead and store them in covered containers in the refrigerator. Peel and devein the shrimp and keep them chilled.

★
★ ★
★ RAZZLE-DAZZLE

Top the shrimp with crumbled bacon along with the parsley and/or scallions.

Lowcountry Shrimp Boil

SERVES: 12
PREP: 25 MINUTES
COOK: 15 TO 18 MINUTES

The variety of seafood boils that exists up and down the East Coast is endless. Popular as festive summertime party dishes, along the Georgia coast the traditional boil consists of cooking the freshest shrimp with potatoes, corn, and smoked sausage. There the resulting dish is called Frogmore Stew. To make it, you'll need to use a very big pot—if you don't own one, borrow one from a friend, the local church or school kitchen, or even a restaurant that you frequent. The same with the serving platter—*big* is the operational word here. If you want to make the boil for fewer people, you can greatly reduce the ingredients to pare it down for a casual supper for four as my friends Jay and Debbie do. They serve this in the summer when corn is at its sweetest and the days are longest. And so should you.

¼ cup seasoned salt or seafood seasoning (see Note)

3 bay leaves

4 pounds small red-skinned potatoes, scrubbed

2 pounds smoked pork or beef sausage, or a mixture of the two, cut into 2-inch pieces

6 ears corn, shucked and cut in half

4 to 5 pounds large shrimp in their shells

Lemon wedges, for garnish

Fresh flat-leaf parsley, for garnish

Cocktail sauce, for serving

1. Fill a large stockpot halfway with water and place it on the stove over medium-high heat. Add the seasoned salt and bay leaves. Cover the pot and let the water come to a boil.

2. Add the potatoes and sausage and cook until the potatoes are nearly tender, 12 to 15 minutes. Add the corn and shrimp and place the lid back on the pot. When the water returns to a boil, cook the shrimp until they turn bright pink, 3 minutes, no more. Turn off the heat.

3. Using a slotted spoon, transfer the potatoes, sausage, corn, and shrimp to a large platter. Garnish with the lemon wedges and parsley. Serve with cocktail sauce.

 SAVE THE DAY NOTE Everyone's got a favorite seafood seasoning. Old Bay is a good standby. I also like Cajun seasonings like Zatarain's and Slap Ya Mama.

I'd serve it with . . .
plenty of napkins, cold beer and iced tea, coleslaw, and garlic bread.

New Year's Eve Lobster with the Kids

SERVES: 4
PREP: 15 TO 20 MINUTES
COOK: 8 TO 9 MINUTES PER POT OF LOBSTERS

A tradition we started when our children were young was to celebrate New Year's Eve at home with them, and cook lobster. Our children are spaced four years apart, and just as soon as one of the girls turned twelve or thirteen and didn't want to welcome in the New Year with her parents, we had an excuse—your little brother really wants you to spend the evening with us, dear. So the pressure was definitely on me to make this evening special and fun and the meal so fabulous no one wanted to miss it. One year it came to me: live lobsters from the market. I could steam them right in the kitchen, serve them with melted butter and lemon, make some crispy roasted potatoes and a green salad, and possibly garlic bread.

I'd set the table with lots of little bowls to hold the lemon butter for dipping and bigger bowls for the shells. Sparkling grape juice was poured into Champagne flutes. There were party hats and favors. It was so much fun, it became the best tradition ever. Yes, one year a lobster got loose in the kitchen before we could wrangle it into the pot. But lobsters on New Year's was a treat for a landlocked Southern family, and it was a lot less expensive than hiring a babysitter and going out.

I'd serve it with . . .
roasted or hash brown potatoes, corn on the cob, a green salad,
garlic bread—but really it doesn't matter because
everyone just wants the lobster.

Sea salt

*4 large live Maine lobsters
(about 1½ pounds each; see Note)*

*8 tablespoons (1 stick) lightly salted
butter*

1 lemon

1. Fill a large stock pot with 3 to 4 quarts of water and season the water with 3 to 4 tablespoons of sea salt. You will be able to cook 2 lobsters at a time in this pot. If you have 2 pots, you can cook all of the lobsters at once.

2. Bring the water to a boil and when boiling grasp one lobster at a time around its back and plunge it head first into the water. Cover the pot. When the water returns to a boil, start timing. You need to cook lobsters 5 to 6 minutes per pound, which is about 8 or 9 minutes for 1½-pound lobsters.

3. To test for doneness, pull one of the antennae on the head of a lobster; it should come out easily. Drain the lobsters well in the sink or in a large colander, so all of the cooking water drains out of them (see Note).

4. Melt the butter in a small saucepan over low heat. Cut the lemon in half and squeeze 1 to 2 tablespoons of lemon juice into the melted butter.

5. Serve the lobsters on a big platter with cracking tools and small forks for picking out the meat. Set a little bowl of the lemon butter at each serving place. Don't forget bowls for the lobster shells and plenty of napkins.

SAVE THE DAY NOTE Many supermarket seafood departments sell live lobsters. Be sure to call ahead and reserve them during peak holiday times. If they are fresh, the lobsters will be active, and the seafood department will pack them into crates for your voyage home. Unless you live near the sea, you are going to have to create sea water for cooking the lobsters by adding sea salt to tap water. Add 1 tablespoon of salt for each quart of water.

To drain a lobster, hold it with tongs upside down over the sink and gently shake it.

★RAZZLE-DAZZLE

It's New Year's Eve! Create some razzle-dazzle. Turn on your favorite music, light the candles, dim the lights, and enjoy a special dinner. Once dinner is through, hand out party hats to everyone and put them on—even if they're silly! Play your favorite games—whether board or card or guessing games, like charades or twenty questions. Be sure to have bowls of favorite snacks set out. Even after a big fancy dinner, games can work up an attack of the nibbles.

Once the clock strikes midnight (watching the ball drop in Times Square is a TV must), a Champagne or apple juice or other favorite drink toast is a great way to welcome in the new year. For those who still feel awake enough to keep the brand-new year company, it's time to turn up the music and dance till you drop—or at least slow dance till it's time to call it a night. Happy Festive New Year!

CHAPTER 6

ON THE SIDE

I've never been a main dish gal. Whether at home or in a restaurant, my eyes follow the sides because they have color, flavor, and excitement. And in writing this cookbook, I fell in love with the sides you'll find here— some wonderful in their own right and others because they work well as a group.

What makes a great side dish? The ability to complement a main dish but not steal the show, for one. These include the potato and rice dishes in this chapter. They are solid recipes, but they step back when roasted turkey or grilled steaks come to the table. They are there to sop up juices, fill hungry stomachs, and marry well with big flavors.

A great side dish also can have a big personality. Take the grilled eggplant slices stacked with tomatoes and feta, the roasted green beans with ginger, and the roasted cauliflower with currants—all exciting flavors, all visually interesting, all able to stand on their own. Add a salad and some bread and you have a meal.

And then there are those sides that are just plain nostalgic. They are a part of your cooking heritage or they should be—White Corn Pudding, Esther's Carrot Soufflé, and John's Scalloped Oysters. Bake them and love them as your own.

I've also included a few breads I love in this chapter. They make wonderful side dishes for buffets and holiday dinners, add interest at brunch, serve you well when baked ahead and stashed in the freezer, and are just plain delicious. You will adore the banana bread and muffins, the breakfast bread, the coffee cake, and the pumpkin bread. The overnight rolls are a godsend for busy families, and Kirsten's Dutch Baby is perfect for long, slow weekend mornings and snow days.

Enjoy every recipe, every bite, every exceptional side. They save an entrée from tasting ho-hum, satisfy your craving for something comforting or nostalgic feeling, and many can be made ahead, taking the rush out of mealtime.

Holiday Buffet Psychology

Planning a perfect holiday buffet is a lot like planning seating at a dinner party with conflicting and complementing personalities to consider. You want a balance of color, texture, and seasoning. Let's say the "host" is the main dish. Depending on the size of the party, "invite" one to three noisy, bossy "guests" (side dishes). Spread them out and let them shine. Invite a needy guest (a fussier side dish) as well. Place the invited needy guest next to the host. This might be the delicate White Corn Pudding, straight from the oven, right next to a ham because it can soak up the ham juices. Or, it might also be Flowerree's Overnight Rolls because they need something like turkey or ham to go with them. When arranging the buffet table, the main dish or dishes and accompaniments come first, then come the vegetable sides, and finally the sweet desserts.

In this chapter, I would say the bossy standalone side recipes are Dave's Ooh-La-La Potatoes, Roasted Cauliflower with Garlic and Currants, Turkish Green Beans with Tomatoes and Mint, Spicy Creamed Spinach Gratin, G's Cheddar Baked Apples, and John's Scalloped Oysters. All the others are complementary and can be arranged most anywhere on the table.

Elaine's Broccoli Jennifer

SERVES: 6 TO 8
PREP: 15 TO 20 MINUTES
BAKE: 35 TO 40 MINUTES

When St. Louis resident Elaine Bly plans her Thanksgiving menu, two things are always on the menu—turkey and Broccoli Jennifer. A throwback casserole recipe containing a can of cream of mushroom soup as well as broccoli and cheddar cheese, Broccoli Jennifer wasn't named for a family member. Instead it was clipped from a fall 1979 *Bon Appétit* magazine column and a variation has worked its way into the Bly family food files, beloved by young and old. Elaine loves how adaptable the recipe is because she can assemble the casserole without adding the cracker and butter topping and freeze it. On Thanksgiving morning she pulls Broccoli Jennifer from the freezer, adds the topping, and places it right into the oven to bake.

1 package (10 ounces) frozen chopped broccoli, thawed and drained

½ cup mayonnaise

½ cup (2 ounces) shredded sharp cheddar cheese

2 tablespoons minced onion (optional; see Note)

1 can (10¾ ounces) cream of mushroom soup

1 large egg

Freshly ground black pepper

½ to 1 cup crushed buttery round crackers (from 9 to 18 crackers)

1 tablespoon butter, cut into small pieces

1. Place a rack in the center of the oven and preheat the oven to 350°F.

2. Place the broccoli, mayonnaise, cheddar cheese, onion, if using, mushroom soup, and egg in a large bowl and stir to combine. Season with pepper to taste. Spoon the broccoli mixture into a 2-quart casserole dish.

3. Top the broccoli mixture with ½ cup of the cracker crumbs (if you want more crumb topping add up to 1 cup). Dot the cracker crumbs with the butter.

4. Bake the broccoli casserole until it is bubbly and golden, 35 to 40 minutes.

Elaine does not add the onion because she has found that her grandchildren are more likely to eat this without onion.

Take the package of broccoli out of the freezer the night before you want to assemble the casserole. Place the broccoli in a bowl in the fridge to thaw overnight. Or, prepare the entire recipe up until adding the cracker crumbs, cover the casserole with aluminum foil, and freeze it for up to a month.

★RAZZLE-DAZZLE

Add mushrooms to the casserole. Cook a cup of sliced mushrooms in a tablespoon of butter until they release their juices and cook down, 4 to 5 minutes, then add them to the casserole along with the broccoli.

Kren's Brussels Sprouts with Toasted Pecans

SERVES: 8
PREP AND COOK: 20 TO 25 MINUTES

Kren Teren of Nashville made this brussels sprouts dish on New Year's Eve several years ago, and everyone at the party begged for the recipe. Kren has a knack for putting together flavors and being on the cutting edge of new food trends. Since that party this recipe has made the rounds for good reason. Kren has a light touch with brussels sprouts. The recipe answers the question as to what green vegetable to serve when you need something extra special. And it's a snap to prepare.

1½ pounds brussels sprouts

½ cup chopped pecans

2 tablespoons (¼ stick) butter

1 cup finely chopped onion

4 cloves garlic, minced

½ cup chicken broth

1½ tablespoons sugar

Salt

① Preheat the oven to 350°F.

② Cut the stem ends off the brussels sprouts and, using a sharp knife, cut them in half lengthwise and then thinly slice the halves crosswise. You should have about 8 cups.

③ Place the pecans in a metal cake pan or pie pan. Place the pecans in the oven to toast until golden, 4 to 5 minutes. Set the pecans aside.

I'd serve it with . . .
grilled or roasted beef fillet, Dave's Ooh-La-La Potatoes
(page 232), or White Corn Pudding (page 214).

④ Melt the butter in a large skillet over medium heat. Add the onion and garlic and cook, stirring, until cooked through and lightly browned, about 4 minutes.

⑤ Add the brussels sprouts to the skillet. Cook, stirring, until they turn bright green, about 2 minutes. Add the chicken broth and sugar and cook until the liquid has almost evaporated, about 5 minutes. Add salt to taste and stir in the pecans, then serve.

Do Ahead You can slice the brussels sprouts early in the day and refrigerate them until you assemble the recipe.

MONEY SAVER: Look at warehouse stores for deals on brussels sprouts in a large bag. Keep them in the fridge, where they will last for 10 days or more.

The Sweet Secret of Cooking Brussels Sprouts

While on book tour in Seattle, I was at a TV station about to go on air to frost a cake, and a fellow TV guest was a dietitian from a local hospital whose segment included cooking brussels sprouts. She was intrigued with my cake, and I was intrigued with her knowledge of cooking brussels sprouts. She advised that roasting brussels sprouts in a hot pan caramelizes them and makes them taste sweeter. I have followed her instructions and can tell you they work. So the next time you roast brussels sprouts cut them in half, toss them with olive oil and a pinch of salt, and then place them on a baking sheet that has been preheating in the oven. Roast the brussels sprouts at 400°F for 7 to 8 minutes and see how much sweeter they taste from the hot baking sheet.

★ RAZZLE-DAZZLE

For a sweet complement to the onion, add a handful of currants to the skillet along with the chicken broth.

Esther's Carrot Soufflé

SERVES: 6
PREP: 15 MINUTES
BAKE: 40 TO 45 MINUTES

Esther Levine of Atlanta loves to bring this soufflé to holiday dinners for several reasons—it is bright and colorful, tastes good with most anything served, and can be made ahead and reheated. Plus, it's good for conversation. "People always think it is sweet potatoes, and I say, 'No, not sweet potatoes. Can you guess what's in it?' And that gets the conversation rolling with everyone trying to guess." This recipe saves Esther's day because she knows it backward and forward. It's a tried-and-true side that's based on canned carrots, making it easy to prepare (the peeling and slicing has already been done for you), with the familiar seasonings of a sweet potato casserole. Through the years she has revised it by decreasing the sugar. It was a recipe she originally received from her friend Ruth Melkonian Jaffe, who got it from her friend Karen Wise—the sign of a great recipe, constantly shared.

5 tablespoons butter, melted, plus 2 teaspoons butter for greasing the casserole dish

2 cans (14½ ounces each) sliced carrots, drained

3 large eggs

⅓ cup sugar

3 tablespoons all-purpose flour

1 teaspoon baking powder

1 teaspoon pure vanilla extract

Splash of fresh orange juice

Dash of ground cinnamon

⅓ cup cornflakes or Honey Bunches of Oats cereal

⅓ cup finely chopped pecans

2 tablespoons light brown sugar

1. Place a rack in the center of the oven and preheat the oven to 350°F. Butter a 1½- to 2-quart casserole dish with the 2 teaspoons of butter and set it aside.

2. Place the drained carrots, melted butter, eggs, sugar, flour, baking powder, vanilla, orange juice, and cinnamon in the bowl of a food processor. Pulse until well combined, about 15 seconds. Pour the carrot mixture into the prepared casserole dish.

3. Place the cereal, pecans, and brown sugar in a small bowl and toss to mix. Scatter the topping over the carrot mixture.

4. Bake the soufflé until the topping is golden and the soufflé has cooked through, 40 to 45 minutes.

Do Ahead Prepare the soufflé but don't make the topping. Cover and freeze the carrot mixture for up to 2 weeks. Just before reheating, remove the casserole from the freezer, preheat the oven, and make the topping. Scatter the topping over the frozen casserole and bake until the topping is golden and the soufflé has cooked through, 50 to 55 minutes.

I'd serve it with . . .
roasted turkey, brisket, or lamb. Even fried chicken.

Pairing Sides and Mains

How many times have you thought you could make a meal of all the side dishes at a buffet or potluck and just skip the main? I am guilty of that. Often the sides are a heck of a lot more interesting than the main course. And if you think this way, then plan your next meal around a favorite side. For example, say you love the flavor of Roasted Green Beans with Fresh Ginger. Both chicken and fish would go nicely with them.

Marinate flattened chicken breasts in a teriyaki marinade from the supermarket, then grill them for 3 to 4 minutes per side. Add steamed rice and you have a meal with those green beans. To the roasted cauliflower side recipe, I would pair roasted chicken. To the spinach gratin, I would pair a small steak. To the roasted ratatouille, I'd add skewers of grilled shrimp. Start with the side and wind up with a meal.

Roasted Cauliflower with Garlic and Currants

SERVES: 6
PREP: 10 MINUTES
BAKE: 20 TO 25 MINUTES
COOLING: 15 TO 20 MINUTES

My family was so excited to pick up our first CSA (Community Supported Agriculture) share on a spring afternoon. Too early for tomatoes, our box contained a huge assortment of greens, a few early peppers, and a massive head of purple-tinged cauliflower. My kids were skeptical, but I could not wait to get home and roast the cauliflower. It was just too precious to steam and serve with cheese sauce as my mother had loved to do. No, it needed just a smidgen of salt, garlic, olive oil, and a little time in the oven. I tossed the hot roasted cauliflower with a few currants and scallions—delicious! This might not have saved my day, but it surely made my day.

1 large head cauliflower

6 cloves garlic

3 tablespoons olive oil, plus olive oil for serving

¼ teaspoon salt, or more to taste

⅓ cup currants

Freshly ground black pepper

White balsamic vinegar or white wine vinegar, for serving

¼ cup chopped scallions, green parts only

I'd serve it with . . . grilled salmon or any fish, baked or grilled pork chops, or grilled steaks.

1. Preheat the oven to 400°F.

2. Cut the florets from the head of cauliflower and separate them into small pieces. Reserve the stems for another use, or discard. Peel and slice the garlic into ¼-inch-thick pieces. Toss the cauliflower and garlic with the olive oil and season it with the salt. Transfer the cauliflower to a rimmed baking sheet and place it in the oven.

3. Roast the cauliflower until it is lightly browned, 20 to 25 minutes. Toss the currants with the hot cauliflower on the baking sheet. Let the mixture cool for 15 to 20 minutes. Taste for seasoning, adding more salt if necessary and pepper to taste.

4. Transfer the cauliflower and currant mixture to a serving bowl or shallow platter. Drizzle some olive oil and a little vinegar on top. Garnish the cauliflower with the scallions and serve.

★ ★ ★
★ **RAZZLE-DAZZLE**

Capers are a salty over-the-top garnish you may or may not like. To add some drama to this dish, add 1 tablespoon of them.

LAST-MINUTE BIRTHDAY PARTY • WEEKNIGHT DINNER • **VERY VEGETARIAN**

White Corn Pudding

SERVES: 8
PREP: 15 MINUTES
BAKE: 30 TO 35 MINUTES

I was having breakfast with the novelist and cookbook author Alice Randall and she described how her daughter living in a small town in Mississippi found the convenience of frozen white corn just too good to pass up. There aren't any farmers' markets

I'd serve it with . . .
pork tenderloin,
baked ham, turkey, or
fried chicken and
sliced tomatoes.

nearby, and supermarket corn on the cob isn't that fresh, but her daughter could always rely on the fresh flavor of frozen corn. Funny, my mother knew this trick as she made a corn pudding any time of the year using frozen white corn. It's a nice change from potatoes or rice. And it is seasonless, too.

2 tablespoons (¼ stick) butter, melted, plus 2 teaspoons butter for greasing the casserole dish

3 packages (10 ounces each) frozen white corn, thawed, or 7 to 8 ears fresh white corn (see Note)

1 tablespoon all-purpose flour

2 large eggs

2 teaspoons sugar

1 teaspoon salt

1¼ cups half-and-half

1. Place a rack in the center of the oven and preheat the oven to 350°F. Lightly butter a 2-quart casserole dish.

2. Place the corn in the prepared casserole dish and stir in the flour. Set the corn aside.

3. Place the eggs, sugar, and salt in a medium-size bowl and whisk to combine. Whisk in the half-and-half. Pour the half-and-half mixture over the corn in the casserole dish and stir to combine. Pour the melted butter over the corn.

4. Bake the corn until the center of the pudding is set, 30 to 35 minutes. Serve hot.

SAVE THE DAY NOTE To cut the kernels off an ear of corn hold it upright on a cutting board and, using a sharp knife, cut close to the cob, slicing off the kernels. You need 4 cups.

★
★ ★
★ RAZZLE-DAZZLE

I love to add a pinch of ground nutmeg or cayenne pepper to the corn pudding.

Grilled Eggplant Stacks

SERVES: 6 TO 12, DEPENDING ON THE HEIGHT OF THE STACKS
PREP: 35 TO 40 MINUTES TO 1 HOUR
GRILL: 7 TO 8 MINUTES
BAKE: 6 TO 7 MINUTES

This recipe has saved me for a number of summers. If friends are coming over for a casual supper of steaks or chicken on the grill, this is the side that I serve. Yes, it takes a little advance preparation to make basil-infused olive oil and grill the egg-plant slices, but once that is done you assemble the stacks and let them rest at room temperature until it's time to heat them through before dining. In fact, it is this do-ahead component that makes the eggplant stacks great for entertaining. Plus, you have options—when made high, the stacks can be a main dish for vegetarians; shorter, they're perfect as a first course at a seated dinner, and a showstopper arranged on a long platter for buffets. And did I mention the flavor? The ingredients make enough for twelve short or six high stacks. One bite says summertime.

FOR THE BASIL OIL

1 cup fresh basil leaves

½ cup olive oil

½ teaspoon salt

FOR THE EGGPLANT STACKS

*2 large or 3 medium-size eggplants
(2 to 3 pounds; for 24 slices)*

Salt and freshly ground black pepper

3 large tomatoes (for 12 slices total)

¾ cup (6 ounces) crumbled feta cheese

Arugula, for serving

Garnish the eggplant stacks with
chopped basil, a few capers, or a
kalamata olive, in addition to the basil oil.

1. Make the basil oil: Place the basil leaves, olive oil, and ½ teaspoon of salt in a food processor. Process the basil until it is finely chopped. Line a sieve with paper towels and place it over a bowl. Pour the basil and oil mixture onto the paper towels and press gently on the mixture to extract the oil from the basil. About ⅓ cup of basil oil will seep into the bowl. Set aside 1 tablespoon of the basil oil for garnishing the eggplant stacks. Set aside the chopped basil leaves on the paper towels.

2. Make the eggplant stacks: Preheat the grill to medium-high. Or preheat an indoor stovetop grill.

3. Trim the ends off the eggplants, then cut them into 24 slices that are a little less than ½ inch thick. Brush the eggplant slices on both sides with the basil oil and season them with salt and pepper to taste. Grill the eggplant slices until they soften and are crisp around the edges, 7 to 8 minutes, turning once. Transfer the grilled eggplant to a platter.

4. Preheat the oven to 400°F.

5. Cut the tomatoes into 12 slices, each about ⅓ inch thick, discarding the end slices or setting them aside for another use.

6. For 12 short stacks, select 12 large slices of grilled eggplant and place them on a baking sheet. Spread each with ½ teaspoon of the reserved chopped basil. Top each with a slice of tomato and add a generous spoonful of feta cheese. Top the cheese with another eggplant slice and finish the stack with another heaping tablespoon of feta.

7. Place the baking sheet in the oven and bake the stacks until the eggplant is warmed through and the feta has melted slightly, 6 to 7 minutes.

8. To serve, line a platter or plate with arugula. Place the eggplant stacks on top of the arugula and drizzle the reserved 1 tablespoon of basil oil over the stacks.

SAVE THE DAY NOTE Use additional eggplant, tomatoes, cheese, and basil to make these stacks even higher. Top the feta cheese with another eggplant slice, more chopped basil, another slice of tomato, a final slice of eggplant, and a final tablespoon of feta.

Do Ahead You can make the basil oil up to 6 hours in advance and leave it at room temperature. You can grill the eggplant up to 6 hours in advance as well.

Turkish Green Beans with Tomatoes and Mint

SERVES: 4 TO 6
PREP: 15 MINUTES
COOK: 10 TO 12 MINUTES
COOL: 15 MINUTES

When you're searching for something different to do with green beans, this dish is fresh and unique on the potluck table or alongside chicken and mashed potatoes in your kitchen. Pairing tomatoes with cinnamon, hot pepper, and mint lends an exotic flavor combo, and it is one I have made often after researching fresh mint for a cooking class years ago. Fresh mint effortlessly adds interest, and along with cinnamon and hot pepper flakes, contributes to the classic Turkish flavor. Another way to season with fresh mint is to make a couscous salad with a Mediterranean vibe—fresh mint, cucumbers, and crumbled feta.

8 ounces thin green beans

¼ cup olive oil

1 cup thinly sliced onion

½ teaspoon salt

1 cup water

1 cup chopped fresh tomatoes

1 large clove garlic, minced

Pinch of cinnamon

Freshly ground black pepper

2 tablespoons fresh lemon juice (from 1 lemon)

1 teaspoon red wine vinegar

Pinch of red pepper flakes

¼ cup chopped fresh mint

I'd serve it with . . .
grilled lamb chops or skewers of
marinated chicken breast.

1. Snip the stem ends off the green beans. Rinse, drain, and set the beans aside.

2. Heat the olive oil in a large skillet over medium heat and add the onion. Cook, stirring, until the onion softens, 2 to 3 minutes. Add the green beans, salt, and ½ cup of water and cover the skillet. Cook the green beans until they turn bright green, about 3 minutes.

3. Place the tomatoes, garlic, and cinnamon in a bowl. Season with black pepper to taste and stir to combine. Add the tomato mixture and ½ cup of water to the skillet with the green beans and stir to combine. Let cook uncovered until the green beans are tender, 4 to 5 minutes.

4. Remove the skillet from the heat. Stir in the lemon juice, wine vinegar, and red pepper flakes. Let the green bean mixture cool to room temperature, about 15 minutes, then stir in the mint. Serve at room temperature.

Do Ahead The green bean mixture can be made early in the day. Don't add the mint until just before serving.

LAST-MINUTE BIRTHDAY PARTY • WEEKNIGHT DINNER • HOLIDAY IDEAS

Roasted Green Beans with Fresh Ginger

SERVES: 6 TO 8
PREP: 10 MINUTES
BAKE: 12 TO 15 MINUTES

Beth Meador asked me to watch these green beans while they were roasting in her oven. She was hosting a going-away party for our friend Dayna, and as can happen at fun parties, everyone congregated in the kitchen and it was easy to forget something was in the oven. So I looked after the beans and, when they were roasted, took them out and tossed them with grated fresh ginger. Those beans were fabulous—I would like to take the credit, but it was not my recipe. Beth was nice enough to share her green bean recipe, something she falls back on a lot.

1 pound green beans (see Note)

2 tablespoons olive oil

1 teaspoon Asian (dark) sesame oil

¼ teaspoon salt

Pinch of dried thyme

1 tablespoon grated peeled fresh ginger

(1) Place a rack in the center of the oven and preheat the oven to 400°F.

(2) Snip the stem ends off the green beans. If they are large and tough, slice them in half. Rinse, drain, and set the beans aside.

(3) Place the olive oil, sesame oil, salt, and thyme on a rimmed baking sheet. Add the green beans and toss to coat them well with the oils.

(4) Bake the green beans until they soften and are cooked through, 12 to 15 minutes. Remove the baking sheet from the oven, toss the green beans with the ginger, and serve.

SAVE THE DAY NOTE This recipe works best with fresh green beans. Select tender medium-size beans. If they have strings, remove them. Do not use the larger pole beans as they do not roast well. You can use tiny slender French-style beans; they will need just 8 to 10 minutes in the oven.

Do Ahead Prepare the green beans, placing them on the baking sheet and coating them with the oils up to 3 hours in advance. Let sit at room temperature and pop them in the oven at the last minute.

I'd serve it with . . . anything, from chicken to fish to beef to lamb to a cheese omelet.

I'd serve it with . . . a grilled steak, burgers, chicken breasts, lamb kebabs, or as the main dish with a plate of sliced ripe tomatoes on the side.

Spicy Creamed Spinach Gratin

SERVES: 6 TO 8
PREP: 10 TO 15 MINUTES
COOK: 9 TO 12 MINUTES
BAKE: 20 TO 25 MINUTES

For years I have yearned for the perfect creamed spinach recipe. My husband is a huge fan, and I have experimented with so many versions: with cream cheese, with a roux, with fresh spinach, with frozen, stirred in a pot, baked in the oven—you name it. When I visited Raleigh, North Carolina, on a book tour I talked food with one of my favorite Southern cooks, Sheri Castle. I asked Sheri what her favorite recipe was to take to potlucks and serve at spur-of-the-moment dinner parties, and Sheri said creamed spinach with jalapeño peppers. Aha! Another twist. So once I was home I experimented with fresh jalapeños sautéed along with the onions in the early stages of this recipe. Loved it! And if you wonder why after years of trials I would use frozen rather than fresh spinach, the reason is that you need far too much fresh spinach to cook down into a manageable gratin. P.S.: My husband loved this version, too.

3 tablespoons unsalted butter

2 cups chopped onion

2 tablespoons minced jalapeño pepper (from 1 large or 2 small peppers)

3 tablespoons all-purpose flour

¼ teaspoon grated nutmeg

1½ cups milk

1½ cups heavy (whipping) cream

3 packages (10 ounces each) frozen chopped or leaf spinach, thawed

1½ cups (6 ounces) grated Parmesan cheese

½ teaspoon salt, or more to taste

¼ teaspoon freshly ground black pepper

1. Place a rack in the center of the oven and preheat the oven to 425°F.

2. Melt the butter in a heavy medium-size saucepan over medium heat. Add the onion and jalapeño pepper and cook, stirring, until the onion is translucent, 5 to 6 minutes. Stir in the flour and nutmeg and cook, stirring, until the mixture pulls together in a mass, 1 to 2 minutes. Pour in the milk and cream and whisk until the mixture thickens, 3 to 4 minutes.

3. Squeeze as much water out of the frozen spinach as you can. Crumble the spinach into the pan. Add 1 cup of the Parmesan cheese, season with the salt and black pepper, and stir to combine. Pour the spinach mixture into a 2-quart baking dish and spoon the remaining ½ cup of Parmesan over the top.

4. Bake the creamed spinach until golden brown on top and bubbly around the edges, 20 to 25 minutes. Serve at once.

How to Cook Any Green Well (and Healthfully, Too)

A prepared refrigerator is a refrigerator filled with greens ready for cooking. Chard, kale, collards, and turnip greens are easily simmered to accompany grilled fish and steaks or roasted chicken or pork, and even make a meal all by themselves when served alongside white beans and a slice of garlic bread or corn bread.

Rinse the greens two or three times to remove any sand or debris, and drain on paper towels. If you buy pre-washed and chopped greens, take care to sort through the bag to remove an excess of chopped tough stem pieces. If the leaves are whole, you can discard the tough stems, and then tear or chop the leaves for cooking.

To cook, heat a tablespoon or two of olive oil in a large heavy pot over medium heat. Add a handful of minced onion and a couple of sliced garlic cloves and cook until soft, 3 to 4 minutes. Add the greens and any water that clings to them after rinsing. Reduce the heat to low and cook, stirring, until the greens begin to wilt, adding a tablespoon or two of water or chicken broth to keep the greens from sticking to the pot. Reduce the heat to very low, cover the pot, and cook the greens until they are very tender, 20 to 30 minutes. If desired, add a handful of fresh spinach leaves at the end of cooking. Unlike the tougher flavorful leaves, spinach is more tender, and it needs to cook only a minute or two to soften to delicious goodness. Season the greens to taste with salt and pepper and lemon juice or hot sauce.

Tana's Roasted Ratatouille

SERVES: 8
PREP: 20 MINUTES
COOK: 15 TO 20 MINUTES
ROAST: 1 HOUR

Tana Comer is a farmer and friend who has supplied our family with an endless array of organic produce for many summers. One of the recipes she shared with us and our fellow shareholders in her CSA (Community Supported Agriculture) was ratatouille. Her secret for making a great ratatouille: Instead of sautéing each vegetable separately, and then combining them at the end—the French way—sauté the vegetables in groups and roast the ratatouille so the liquid from the veggies evaporates and makes the flavors more pronounced. I love the latter method. For years I had laboriously made ratatouille the French way, but the result was often watery. Now I first sauté and then roast them, which makes for a side dish that will save your day in the summertime.

FOR THE RATATOUILLE

About ¾ cup olive oil

2 large eggplants, peeled and cut into ½-inch cubes (6 cups)

Salt and freshly ground black pepper

1 large zucchini, cut lengthwise in half, then cut crosswise into ½-inch-thick half moons (2 cups)

1 green or red bell pepper, stemmed, seeded, and cut into ½-inch-wide strips

2 small onions, peeled and quartered

4 large tomatoes, peeled, seeded, and coarsely chopped

4 cloves garlic, finely minced or crushed in a garlic press

1 tablespoon minced fresh flat-leaf parsley or fresh thyme leaves

FOR THE GARNISHES (optional)

My Easy Pesto (page 35)

Kalamata olives

Feta cheese, crumbled

1. Place a rack in the center of the oven and preheat the oven to 350°F.

2. Place 2 or 3 tablespoons of the olive oil in a large skillet over medium-high heat. Working in batches, add the eggplant and cook it until it is golden brown, adding more olive oil as needed. This will take a total of 8 to 10 minutes. As the eggplant cooks and browns, using a slotted spoon, transfer it to a 3-quart baking dish. Season the eggplant with salt and black pepper to taste.

3. Add 1 to 2 more tablespoons of olive oil to the skillet and cook the zucchini over medium-high heat until it is lightly browned, 4 to 5 minutes. Add the zucchini to the baking dish with the eggplant.

4. Add more olive oil to the skillet and add the bell pepper and onions, cooking them until they are soft, 3 to 4 minutes. Transfer the bell pepper and onions to the baking dish. Add more olive oil to the skillet, reduce the heat to low, then add the tomatoes and garlic and cook them gently until the tomatoes soften, 1 to 2 minutes. Transfer the tomatoes and garlic to the baking dish. Add the parsley or thyme and season with salt and black pepper to taste. Stir to combine.

5. Bake the ratatouille uncovered until the liquid evaporates from the vegetables and they are cooked through, about 1 hour. Serve the ratatouille with pesto, olives, and feta cheese, if desired.

Do Ahead By all means, make the ratatouille a day or two in advance and refrigerate it, covered. Ratatouille tastes better the next day. In the summer months, just remove it from the refrigerator and let it come to room temperature before serving.

I'd serve it with . . .
crusty bread and maybe some grilled chicken or fish.

Missy's Make Ahead Mashed Potatoes

SERVES: 10
PREP: 25 MINUTES
BAKE: 85 TO 95 MINUTES

Missy Myers of Nashville serves this easy do-ahead potato recipe once a year—on Christmas Day. She loves how easy it is to prepare the potatoes the day before and have them ready and waiting in the fridge to bake on Christmas. Her father loves garlic, so Missy roasts whole heads of garlic and squeezes the pulp into the potatoes, just for her dad. If you are not a fan of garlic, you can easily omit the roasted garlic step. But roasting garlic sweetens it, and the garlic does make the flavor of the potatoes particularly special.

FOR THE ROASTED GARLIC

3 heads garlic

1 tablespoon olive oil

FOR THE POTATOES

4 pounds potatoes, peeled and cut into 2-inch chunks

4 tablespoons (½ stick) unsalted butter, at room temperature, plus 2 tablespoons (¾ stick) butter, melted

1 package (8 ounces) cream cheese, cut into 8 pieces

1 cup sour cream

⅓ cup milk

1 teaspoon salt

1 teaspoon freshly ground black pepper

Choosing the Best Potato for the Job

Ever wonder what potato makes the best potato salad? For so many years I thought it was the waxy, firm red potato because it held up well to cooking and dressing. But now I think otherwise. The best potato for potato salad is a softer potato like a russet potato that absorbs seasonings well. The flavor of a potato salad comes from the seasonings that are added while the potatoes are warm, long before you stir in the mayonnaise. Cook potatoes in large pieces (cut medium-size potatoes in half), and then after they are just tender, cut them into 1-inch pieces and season them while hot with salt, garlic or onion salt, or just an all-purpose seasoned salt. Let the potatoes cool completely before adding chopped onion and celery and mayonnaise.

And what potato makes the best mashed potato? Also a russet because this potato is fluffy and light and absorbs the seasonings and add-ins that make mashed potatoes interesting. And, of course, the best potato for baking is . . . the russet.

But the best potato for roasting is still the red potato or the Yukon Gold because it is starchy and moist in the center and can be crisped up around the edges with a little oil and high heat in the oven.

① Roast the garlic: Preheat the oven to 375°F.

② Cut ½ inch off the top of each head of garlic so the garlic cloves are exposed. Place the garlic heads in a small baking pan and peel away as much of the papery outside as possible while keeping the heads intact. Drizzle the olive oil over the heads of garlic and cover each head with aluminum foil. Bake the garlic until it is quite soft, 45 to 50 minutes. Set the baking pan aside so the garlic can cool.

③ Meanwhile, prepare the potatoes: Place the potato chunks in a large saucepan and add cold water to cover. Let come to a boil over medium-high heat, then reduce the heat to low and cover the pan. Let the potatoes simmer until they are tender, 15 to 20 minutes. Drain the water from the potatoes and mash the potatoes with a potato masher.

④ Add the 4 tablespoons of butter and the cream cheese, sour cream, milk, salt, and pepper to the mashed potatoes. Squeeze the roasted garlic cloves out of the garlic heads into the potato mixture and stir to combine. Mix well with a wooden spoon or, using an electric mixer, beat on low speed. Brush a 3-quart or 13-by-9-inch glass baking dish with a little of the melted butter. Spoon the potato mixture into the baking dish, smoothing the top. Drizzle the remaining melted butter over the potatoes. Cover the baking pan with aluminum foil and place in the refrigerator overnight. (Or, you can bake the potatoes immediately. Omit the chilling and bake as directed below.)

⑤ The next day, remove the potatoes from the refrigerator and let them come to room temperature, about 1 hour. Preheat the oven to 350°F.

⑥ Place the covered baking pan in the oven and bake the potatoes until they are heated through, 40 to 45 minutes. Serve.

 If there are potatoes left over, wrap the baking dish with aluminum foil and refrigerate for up to 1 day. To reheat, pour ½ cup milk over the top of the potatoes and toss. Reheat, covered, in a 325°F oven for 30 minutes.

I'd serve it with . . .
beef tenderloin, barbecue ribs, pork chops, or roasted lamb.

Dave's Ooh-La-La Potatoes

SERVES: 8
PREP: 40 TO 45 MINUTES
BAKE: 35 TO 40 MINUTES

These potatoes always draw rave reviews, and thus the name. Dave Mullendore coined the phrase after his jazzed-up version of mashed potatoes was getting a lot more attention at dinner parties than anything else he cooked. "No matter what else you have on the table, people always chow down on the potatoes." Through the years he has added onions, as well as garlic, goes heavy on the cheddar cheese, and grinds enough pepper on top "until your wrist starts to hurt." The skins get mashed into the potatoes, which totally threw his wife, Karen, for a loop the first Thanksgiving meal they shared together. But she has gotten used to Dave's method and his ritual of making them during the holidays. Their forgiving nature is what makes these potatoes save the day: "If dinner is late, keep the cover on and don't worry about the potatoes. It's very hard to overcook them no matter how much fun you are having."

3 pounds red new potatoes

8 tablespoons (1 stick) lightly salted butter

1 cup shredded sharp cheddar cheese, plus 1 to 2 cups shredded sharp cheddar cheese for topping the potatoes

1 clove garlic, minced or crushed in a garlic press

1 cup sour cream or plain yogurt

1 cup milk

¼ cup minced onion (optional)

Salt and freshly ground black pepper

① Rinse the potatoes under warm running water and scrub them to remove any grit. Place the potatoes in a pot and add cold water to cover. Bring to a boil

I'd serve it with . . .
roasted turkey, baked ham, steaks on the
grill, brisket, pork barbecue—whatever
your heart desires.

over medium-high heat, then reduce the heat and let simmer until the potatoes are cooked through but not mushy, 20 to 25 minutes. Using a slotted spoon, transfer the potatoes to a large bowl. Cut the butter into pieces and add them to the potatoes.

(2) Preheat the oven to 350°F.

(3) Using a potato masher or a large fork, coarsely mash the potatoes, skins and all. Add the 1 cup of cheddar cheese and the garlic and mix well. Add the sour cream and mix well. Add the milk and mix well. Mix in the onion, if using, and season the potatoes with salt and pepper to taste. Transfer the potatoes to a baking dish. Sprinkle anywhere from 1 to 2 cups of cheddar cheese on top of the potatoes, depending on your taste. Cover the dish, and place it in the oven.

(4) Bake the potatoes until they are heated through, 35 to 40 minutes. Uncover the potatoes for the last 15 minutes of baking to let the cheese bubble and lightly brown.

★ RAZZLE-DAZZLE

Instead of sour cream use an herb-flavored fresh cheese, such as Boursin. Garnish the potatoes with minced fresh chives.

Henrietta's Rice Chantilly

SERVES: 6 TO 8
PREP: 15 TO 20 MINUTES
BAKE: 30 TO 35 MINUTES

Tish Elliott remembers how her Aunt Ret, Henrietta Crosland of Bennettsville, South Carolina, used to make this fancy rice dish when family came for Sunday dinner. She would go to Aunt Ret's and no matter what else was on the table, the rice was always her favorite dish. When Aunt Ret died Tish thought the rice recipe would be lost, but thankfully a cousin had a copy of it and sent it to Tish. When plain steamed rice isn't fancy enough for the occasion, this recipe is just the thing.

1 teaspoon butter, at room temperature

3 cups freshly cooked rice

Salt

⅛ teaspoon freshly ground black pepper

⅛ teaspoon cayenne pepper

1 cup heavy (whipping) cream, chilled

1 cup (4 ounces) shredded sharp cheddar cheese

1. Place a rack in the center of the oven and preheat the oven to 350°F. Grease a 2-quart casserole dish with the butter.

2. Stir 1 teaspoon of salt and the black pepper and cayenne pepper into the cooked rice. Spoon the rice into the prepared casserole dish.

3. Place the cream in a large bowl and beat it with an electric mixer on high speed until stiff peaks form, 3 to 4 minutes. Stir in ¼ teaspoon of salt and the cheddar cheese. Spread the whipped cream mixture over the rice.

④ Bake the casserole until the topping browns and puffs up, 30 to 35 minutes. Remove it from the oven and serve at once. The topping will fall as it cools.

Do Ahead Cook the rice early in the day following package directions (2 cups raw rice equals 3 cups cooked when boiled in 2 to 2½ cups water) and it will keep covered on the kitchen counter until you assemble the casserole.

I'd serve it with . . .
simple main dishes like roast chicken, broiled or grilled fish, or roasted pork.

A Blueprint for Fried Rice

Leftover rice does not go unnoticed in my fridge, for within a couple of minutes it can be turned into my son's favorite fried rice.

Start with a sauté of a little chopped onion in vegetable oil, then add a handful of chopped fresh veggies from your fridge—carrots, peppers, green beans—or frozen veggies (even that ubiquitous corn, carrot, and pea mix works great). While this is warming in the pan, season it with a little soy sauce or teriyaki sauce and a dash of hot sauce if you like. Add about 2 cups of cooked rice to the pan and stir to combine. Add a little more oil if the rice sticks to the pan. Add another dash of soy sauce or teriyaki sauce. Now grab an egg from the fridge, crack it into a small bowl, and beat it with a fork. Gradually stir the egg into the rice, stirring as the egg hits the rice so that it blends throughout. Season the rice again with soy sauce or teriyaki sauce and serve. And feel free to add a little chopped leftover chicken or pork chop in addition to those veggies.

John's Scalloped Oysters

SERVES: 8 TO 12
PREP: 15 MINUTES
COOK: 40 TO 45 MINUTES

This recipe is as much a part of the Thanksgiving feast for my husband's family as the turkey and dressing. There simply isn't Thanksgiving without scalloped oysters, and much fuss goes into the planning of this recipe because in Chattanooga, Tennessee, oysters have to be ordered ahead of time at the supermarket seafood department, and the right crackers, seasoning, and half-and-half stocked in house. But then that's it. Because my husband, John, goes into the kitchen in buzz saw mode and twenty minutes later, the oysters are in the oven. They bake with no fuss and Thanksgiving and all holiday meals just get a little bit better.

2 tablespoons (¼ stick) butter cut into pieces, plus 2 teaspoons butter for greasing the baking dish

1 quart (32 ounces) top-quality shucked oysters

2 tablespoons minced celery

2 tablespoons minced shallots

2 tablespoons minced fresh flat-leaf parsley

2 tablespoons fresh lemon juice (from 1 lemon)

Cayenne pepper

1½ cups cracker crumbs (from about 30 buttery round crackers; see Note)

Pinch of ground mace

¾ cup half-and-half

1. Place a rack in the center of the oven and preheat the oven to 375°F. Butter a 13-by-9-inch glass or ceramic baking dish with the 2 teaspoons of butter and set it aside.

2. Drain the juice (liquor) from the oysters, setting aside 2 tablespoons and discarding the rest. Place half of the oysters in the bottom of the prepared baking dish. Sprinkle 1 tablespoon each of the celery, shallots, parsley, and lemon juice and a dusting of cayenne pepper over the oysters. Scatter ¾ cup of the cracker crumbs on top of the oysters. Place the remaining oysters on top of the cracker crumbs. Sprinkle the remaining 1 tablespoon each of celery, shallots, parsley, and lemon juice and another dusting of cayenne pepper over the oysters. Add the pinch of mace. Scatter the remaining ¾ cup of cracker crumbs on top.

3. Dot the cracker crumbs with the butter. Stir the reserved oyster juice into the half-and-half and pour the mixture over all, letting it settle down into the oysters.

4. Bake the oysters until the cracker crumbs are golden brown and the juices bubble up around the edges of the baking dish, 40 to 45 minutes.

SAVE THE DAY NOTE John likes Ritz crackers, but use saltines if you like. He also prefers to crush the crackers by hand or with the back of a spoon in a bowl so that the crumbs are coarse and uneven. If you are in a hurry, you can throw the crackers in a food processor and pulse it 8 to 12 times.

Do Ahead You can do the prep work up to 8 hours in advance. Do your mincing ahead of time, and have all those ingredients plus the cracker crumbs arranged and ready to go. Have your baking dish buttered and ready. Then the process is simply layering.

I'd serve it with . . .
Thanksgiving dinner, or any other holiday feast.
Or, as a main course for a weeknight dinner with steamed rice and
a green salad. It will serve four.

G's Cheddar Baked Apples

SERVES: 8 TO 10
PREP: 10 MINUTES
BAKE: 40 TO 45 MINUTES

When Atlanta resident Tish Elliott needs to bring a dish for Thanksgiving and Christmas she always brings G's apples, an irresistible cross between a side dish and a cobbler that can really blur the line on the buffet table. G was her sister-in-law's mother-in-law from Valdosta, Georgia. She always arrived with baked apples in hand. They became known as G's apples, and her family adores them.

Vegetable oil spray, for misting the baking dish

2 cans (about 20 ounces each) apple pie filling

1 cup all-purpose flour

8 tablespoons (1 stick) butter, at room temperature

¾ to 1 cup sugar

2 cups finely shredded cheddar cheese

① Place a rack in the center of the oven and preheat the oven to 350°F. Lightly mist a 13-by-9-inch glass baking dish with vegetable oil spray.

② Spread the apple pie filling in the prepared baking dish. Place the flour in a large bowl or the bowl of a food processor. Cut the butter into tablespoons and place these on top of the flour. Using 2 knives, cut the butter into the flour until the pieces are the size of large peas, or

I'd serve it with . . . turkey or ham.

pulse in the processor until the mixture is the size of peas, 7 to 8 pulses. Stir in or pulse in the sugar and cheddar cheese. Spoon the cheddar mixture over the apple pie filling.

③ Bake the apple pie filling until the topping is golden brown and the filling bubbles up around the edges, 40 to 45 minutes. Remove from the oven and serve warm.

Starting from Scratch

Tish says it is likely the original version of this recipe called for fresh apples. Here is how to do this, although the preparation takes a little longer: Begin with 8 to 10 medium-large tart apples. Peel, core, and slice them into a saucepan and add water to a depth of ½ inch. Add ¼ cup of sugar, or to taste. Let come to a boil over medium-high heat, then reduce the heat to low and let simmer until the apples have cooked down and are soft, 18 to 20 minutes. Add a little more water as needed and sweeten the apples with a little more sugar, if desired. This makes 4 to 5 cups of apples. Substitute the cooked apples for the apple pie filling in G's Cheddar Baked Apples.

Kirsten's Dutch Baby

SERVES: 2 OR 3
PREP: 10 MINUTES
BAKE: 25 TO 30 MINUTES

Every time it snows, Kirsten Madaus of Dayton, Ohio, fondly remembers her days working on a small dairy farm in Finland after college. It was there she was introduced to the Finnish oven pancake called *pannukakku*, which she continued making when she returned to the States and which would turn out to be her children's favorite snow day food. "This takes too much time to make on a regular school day," says Kirsten, "but if school's canceled there's a good bet I've got the ingredients at the ready in the pantry." Her children are teenagers now and sleep through much of their snow days, but when they were young, they looked forward to the pancakes spread with butter and jam. Or dusted with powdered sugar to look like new fallen snow. Almost flanlike in the center with its custardy texture, her Dutch baby is a little different from the German-style oven pancakes, which are lighter and contain less liquid.

2 tablespoons (¼ stick) unsalted butter

3 large eggs

2 cups half-and-half or whole milk

1 cup unbleached all-purpose flour

2 tablespoons sugar

1 teaspoon salt

① Place a rack in the center of the oven and preheat the oven to 375°F.

② Place the butter in a 10-inch cast-iron skillet and place the skillet in the oven to let the butter melt.

③ Place the eggs, half-and-half, flour, sugar, and salt in the large bowl of an electric stand mixer. Beat on medium speed until the batter is thickened and smooth, 9 to 10 minutes. Check on the skillet frequently while the batter is beating, making sure the butter isn't getting too brown. If it turns dark brown, wipe out the skillet and begin again with fresh butter.

④ When the batter is thick and smooth, remove the skillet from the oven and pour in the batter. Place the skillet back in the oven and bake the batter until it is puffed and golden brown, 25 to 30 minutes. Slice into wedges and serve hot.

I'd serve it with . . .
crisp slices of bacon and fresh raspberries.

Dutch Baby Take #2

For another favorite—a more soufflé-like version of the Dutch baby—make a batter the night before by combining 3 eggs, ⅔ cup of half-and-half, 2 tablespoons of sugar, ¼ teaspoon of salt, and ½ cup of all-purpose flour in a mixing bowl and beat with an electric mixer until smooth, about 5 minutes. Refrigerate the batter, covered.

The next morning, preheat the oven to 475°F. Place 2 tablespoons of butter in a 10-inch cast-iron skillet and put it in the oven for the butter to melt. Remove the batter from the fridge and pour it into the hot skillet with the melted butter. Bake the pancake until it bubbles up in the center and is browned around the edge, 10 to 15 minutes. Serve the pancake with lemon wedges and powdered sugar.

Fresh Banana Muffins

MAKES: 12 MUFFINS
PREP: 15 MINUTES
BAKE: 20 TO 25 MINUTES

If you walked in my kitchen today, there would be black overripe bananas on the counter. Sad but true. Maybe it is the Scottish frugality I inherited from my father and my love of homemade banana bread, but whatever the reason, I just can't bring myself to toss out this very overripe fruit. Actually, my favorite save-the-day way to use them is in this muffin recipe. These muffins take less time to bake than a loaf of banana bread, and if I bake more than I need I freeze them to pull out later for bake sales and friends in need. Overripe bananas are sweeter and more flavorful than regular bananas in baking. They don't look pretty, but boy do they taste good in these muffins.

12 paper liners for the muffin tin

1½ cups all-purpose flour

¾ teaspoon baking soda

½ teaspoon salt

1 cup sugar

¾ cup vegetable oil

3 tablespoons buttermilk (see Note)

2 large eggs, lightly beaten

*1 cup mashed bananas
(from 2 large or 3 small bananas,
see Note)*

① Place a rack in the center of the oven and preheat the oven to 350°F. Line a muffin tin with 12 paper liners.

② Place the flour, baking soda, and salt in a large mixing bowl and stir with a wooden spoon to combine. Add the sugar and stir to combine. Add the oil, buttermilk, eggs, and mashed bananas and stir until the batter is smooth but just blended, 50 to 60 strokes. Scoop the batter into the muffin tin liners, filling them very full.

③ Bake the muffins until they are golden brown and the tops spring back when

lightly pressed with your finger, 20 to 25 minutes. Let the muffins cool in the muffin tin for 2 to 3 minutes, then carefully transfer the muffins to a wire rack until cool enough to eat.

 If you don't regularly keep fresh buttermilk in your refrigerator, to help keep a container of buttermilk powder on hand on a pantry shelf. I use 1 tablespoon of buttermilk powder mixed with 3 tablespoons of water when I don't have 3 tablespoons of fresh buttermilk. Or you can substitute 3 tablespoons of regular milk mixed with ½ teaspoon of fresh lemon juice.

You need about a cup of mashed ripe bananas—that's 2 large or 3 small bananas—to make a dozen muffins. Don't worry if you have a little less or a little more than a cup; the recipe will turn out just fine.

 Once the muffins are cool, you can place them in resealable plastic freezer bags and freeze them for up to 6 months.

★ ★ ★ ★ RAZZLE-DAZZLE

Add a pinch of grated nutmeg to the muffin batter and scatter finely ground pecans over the tops of the banana muffins before they bake. Sometimes I add ¼ teaspoon of cinnamon to the batter to give the muffins a morning pick-me-up.

Hawaiian Banana Bread

MAKES: 1 LARGE LOAF
PREP: 10 TO 15 MINUTES
BAKE: 52 TO 56 MINUTES
COOL: 45 MINUTES

Sorry to disappoint, but this recipe didn't originate in Hawaii. My friend Katharine Ray passed along the recipe years ago and could only offer that the name was coined by her mother, Honey Lou Glasscock of Shelbyville, Tennessee, or one of her mother's friends. "I guess it's just one of those recipes that seems exotic in Shelbyville," mused Katharine, who has been making this bread for decades. It was one of the few recipes she took with her when she left home and married. And what makes the recipe perfect for a new cook is its ease of preparation. Plus it makes good use of those overripe, blackened bananas that sit on the kitchen counter. Come to think of it, the flavor is pretty exotic, thus the name.

Vegetable oil spray, for misting the loaf pan

1¼ cups all-purpose flour, plus flour for dusting the loaf pan

1 cup sugar

1 teaspoon baking soda

½ teaspoon salt

½ cup vegetable oil

2 large eggs, lightly beaten

3 very ripe bananas, mashed (1 heaping cup)

① Place a rack in the center of the oven and preheat the oven to 350°F. Lightly mist a 9-by-5-inch loaf pan with vegetable oil spray and dust it with flour. Set the loaf pan aside.

2. Place the flour, sugar, baking soda, and salt in a large bowl and stir to combine well. Make a well in the center of the dry ingredients and add the oil, eggs, and mashed bananas. Stir with a wooden spoon until the ingredients are well combined, 1 to 2 minutes. Spoon the batter into the prepared loaf pan.

3. Bake the banana bread until it is golden brown and the top springs back when lightly pressed with your finger, 52 to 56 minutes. Let the banana bread cool on a wire rack for about 15 minutes, then run a knife around the edges and turn the loaf out right side up to cool completely, about 30 minutes. Slice and serve.

Do Ahead The banana bread can be frozen for up to 3 months. Let thaw on the kitchen counter for about 2 hours.

MONEY SAVER: Banana bread is very inexpensive to make. Use bananas that are very ripe and dark in color, which means the bananas that are too dark for most people to enjoy eating out of hand.

★★★ RAZZLE-DAZZLE

You can add a half cup of finely chopped pecans to the batter.

Marion's Pumpkin Bread with Chocolate Chips

MAKES: 2 LOAVES
PREP: 15 TO 20 MINUTES
BAKE: 50 TO 55 MINUTES
COOL: 45 MINUTES

Marion Martignetti, who lives in Hingham, Massachusetts, has been baking this pumpkin bread religiously since her children were in high school. It was the snack she brought to sporting events, and she thanks Marilyn Cheney, a teacher at Milton Academy, for first sharing the recipe. When Marion's daughter played lacrosse for Harvard, Marion baked pumpkin muffins for her daughter's tailgate parties, and now that Marion is in the clothing business, she bakes loaves for her trunk shows. Which is where I tasted this bread—at a trunk show in Nashville at her cousin Judy's home.

What I love about this pumpkin bread recipe is that it is different from the norm. It has a generous amount of spices and those flavors play well with the chocolate chips. Plus, the bread has a lot less sugar than many pumpkin breads, and you don't miss it—largely because you have two cups of chocolate chips in the batter. And with a mixture of oil and applesauce you feel a bit better about slicing a second piece on a rainy afternoon. I have decided that this bread is the perfect save-the-day recipe—it makes a great gift and it feeds crowds.

RAZZLE-DAZZLE

Add chopped dried cherries to the chocolate chips, using 1½ cups of chocolate chips and ½ cup of dried cherries. Or, omit the chocolate chips and use 1 to 2 cups of raisins.

Vegetable oil spray, for misting the loaf pans

4 large eggs

1½ cups sugar

½ cup vegetable oil

½ cup unsweetened applesauce

1 can (15 ounces) pumpkin

2 cups all-purpose flour, plus flour for dusting the loaf pans

2 teaspoons baking soda

1 teaspoon ground cinnamon

1 teaspoon ground nutmeg

1 teaspoon ground cloves

1 teaspoon ground ginger

2 cups semisweet chocolate chips

① Place a rack in the center of the oven and preheat the oven to 350°F. Lightly mist two 9-by-5-inch loaf pans with vegetable oil spray and dust them with flour. Set the loaf pans aside.

② Place the eggs, sugar, and oil in a large mixing bowl and beat with an electric mixer on low speed to combine, then increase the speed to medium and beat until thickened and the mixture doubles in size. Add the applesauce and pumpkin and beat on low speed until just incorporated.

③ Place the flour, baking soda, cinnamon, nutmeg, cloves, and ginger in a separate bowl and stir to combine. Stir in the chocolate chips. Add the flour mixture to the pumpkin mixture and beat on low speed until the flour is well combined, 30 to 45 seconds.

④ Spoon the batter into the 2 prepared loaf pans and smooth the tops. Bake the loaves until they test done, 50 to 55 minutes; when you press the tops of the loaves lightly with your finger they will feel firm.

⑤ Let the loaves rest in the pans on a wire rack to cool for about 15 minutes. Then, run a knife around the edges of the pans, loosen the loaves by gently shaking them, and turn them out, placing the loaves right side up on the rack to finish cooling for about 30 minutes before slicing.

Do Ahead The pumpkin bread loaves freeze beautifully for up to 6 months. Wrap them in aluminum foil and place them in plastic freezer bags. Let thaw on the kitchen counter for about 2 hours.

Charlot's Breakfast Bread

MAKES: 1 LARGE LOAF
PREP: 25 MINUTES
RISE: 2 HOURS
BAKE: 35 TO 38 MINUTES

Charlot Schaffner was one of my mother's closest friends, and during the busy Christmas season she always brought us a loaf of her breakfast bread. It saved our busy holidays. Crammed with dried cranberries, pecans, and raisins, this bread, toasted and buttered, was just what we craved on those cold winter mornings when there were so many tasks to get done preparing for Christmas. It's also a cheery bread to serve up when your children are leaving the house bleary-eyed to take exams and you have a long to-do list for work and family life.

Charlot was very proud of the fact that she made this bread in a bread machine, dropping the "goodies" as she called them—the cranberries, nuts, and raisins—into the machine while the dough was blending. I wanted to convert this recipe to a traditional method of making bread so that everyone might enjoy it, whether or not they have a bread machine. I use a stand mixer to mix the dough, which is sticky. Don't be tempted to add more flour as this will dry out the bread.

3 cups bread flour

2 tablespoons nonfat dry milk

1 tablespoon dark brown sugar

1¼ teaspoons salt

½ cup dried cranberries

½ cup finely chopped pecans

¼ cup raisins

1 cup plus 2 tablespoons water

2 tablespoons (¼ stick) butter

1 package active dry yeast
(2¼ teaspoons)

Vegetable oil spray, for misting the loaf pan

1. Place the flour, dry milk, brown sugar, and salt in the large bowl of an electric stand mixer. Beat on low speed until just combined. Add the cranberries, pecans, and raisins and beat on low until just combined. Set the flour mixture aside.

2. Place the water and the butter in a small saucepan over low heat. Cook, stirring, until the butter has melted, then remove the pan from the heat. Let the water and butter cool until warm to the touch. Stir in the yeast to dissolve it.

3. Turn on the mixer to low speed and pour the water and yeast mixture into the flour mixture. Increase the mixer speed to medium and beat until the dough comes together in a mass, 3 to 4 minutes. Transfer the dough to a large bowl, cover it with a kitchen towel, and place it in a warm place to rise until doubled in size, about 1 hour.

4. When the dough has risen, lightly mist a 10-by-5-inch loaf pan with vegetable oil spray. Using lightly oiled fingers, punch down the dough. Form it into a loaf and place it in the prepared loaf pan. Cover the loaf pan with the kitchen towel, place it in a warm place, and let the dough rise again until doubled in size, about 1 hour.

5. Place a rack in the center of the oven and preheat the oven to 350°F.

6. Uncover the loaf pan and place it in the oven. Bake the bread until it is well browned on top and tests done (thump it gently with your thumb and pointer finger; if it sounds hollow, it's done), 33 to 38 minutes. Remove the bread from the oven and let it rest in the loaf pan on a wire rack to cool for about 5 minutes, then invert the pan and remove the bread. Let the bread cool on its side on the rack for about 1 hour, then slice it and serve.

Do Ahead Yes, bake this bread ahead of time, let it cool, then wrap it in aluminum foil and freeze it for the busy months ahead. It will keep for up to 3 months. Let thaw on the kitchen counter for 3 to 4 hours.

★ RAZZLE-DAZZLE

Use this bread recipe as a basic template. You can substitute other nuts and dried fruit, even chocolate chips, pumpkin seeds, orange zest, and a smidgen of cinnamon.

Nashville Sour Cream Coffee Cake

SERVES: 12
PREP: 20 MINUTES
BAKE: 28 TO 33 MINUTES

This recipe was such a huge part of my food memories growing up in Nashville. I am sure that sour cream coffee cake existed in other parts of the country, too, but I knew the recipe backward and forward from the Junior League cookbook. However, years later I revisited the recipe and the loaves didn't rise. So I tested and retested this recipe, and what you have today is a different version from the one I remember. The new cake is baked in a nine-inch square pan, and is delicious and moist, perfect for breakfast and brunch and giving to friends when the need arises.

FOR THE COFFEE CAKE BATTER

Vegetable oil spray, for misting the baking pan

1¾ cups sifted all-purpose flour (see Note), plus flour for dusting the baking pan

8 tablespoons (1 stick) unsalted butter, at room temperature

1 cup sugar

2 large eggs

1 teaspoon pure vanilla extract

1½ teaspoons baking powder

¼ teaspoon salt

1 cup sour cream, at room temperature

FOR THE TOPPING

⅓ cup sugar

2 teaspoons ground cinnamon

⅓ cup finely chopped pecans (optional)

To bake this coffee cake as a loaf, assemble it in a 9-inch loaf pan and bake for 55 minutes to 1 hour at 350°F.

1. Place a rack in the center of the oven and preheat the oven to 350°F. Lightly mist a 9-inch-square metal baking pan with vegetable oil spray and dust it with flour. Set the baking pan aside. (This cake can also be baked as a loaf; see the photo on the facing page.)

2. Make the coffee cake batter: Place the butter and the 1 cup of sugar in a large mixing bowl and, using an electric mixer, beat on medium-high speed until the mixture is well creamed and fluffy, 2 to 3 minutes. Reduce the mixer speed to medium and add the eggs, one at a time, beating until just incorporated. Add the vanilla and beat until smooth, about 30 seconds.

3. Place the flour, baking powder, and salt in a bowl and stir to combine. Add a third of the dry ingredients to the batter, and beat on low speed until just combined, about 15 seconds. Add ½ cup of the sour cream and beat on low speed until just combined. Add another third of the dry ingredients, then the remaining ½ cup of sour cream, and the remaining dry ingredients, beating on low speed until smooth. Set the batter aside.

4. Make the topping: Place the ⅓ cup of sugar and the cinnamon in a small bowl and stir to combine. Fold in the pecans, if using. Spoon about 1 tablespoon of the topping mixture over the bottom of the prepared baking pan. Spoon half of the batter on top, carefully spreading it to the edges of the pan with a small spatula. Sprinkle half of the remaining topping mixture evenly over the batter. Spoon the rest of the batter evenly over the topping, spreading it to the edges of the pan. Sprinkle the remaining topping over the top, pressing the pecans into the batter with your fingers, if using.

5. Bake the coffee cake until it is a light golden brown, 28 to 33 minutes. Transfer the baking pan to a wire rack for the coffee cake to cool for about 30 minutes, then serve it while still a little warm.

SAVE THE DAY NOTE Sift the flour before measuring it. This makes the coffee cake lighter.

Do Ahead You can bake the coffee cake ahead and freeze it, wrapped in aluminum foil. It will keep frozen in the pan for up to a month. Let it thaw, uncovered, on the kitchen counter for 2 to 3 hours.

Mini Cinnamon Rolls

MAKES: 40 MINI ROLLS
PREP: 15 MINUTES
BAKE: 20 TO 25 MINUTES

On a church retreat many years ago Veronica Young, who lives in Greenville, South Carolina, first tasted a miniature cinnamon roll that would work its way into her collection of most cherished recipes. A mom had brought along the rolls to share for breakfast. "They simply melted in my mouth," says Veronica, who begged for the recipe from Liz Harbaugh of Collierville, Tennessee. Veronica then made them for her children's sleepovers and out-of-town weekend guests, and everyone came to expect them when they visited her. I love how easily the sweet rolls can be assembled from an ingredient you pick up for cooking emergencies—refrigerated crescent roll dough.

FOR THE ROLLS

2 cans (8 ounces each) refrigerated reduced-fat crescent roll dough

6 tablespoons (¾ stick) unsalted butter, at room temperature

¼ cup granulated sugar

1 teaspoon ground cinnamon

¼ cup golden raisins (optional)

FOR THE GLAZE

1 cup confectioners' sugar

2 tablespoons milk or orange juice

① Make the rolls: Place a rack in the center of the oven and preheat the oven to 350°F.

② Open a can of dough and separate it into 4 rectangles. You will see the dough stamped into triangles, but instead of tearing it into those triangles, press the perforations in the dough together, joining the triangles to form 4 rectangles. Repeat with the second can of dough for a total of 8 rectangles. Spread the butter on the dough rectangles.

③ Place the granulated sugar and cinnamon in a small bowl and stir to combine.

Bake the cinnamon rolls in 2 disposable aluminum foil baking pans, glaze them, then cover the pans with foil. The rolls make a wonderful gift for a friend or as a bake sale offering. Reheat them covered with foil in a 300°F oven for 15 minutes.

Sprinkle the cinnamon sugar evenly over the buttered rectangles of dough. If desired, press the raisins into the dough. Starting from a short end, roll each rectangle of dough up into a cylinder. Cut each roll into 5 equal slices.

④ Place the slices cut side down in an ungreased 13-by-9-inch metal baking pan. Bake the rolls until they are golden brown, 20 to 25 minutes. Let the rolls cool in the baking pan while you make the glaze.

⑤ Make the glaze: Place the confectioners' sugar in a small bowl and whisk in the milk or orange juice. Using a knife or spoon, drizzle the glaze over the warm rolls. Serve the cinnamon rolls warm.

Do Ahead

Bake the cinnamon rolls ahead of time and freeze the unglazed rolls in the baking pan covered with aluminum foil for up to 2 months. Reheat the unglazed rolls, covered, in the oven at 350°F until warmed through, about 10 minutes. Uncover the rolls and glaze them before serving.

I'd serve it with . . . omelets, bacon, and anything else for brunch.

Flowerree's Overnight Rolls

MAKES: 6 DOZEN ROLLS (see Note)
PREP: 20 MINUTES
RISE: 1½ HOURS
BAKE: 10 TO 12 MINUTES

It is no coincidence that save-the-day recipes are popular for the holidays. After all, during the peak busy periods in our lives we need to fall back on those recipes we know by heart. And, rely on recipes that can be made in advance so there is less work to do when the kitchen is frantic. This is one such recipe. It belongs to my mother-in-law Flowerree, and for many years when we went to Chattanooga for Thanksgiving, this roll dough was already made when we arrived. The warm kitchen with the turkey roasting and casseroles baking made a nice and cozy temperature for the rolls to rise before baking. And if the aroma of the roasted turkey wasn't intoxicating enough, you had the scent of yeasty rolls baking in the oven while the turkey rested, waiting to be carved. It doesn't get much better than this.

1 cup vegetable shortening or margarine

¾ cup sugar

2 cups boiling water

2 packages active dry yeast (2¼ teaspoons each)

¼ teaspoon salt

2 large eggs, beaten

6 cups unsifted all-purpose flour (see Note), plus flour for rolling out the rolls

8 tablespoons (1 stick) butter

1. Place the vegetable shortening or margarine and sugar in a large bowl. Pour the boiling water on top and stir until the shortening melts and the sugar dissolves. Let the mixture cool for about 10 minutes; it will still be warm. Add the yeast and stir until it dissolves. Stir in the salt and eggs. Stir in the flour, gradually, until the mixture comes together in a mass. The dough will be thick and sticky. Cover the bowl with plastic wrap and refrigerate it overnight. It will double in size.

2. The next morning, melt the butter in a small saucepan over medium-low heat. Brush a little of the melted butter onto 1 or 2 large rimmed baking sheets and set it aside. Place the dough on a generously floured work surface. Using a floured rolling pin, roll the dough out until it is about ⅓ inch thick. Using a glass dipped in flour or a floured biscuit cutter, cut the dough into 2-inch rounds. Dip the rounds of dough in the melted butter, fold them in half, and place the folded rolls in tight rows on the prepared baking sheet(s). Brush the rolls with more melted butter, if desired. Cover the baking sheet(s) with a light kitchen towel and place it (them) in a warm place for the rolls to rise until doubled in size, about 1½ hours.

3. Place a rack in the center of the oven and preheat the oven to 400°F.

4. Uncover the rolls and place the baking sheet(s) in the oven. Bake the rolls until they are lightly browned and cooked through, 10 to 12 minutes. If you're using more than 1 baking sheet, you may have to bake the rolls in batches. Place the baking sheet on a rack to cool, then serve the rolls warm.

★ RAZZLE-DAZZLE

For easy gift giving, bake the rolls in small disposable aluminum pans that have plastic lids. Tie a festive bow around the package of rolls and give them along with a jar of your favorite preserves.

If 6 dozen rolls seems over-whelming even for holiday season (remember, you can freeze these; see below), all the ingredients are easy to halve.

For the best results, use half White Lily and half Gold Medal flours.

The dough can be made a day in advance. And it is easy to transport. In fact, at this writing, I have been assigned to make this dough in Nashville, tote it to Chattanooga, and roll it out for the upcoming Thanksgiving dinner. I just keep the dough cold during the car ride and place it back in the fridge once I am at my destination. Then I proceed with the recipe.

Another plus is that the rolls may be baked and frozen, where they will keep wrapped in aluminum foil for up to 3 months. To reheat frozen rolls, open up the foil, and place the rolls in a 350°F oven to warm through, 8 minutes.

CHAPTER 7

SWEET ENDINGS

It's no secret—I love dessert.

Cakes were the first recipes I baked, and pies were a close second. And in keeping with this book, desserts are critical for saving the day. Great pies, puddings, cakes, and cookies can salvage a ho-hum meal. You can get away with just about anything if you have baked a fresh peach pie.

Years ago, before airport security was as ramped up as it is today, I was able to pack cake layers in my bags and roll them through security. If anyone questioned or searched they might find fresh layers of banana cake or chocolate or carrot. Frowns turned into smiles, the conversation turned to baking, and I made my flight.

A store-bought dessert will never save the day. It isn't yours. It was baked by someone else. It doesn't have a story. To name just a few recipes with stories, this chapter includes the Little St. Simons Apricot Oatmeal Bars, John's Little Fried Apple Pies, Graduation Pound Cake Bites with Caramel Frosting, and Veronica's Mocha Cake. Great desserts come to the rescue and give people something to talk about—like Lemon Snow Pudding, Ole Miss Fudge Pie, Aunt Cathleen's Blueberry Snack Cake, and Kentucky Brown Sugar Pie.

Great desserts not only have a story, they are fresh and local. This describes Ella's Easy Peach Pie, Fresh Fig Pound Cake, Roasted Peaches with Brown Sugar and Spices, and Fresh Blueberry and Lemon Tart. And they make memories. So get out the pans, bowls, and beaters, for this chapter is a sweet reminder of how desserts can save your day.

Veronica's Mocha Cake

MAKES: ONE 12-INCH BUNDT CAKE
PREP: 20 MINUTES
BAKE: 45 TO 50 MINUTES
COOL: 70 MINUTES

Veronica Young, who lives in Greenville, South Carolina, is known for her mocha cake. She says it has saved her numerous times when entertaining. In spite of thinking about the appetizers, drinks, and the main course, Veronica invariably forgets to plan dessert when company is coming. But this cake can be pulled together in a little more than an hour. Veronica loves how pretty it looks on a cake stand, and everyone begs her for the recipe. She says the recipe originally came from Aimee Fountain of Simpsonville, South Carolina, who shared it with Veronica after being hounded much too long for the recipe.

★
 ★ ★
★RAZZLE-DAZZLE

Make a quick Kahlúa glaze for drizzling over the mocha cake. Whisk together ½ cup of confectioners' sugar and 1 to 2 tablespoons of Kahlúa and drizzle this on top of the cake when it has cooled. Garnish the cake with chocolate shavings.

Vegetable oil spray, for misting the pan

6 tablespoons all-purpose flour, plus flour for dusting the Bundt pan

1 package (about 16 ounces) devil's food cake mix (see Note)

2 cups sour cream

½ cup Kahlúa or other coffee liqueur

¼ cup vegetable oil

2 large eggs

2 cups (one 12-ounce package) semisweet chocolate chips

½ cup almond toffee bits, such as Heath

Confectioners' sugar, for dusting

Vanilla or salted caramel ice cream, for serving

① Place a rack in the center of the oven and preheat the oven to 350°F. Generously mist a 12-inch Bundt pan with vegetable oil spray, then dust it with flour. Shake out the excess flour. Set the pan aside.

② Place the cake mix and the 6 tablespoons flour in a large bowl and stir to combine. Add the sour cream, Kahlúa, oil, and eggs. Beat with an electric mixer on low speed until the ingredients come together, 30 seconds, then increase the speed to medium and beat until smooth, about 1 minute. Scrape down the side of the bowl with a rubber spatula and fold in the chocolate chips and toffee bits.

③ Pour the batter into the prepared pan and smooth the top with the spatula. The batter will be very thick. Bake the cake until the top springs back when lightly pressed with a finger in the center, 45 to 50 minutes.

④ Transfer the pan to a wire rack and let the cake cool for about 10 minutes. Run a long sharp knife around the edges of the pan, shake the pan gently to release the cake, and invert it onto the wire rack to cool completely, 1 hour.

⑤ To serve, transfer the cake to a plate and dust it with the confectioners' sugar. Serve slices of the cake with ice cream.

SAVE THE DAY NOTE As cake mix packages have been downsized, it is necessary to add some flour to the smaller mixes so that they work with the recipes you love. If you can find a cake mix that is around 18¼ ounces, there is no need to add the 6 tablespoons of flour.

Do Ahead This cake freezes well in a cake saver or place it on a cardboard cake round and cover it with heavy-duty aluminum foil. The cake can be frozen for up to 3 months. Let it thaw for 2 to 3 hours before serving. It also keeps at room temperature for up to 4 days.

Eugenia's Italian Cream Cake

MAKES: ONE 9-INCH ROUND LAYER CAKE
PREP: 1 HOUR
BAKE: 22 TO 25 MINUTES
COOL: 40 MINUTES

This recipe has been floating around American kitchens for the past thirty plus years, and it is doubtful there is anything truly Italian about it. Pecans and coconut? But no matter the name, Nashville cook Eugenia Moore loves this cake and everything Italian. She started cooking Italian after trips to Italy, traveled to Chicago for ingredients she couldn't find in Nashville, and baked this cake as the signature dessert for her Italian dinner parties. "People went wild about it." So Eugenia kept baking it. Not last minute at all, this cake is planned. It is anticipated. It is celebrated. If you are looking for a fabulous, out-of-the-ordinary scratch cake to make for those special people on your guest list, bake this one and watch them go wild about it.

★
★ ★
★ RAZZLE-DAZZLE

Lightly toast the coconut for garnishing the cake. Place the coconut on a rimmed baking sheet and toast it in a 350°F oven until lightly browned, 4 to 5 minutes.

FOR THE CAKE

8 tablespoons (1 stick) unsalted butter, at room temperature, plus butter for greasing the cake pans

2 cups all-purpose flour, plus flour for dusting the cake pans

½ cup vegetable shortening

2 cups granulated sugar

5 large eggs, at room temperature, separated

2 teaspoons pure vanilla extract

1 teaspoon baking soda

1 cup buttermilk, at room temperature

1 cup sweetened flaked coconut

¾ cup finely chopped pecans

FOR THE FROSTING

¼ cup finely chopped pecans

8 tablespoons (1 stick) unsalted butter, at room temperature

1 package (8 ounces) cream cheese, at room temperature

2 teaspoons pure vanilla extract

4 to 4¾ cups confectioners' sugar, sifted

Dash of salt

Sweetened flaked coconut (optional), for garnish

① Place 1 rack in the center of the oven and 1 rack above it. Preheat the oven to 325°F. Grease three 9-inch round cake pans with butter, then dust them with flour. Shake out the excess flour. Set the pans aside.

② Make the cake: Place the 8 tablespoons of butter and the vegetable shortening in a large bowl and beat with an electric mixer on high speed until creamy, about 1 minute. Gradually add the granulated sugar, beating on medium speed. Add the egg yolks, one yolk at a time, beating until just combined before adding the batter. Add the 2 teaspoons of vanilla and beat on low speed to combine, 5 seconds.

③ Sift the 2 cups of flour with the baking soda to combine well. Spoon a third of the flour mixture into the butter mixture and beat on low speed, then add ½ cup of the buttermilk and beat. Add another third of the flour mixture, followed by the remaining ½ cup of buttermilk, beating to combine. Add the remaining flour mixture. Fold in the 1 cup of coconut and ¾ cup of pecans until just combined and set the cake batter aside.

④ Place the egg whites in a large bowl and beat with an electric mixer on high speed until stiff peaks form, about 4 minutes. Fold the beaten whites into the cake batter until they are well combined. Divide the batter among the

3 prepared cake pans, smoothing the tops with a rubber spatula. Place the pans in the oven. If your oven is not large enough to hold 3 pans on the center rack, place 2 pans on that rack and 1 in the center of the rack above it.

5. Bake the cake layers until they are golden brown and just pull away from the side of the pans, 22 to 25 minutes. Transfer the pans to a wire rack and let the cakes cool for about 10 minutes. Leave the oven on. Run a knife around the edge of each cake, shake the pans gently to release the cakes, then invert them onto a rack right side up to cool completely, about 30 minutes longer.

6. Make the frosting: Place the ¼ cup of pecans in a metal cake pan or pie pan in the oven to toast until golden, 3 to 4 minutes. Set the pecans aside to cool.

7. Place the 8 tablespoons of butter and the cream cheese in a large bowl and beat with an electric mixer on medium speed until creamy, about 1 minute. Add the 2 teaspoons of vanilla and 2 cups of confectioners' sugar, beating on medium speed until combined. Add 1 more cup of confectioners' sugar and the salt and beat on medium-high speed until smooth and spreadable, 30 to 45 seconds. Add as much of the remaining 1¾ cups of confectioners' sugar as needed to lighten the frosting and beat on medium-high speed. Fold in the toasted pecans.

8. To assemble the cake, place one cooled layer on a serving platter or cake stand and spread ¾ cup of the frosting over the top. Place a second layer on top of the first and spread ¾ cup of the frosting over it. Place the third layer on top and add 1 cup of frosting to the top of the cake, spreading it decoratively across the cake. Use the remaining frosting to frost the side of the cake, using smooth, clean strokes. Pat coconut on top of the cake for garnish, if desired.

Do Ahead You can chop and toast the pecans ahead of time. Remove the eggs from the refrigerator about 30 minutes before starting to make the cake so they come to room temperature. This will give the batter better volume. And remove the butter and cream cheese from the fridge at least 30 minutes ahead of time so they come to room temperature and can blend well with the other ingredients. The cake will keep on the counter in a cool kitchen for 3 hours. After that, it needs to be refrigerated.

Aunt Cathleen's Blueberry Snack Cake

MAKES: ONE 8- OR 9-INCH SQUARE CAKE
PREP: 20 MINUTES
BAKE: 27 TO 37 MINUTES, DEPENDING ON PAN SIZE
COOL: 25 MINUTES

One of Martha Bowden's favorite dessert memories is eating a blueberry cake named for her great-aunt Cathleen. Martha's grandmother Catherine and her twin sister Cathleen were raised on a family farm in Franklin, Massachusetts, in the early 1900s. This cake was made from local berries, and it was baked for Sunday afternoon picnics and potlucks. Even after the sisters married and had their own families, the story goes that without consulting each other, the twins would often bring an identical dish to a potluck gathering. Often, it was this blueberry cake. Martha's grandmother passed along the recipe to Martha's mother, and Martha shared it with me.

Vegetable oil spray, for misting the cake pan

1¾ cups sifted all-purpose flour (see Note), plus 2 teaspoons flour, plus flour for dusting the cake pan

1 cup granulated sugar

4 tablespoons (½ stick) unsalted butter, at room temperature

½ teaspoon pure vanilla extract

1 large egg

1 teaspoon baking powder

¼ teaspoon salt

¾ cup milk (see Note)

1 heaping cup fresh blueberries, rinsed and drained well

Confectioners' sugar, for dusting the cake

1. Place a rack in the center of the oven and preheat the oven to 350°F. Lightly mist an 8- or 9-inch square metal cake pan with vegetable oil spray, then dust it with flour. Shake out the excess flour. Set the pan aside.

2. Place the granulated sugar and butter in a large bowl. Beat with an electric mixer on medium-high speed until creamed, about 1 minute. Add the vanilla and egg and beat on medium-low speed until the egg is just blended, about 30 seconds. Set the sugar and butter mixture aside.

3. Place the 1¾ cups of flour and the baking powder and salt in a medium-size bowl and stir to combine. Warm the milk over low heat or in a microwave until warm to the touch. Add a third of the dry ingredients mixture to the sugar and butter mixture, followed by a little warm milk, blending with a wooden spoon. Add another third of the dry ingredients, the rest of the milk, and then the remaining dry ingredients, blending only until the ingredients just come together. Toss the blueberries in the remaining

2 teaspoons of flour and gently fold them into the batter.

4. Pour the batter into the prepared cake pan, smoothing the top with a rubber spatula. Bake the cake until it is golden brown and the top springs back when lightly pressed with a finger, 27 to 32 minutes for a 9-inch pan, 32 to 37 minutes for an 8-inch pan.

5. Transfer the pan to a wire rack and let the cake cool for about 10 minutes. Run a knife around the edges of the cake, shake the pan gently to release the cake, then invert it onto the rack right side up to cool for about 15 minutes longer. Dust the top of the cake with confectioners' sugar and slice it. Or just serve the cake straight from the pan, slicing it into pieces. This cake tastes best on the day it is baked, but will keep on the counter wrapped in plastic wrap for 1 day.

SAVE THE DAY NOTE For a richer, more tender cake, sift the flour before measuring. And use milk that has a little fat in it, either 2 percent or whole milk.

★ RAZZLE-DAZZLE

Add 1 teaspoon of grated lemon or orange zest to the cake batter. And make an easy glaze by whisking together ½ cup of confectioners' sugar and 1 to 2 tablespoons of fresh lemon or orange juice. Drizzle the glaze over the cooled cake.

If desired, you can use raspberries or blackberries instead of the blueberries. Or use almond extract instead of the vanilla.

Zucchini Cake
with
Brown Sugar Frosting

MAKES: ONE 9-INCH ROUND LAYER CAKE
PREP: 45 TO 50 MINUTES
BAKE: 30 TO 35 MINUTES
COOL: 45 MINUTES

Kathy Lambert surprised me not long ago with a recipe for a brown sugar cream cheese frosting that she wanted me to try. She said the brown sugar would dissolve and give the frosting a deep and rich taste. I was fascinated and couldn't get it out of my mind. Kathy uses the frosting for carrot cake, but just that week our zucchini were coming in strong from the backyard garden, and it was also my birthday. My daughter, Litton, asked what kind of birthday cake I wanted, so I handed her an old zucchini bread recipe I had cherished for years. Instructions—please make the bread into a layer cake, and try out Kathy's frosting. Litton grated the zucchini and folded them into the batter. The cake and frosting were moist, distinctive, and memorable— and the birthday cake Litton baked for her mom was a big hit.

★ ★ ★
★ **RAZZLE-DAZZLE**

Fold 1/2 cup of miniature semisweet chocolate chips into the zucchini cake batter before baking it.

FOR THE CAKE

Vegetable oil spray, for misting the cake pans

3 cups all-purpose flour, plus flour for dusting the cake pans

1 tablespoon ground cinnamon

1 teaspoon baking soda

¾ teaspoon salt

½ teaspoon baking powder

2 large eggs

2 cups granulated sugar

1 cup vegetable oil

1 teaspoon pure vanilla extract

½ cup finely chopped walnuts (optional)

2 packed cups grated zucchini (about 1 pound)

FOR THE FROSTING

1 package (8 ounces) cream cheese, at room temperature

8 tablespoons (1 stick) lightly salted butter, at room temperature

1 cup firmly packed light brown sugar

1 teaspoon pure vanilla extract

Chopped toasted walnuts or pecans (optional), for garnish

1. Make the cake: Place a rack in the center of the oven and preheat the oven to 350°F. Lightly mist two 9-inch round cake pans with vegetable oil spray, then dust them with flour. Shake out the excess flour. Set the pans aside.

2. Place the flour, cinnamon, baking soda, salt, and baking powder in a medium-size bowl and stir to combine well. Set the dry ingredients aside.

3. Place the eggs and granulated sugar in a large mixing bowl and beat with an electric mixer on low speed until combined, 30 seconds. Increase the speed to medium and beat until lemon colored, about 2 minutes. Add the oil and 1 teaspoon of vanilla and beat until combined, about 1 minute. Fold in the dry ingredients and the walnuts, if desired. Fold in the zucchini. Stir with a wooden spoon until the ingredients are well combined. Divide the batter between the 2 prepared pans.

4. Bake the cake layers until the tops spring back when lightly pressed with a finger, 30 to 35 minutes. Transfer the pans to a wire rack and let the cakes cool for about 15 minutes. Run a knife around the edge of each cake, shake the pans gently to release the cakes, then invert them onto the rack to cool right side up. Let the cakes cool for about 30 minutes before frosting.

5. Make the frosting: Place the cream cheese and butter in a bowl and, using an electric mixer, beat them together on low speed until fluffy. Add the brown sugar and 1 teaspoon of vanilla and beat on medium speed until well combined, 2 to 3 minutes.

6. To assemble the cake, place one cake layer on a serving platter or cake stand and spread about ⅓ cup of frosting over the top, spreading it evenly to the edge. Place the second layer on top of the first and spread 1 cup of frosting on the top of the cake in a decorative fashion. Then spread the remaining frosting over the side of the cake, working with smooth, clean strokes. If desired, press toasted chopped walnuts on the sides of the cake. Slice and serve.

Do Ahead The zucchini can be grated up to 8 hours ahead of time and refrigerated, covered. The cake keeps for up to 1 day in a cake saver or in the refrigerator for up to 3 days.

Fresh Fig Pound Cake

MAKES: ONE 12-INCH BUNDT CAKE
PREP: 15 TO 20 MINUTES
BAKE: 45 TO 50 MINUTES
COOL: ABOUT 1 HOUR

Late in the summer, Linda Coviello of Maiden, North Carolina, waits for the figs on her Brown Turkey fig tree to ripen so she can bake them into a pound cake. The figs are rich and sweet, just like honey, she says, and no frosting is needed to top this naturally sweet cake. You can use figs from your own trees or from the supermarket. Either way, this cake offers up something different for the summertime palate.

7 to 8 large Brown Turkey figs (about 12 ounces) rinsed, dried, and stemmed

12 tablespoons (¾ cup; 1½ sticks) unsalted butter, at room temperature, plus butter for greasing the Bundt pan

3 cups sifted all-purpose flour, plus flour for dusting the Bundt pan

4 large eggs, at room temperature

1½ cups granulated sugar

1 teaspoon grated lemon zest (from 1 lemon)

4 teaspoons baking powder

½ teaspoon salt

1 cup whole milk, at room temperature

1 tablespoon molasses

1 teaspoon ground cinnamon

Confectioners' sugar, for dusting

★
★ ★
★ RAZZLE-DAZZLE

Whisk the juice from the lemon you zested into ¾ cup confectioners' sugar for an easy glaze to spoon over the cake.

1. Chop the figs into small pieces and measure to make sure you have 2 cups. Set the figs aside in a small bowl.

2. Place a rack in the center of the oven and preheat the oven to 350°F. Lightly grease a 12-inch Bundt pan with butter, then dust it with flour. Shake out the excess flour. Set the Bundt pan aside.

3. Separate the eggs, placing the whites in a large stainless steel or glass bowl and the yolks in a smaller bowl. Set the egg yolks aside. Using an electric mixer, beat the whites on high speed until they are stiff, 4 to 5 minutes. Set the beaten egg whites aside.

4. Place the butter and granulated sugar in another large bowl and beat with the electric mixer on medium-high speed until light and fluffy, about 2 minutes. Add the egg yolks, one at a time, and beat on low speed until combined. Fold in the lemon zest and set the egg yolk mixture aside.

5. Set aside 2 tablespoons of the flour. Place the remaining flour in a medium-size bowl and stir in the baking powder and salt. Sift a third of the flour mixture over the egg yolk mixture and beat on medium speed until just combined. Add ½ cup of milk and beat to combine. Sift another third of the flour mixture over the batter and beat to combine. Add the remaining ½ cup of milk, beating until combined. Fold the beaten egg whites into the batter just to combine, then fold in the remaining flour mixture. Pour about a third of this batter into a small bowl and set it aside.

6. Toss the chopped figs with the reserved 2 tablespoons of flour and the molasses and cinnamon. Fold the fig mixture into the reserved two thirds of the batter and spoon this into the prepared Bundt pan. Dollop the plain third of the batter on top. Swirl the batter with a knife to create a marbled effect.

7. Bake the cake until it is golden brown and the top springs back when lightly pressed with a finger, 45 to 50 minutes. Transfer the Bundt pan to a wire rack and let the cake cool for about 10 minutes. Run a long sharp knife around the edges of the cake, shake the pan gently to release the cake, and invert it onto the wire rack to cool completely, about 1 hour. Just before serving, dust the cake with confectioners' sugar.

Do Ahead This and all Bundt cakes can be baked ahead. It will keep for up to 3 days in a cake saver or wrapped in plastic wrap. To freeze, wrap the cooled cake in heavy-duty aluminum foil, then slide it into a large plastic freezer bag or sturdy plastic container with a lid. The cake will keep for 4 months. Thaw it on the kitchen counter, about 2 hours.

Orange Marbled Angel Food Cake

MAKES: ONE 10-INCH ANGEL FOOD CAKE
PREP: 20 TO 25 MINUTES
BAKE: 25 TO 30 MINUTES
COOL: 1 HOUR

Tired of the same old angel food cake recipe? Shirley Hutson of Nashville has had this recipe in her repertoire for decades. And her children love it because it is different, as well as beautiful. This is the springtime cake for bridal showers and christenings, for graduation parties, and for anniversaries. It is light and delicate but deliciously different, with waves of orange batter striping what is normally a simple cake.

FOR THE CAKE

1 cup plus 2 tablespoons sifted all-purpose flour (see Note)

1½ cups granulated sugar

11 large eggs, at room temperature

1¼ teaspoons cream of tartar

¼ teaspoon salt

½ teaspoon pure vanilla extract

2 tablespoons fresh orange juice

1 teaspoon grated orange zest

FOR THE ORANGE GLAZE

½ cup confectioners' sugar

1 to 2 tablespoons fresh orange juice

1. Place a rack in the center of the oven and preheat the oven to 375°F.

2. Make the cake: Sift the 1 cup of the flour and ½ cup of the granulated sugar into a medium-size bowl and set the bowl aside.

3. Separate the eggs, placing the whites in a large bowl and 4 of the yolks in a medium-size bowl. Set the remaining 7 yolks aside for another use.

4. Add the cream of tartar, salt, and vanilla to the egg whites. Beat with an electric mixer on high speed until the whites are soft, 4 to 5 minutes. Add the remaining 1 cup of sugar, about 2 tablespoons at a time, while beating on high speed. Continue beating until the egg whites are stiff, about 2 minutes longer. Fold in the flour and sugar mixture, ¼ cup at a time, with a rubber spatula until just combined.

5. Place half of the egg white mixture in each of 2 medium-size bowls. Set aside 1 bowl for the white batter.

6. Add the 2 tablespoons of orange juice and the orange zest to the bowl with the egg yolks. Using a whisk or electric mixer, beat the yolks until they are lemon colored, about 2 minutes by hand, about 30 seconds at medium speed using an electric mixer. Beat in the remaining 2 tablespoons of flour. Fold the orange mixture into the second bowl of egg white mixture until well combined.

7. Dollop 5 large tablespoons of the white batter in the bottom of an ungreased 10-inch tube pan, evenly spacing the dollops so they don't touch. Between each dollop of white batter, dollop 5 spoonfuls of the orange-flavored batter. For the second layer, dollop the same amount of batter in the reverse pattern, placing orange on top of white and white on top of orange. You will have orange batter left over so just dollop it on top of the second layer. Using a knife or a thin icing spatula, gently swirl the batter to create a marbled effect.

8. Bake the cake until it is golden brown on top and the top springs back when very lightly pressed with your finger, 25 to 30 minutes. Place the cake pan upside down on a wire rack to completely cool the cake in the pan, about 1 hour.

9. Meanwhile, make the orange glaze: Place the confectioners' sugar and 1 tablespoon of the orange juice in a small bowl and whisk until smooth, adding more orange juice as necessary to obtain a drizzling consistency.

10. Run a sharp knife around the edge of the pan to loosen the cooled cake, invert it once, then again, and place on the rack right side up. Drizzle the orange glaze over the top of the cake. Let it rest 20 minutes before slicing. The cake will keep, lightly covered, at room temperature for up to a week.

 SAVE THE DAY NOTE For a lighter, more tender angel food cake, use a soft, low-gluten flour such as White Lily. Or use cake flour.

Bette's Strawberry Angel Food Cake Roulade

MAKES: ONE 12-INCH ROULADE
PREP: 20 TO 25 MINUTES
BAKE: 18 TO 20 MINUTES
COOL: 10 MINUTES
FREEZE: 2 WEEKS

Some of the best recipes I have ever received have been scribbled on napkins. When I told my friend Bette about this book idea and how the recipes were meant to come to the rescue, I could see she already knew what her save-the-day recipe was—this frozen roulade. Quick to prepare using an angel food cake mix, it goes with any flavor ice cream that you like. Bette is partial to strawberry and likes how the almond flavor of the amaretto plays well with the strawberry. This makes a big roulade, perfect for dinner parties and brunches with ten or more people in the house. But if you entertain a smaller crowd, just return the leftover roulade to the freezer, where it can stay frozen for up to two weeks.

Vegetable oil spray, for misting the jelly roll pan

1 package (16 ounces) angel food cake mix (see Note)

1 carton (1½ quarts) strawberry ice cream

¼ cup amaretto

Sliced or chopped fresh strawberries (optional), for garnish

Chocolate sauce (optional), for garnish

① Place a rack in the center of the oven and preheat the oven to 350°F. Place an 18-by-12-inch jelly roll pan on top of a piece of parchment paper. Using a pencil, trace the edge of the pan onto the parchment paper and cut this out. Repeat with a second piece of parchment paper. Lightly mist the bottom of the jelly roll pan with vegetable oil spray

★
★ ★
★ RAZZLE-DAZZLE

Spoon sliced or chopped fresh strawberries over the roulade slices in spring, when the berries are at their best. Top with toasted almond slices.

and press one piece of parchment paper into the bottom of the pan. Set the second piece of parchment paper aside.

2. Follow the directions on the package to make the angel food cake batter. Pour the batter into the prepared pan, smoothing the top with a rubber spatula. Bake the cake until it is golden brown and the top springs back when lightly pressed in the center with a finger, 18 to 20 minutes.

3. While the cake is baking, remove the ice cream from the freezer. Spoon the ice cream into a large mixing bowl. Let it soften while the cake bakes.

4. Transfer the cake pan to a wire rack to cool for about 10 minutes. Run a knife around the edges of the cake and invert it onto a clean kitchen towel placed on the counter. Peel off the parchment paper. Let the cake cool completely, then using a serrated knife, trim off the browned edges. Wash and dry the jelly roll pan. Lightly mist the pan with vegetable oil spray and line it with the second piece of parchment paper.

5. Pour the amaretto in the bowl with the ice cream. Stir well with a wooden spoon until smooth. Spoon the ice cream into the lined jelly roll pan and spread it evenly to the edges. Place the

pan in the freezer to chill the ice cream, 40 to 45 minutes.

6. When the ice cream has frozen, remove the pan from the freezer. Carefully place the ice cream on top of the angel food cake and peel the parchment paper off of the ice cream. Immediately begin to roll up the roulade, starting at a short end of the cake. Place the roulade on a piece of aluminum foil, roll the foil up around the cake, and seal the ends. Place it in the freezer for at least 8 hours, or overnight.

7. When ready to serve, unwrap the roulade and slice it with a serrated knife into slices that are 1 to 1½ inches thick. Place the roulade slices on dessert plates and garnish them with strawberries and chocolate sauce, if desired.

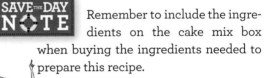

SAVE THE DAY NOTE Remember to include the ingredients on the cake mix box when buying the ingredients needed to prepare this recipe.

Do Ahead By all means, make the roulade ahead. It can be frozen in the aluminum foil for up to 2 weeks. Thaw on the kitchen counter for 2 to 3 hours.

Graduation Pound Cake Bites with Caramel Frosting

MAKES: 4 DOZEN
PREP: 1 HOUR, 20 MINUTES
BAKE: 40 TO 45 MINUTES
COOL: AT LEAST 4 HOURS
FREEZE: 3 HOURS TO OVERNIGHT
THAW: 20 TO 25 MINUTES

When my older daughter graduated from college, we hosted a party near the college for her friends and professors. Kathleen told us the starving college students would most appreciate a meal of steak, sushi, and cake. My husband took charge of grilling the fillets, I picked up the sushi, and I made the cake, actually bites of cakes, a riff on the petits fours of old. Instead of white bakery frosting and piped flowers, these bites were cloaked in my quick caramel frosting. They looked spectacular on the platter, with the caramel cascading down the sides of the little homemade pound cakes, and were pretty wonderful to eat. And to save time on party day, I was able to bake them ahead and tote them with us for graduation.

★★★RAZZLE-DAZZLE

Instead of my caramel frosting, make a lemon glaze: Whisk together 1½ cups of confectioners' sugar and 2 to 3 tablespoons of fresh lemon juice.

SAVE THE DAY NOTE If tight for time, drizzle a store-bought caramel glaze over the cake bites and top with the chopped pecans.

FOR THE CAKE

Vegetable oil spray, for misting the pan

1½ cups (3 sticks) unsalted butter, at room temperature

2¾ cups granulated sugar

6 large eggs

2 teaspoons pure vanilla extract

½ teaspoon pure almond extract

3 cups all-purpose flour

½ teaspoon salt

½ teaspoon baking powder

1 cup sour cream

FOR THE CARAMEL FROSTING

8 tablespoons (1 stick) unsalted butter

½ cup packed light brown sugar

½ cup packed dark brown sugar

¼ cup milk

¼ teaspoon salt

2 cups confectioners' sugar, sifted

1 teaspoon pure vanilla extract

½ cup chopped toasted pecans (optional; see Note), for garnish

① Make the pound cake: Place a rack in the center of the oven and preheat the oven to 350°F. Lightly mist a 13-by-9-inch metal pan with vegetable oil spray and line the bottom of the pan with parchment paper.

② Place the 1½ cups of butter and the granulated sugar in a large mixing bowl and beat with an electric mixer on low speed until the mixture comes together in a mass and is fluffy, 2 to 3 minutes. Add the eggs, one at a time, followed by the 2 teaspoons of vanilla and the almond extract and beat until the mixture is creamy and lemon colored, about 2 minutes in all. Scrape down the side of the bowl.

③ Place the flour in another bowl and stir in the salt and baking powder. Using the electric mixer, add the flour mixture to the butter and egg mixture alternately with the sour cream, beating on low speed. Beat the cake batter until it is well blended and light, about 1 minute longer.

④ Spread the batter evenly in the prepared pan. Bake the pound cake until it is golden brown and the top springs back when lightly pressed in the center with a finger, 40 to 45 minutes.

⑤ Transfer the pan to a wire rack and let the cake cool in the pan for about 10 minutes. Run a knife around the edges of the cake and invert it onto the wire rack. Peel off the parchment paper. Let the cake cool on the rack for 1 hour.

6 After 1 hour wrap the cake in plastic wrap and place it in the freezer so that it is easier to slice, at least 3 hours and preferably overnight.

7 Remove the cake from the freezer. Let it sit on the counter until it softens enough to slice, 20 to 25 minutes. Using a serrated knife, trim a thin layer of crust off each the side of the cake. Cut the cake rectangle into 1½-inch cubes. (To measure exactly, place a ruler on the long side of the cake. Make small slits every 1½ inches along the edge. Repeat with the other long side. Connect the slits and cut through the cake to get 8 strips. Slice each strip into six 1½-inch cubes. There may be a half inch or so of cake left over from one end.)

8 Make the caramel frosting: Place the 8 tablespoons of butter and the light and dark brown sugars in a heavy saucepan over medium heat. Cook, stirring, until the mixture comes to a boil, about 2 minutes. Add the milk and salt, stir, and let come back to a boil, then remove the pan from the heat. Whisk in about 1½ cups of the confectioners' sugar and the 1 teaspoon of vanilla. Whisk until smooth, and add up to ½ cup more sugar if the frosting is too thin.

9 To assemble the cake bites, place them on a rack set over a piece of waxed paper or parchment paper. Using a teaspoon, slowly drizzle the warm caramel frosting over each bite, letting the frosting drip down the sides. While the frosting is warm press toasted pecans on top of each bite, if desired. Let the frosting set for about 1 hour before serving the cake bites.

SAVE THE DAY NOTE To toast the pecans, spread them out on a rimmed baking sheet and bake them in a 350°F oven for 3 to 4 minutes.

Do Ahead Bake the pound cake ahead, wrap it in aluminum foil, and freeze it. It will keep for up to 4 months. Remove the cake from the freezer, cut it into bites, make the frosting, and assemble the cake bites. The cake will keep, unfrosted, at room temperature lightly wrapped in plastic wrap for up to 4 days.

Karen's Molten Chocolate Cakes

**MAKES: 8 INDIVIDUAL CAKES
PREP: 20 MINUTES
BAKE: 8 TO 10 MINUTES**

My friend Karen is kept really busy at work, but in her downtime away from the job she enjoys baking and bakes a mean molten chocolate cake. I learned about these cakes when I had dinner at her house. While everyone at the table was deep in conversation, Karen quietly slipped into the kitchen to pop the cakes in the oven. They emerged cakelike on the outside, and warm and runny in the center—unexpected and fabulous. And she emerged all smiles, as this recipe is her lifesaver. The batter can be made a day ahead. Repeat—the batter can be made a day ahead. I tried that out at my house, baking one or two ramekins one day and a couple more the day after that. Plus, Karen knows the beauty of this recipe is that the ingredients are already in house—pantry staples. Yum!

Vegetable oil spray, for misting the ramekins or muffin tin

1 cup (2 sticks) unsalted butter

1⅓ cups (8 ounces) semisweet chocolate chips

5 large eggs

½ cup granulated sugar

Pinch of salt

4 teaspoons all-purpose flour

Vanilla ice cream, for serving

Fresh raspberries and blackberries, for garnish

Confectioners' sugar, for dusting

1. Place a rack in the center of the oven and preheat the oven to 450°F. Lightly mist eight 6-ounce ramekins or 8 muffin tin cups with vegetable oil spray. Set the ramekins or muffin tin aside.

2. Place the butter and chocolate chips in a medium-size microwave-safe glass bowl. Microwave on high power until melted, 2½ to 3 minutes, stirring halfway through. Remove the bowl from the microwave and stir the chocolate mixture until smooth. Set the chocolate mixture aside.

3. Place the eggs, granulated sugar, and salt in a large bowl. Beat with an electric mixer on medium-high speed until the mixture lightens in color and texture, about 1½ minutes. Fold in the chocolate mixture and the flour by hand, until well blended, 30 seconds. Scoop ½ cup of batter into each ramekin or muffin cup. Place the ramekins on a baking sheet, and place the baking sheet or muffin tin in the oven. Bake the cakes until puffy but still soft in the center, 8 to 10 minutes.

4. Remove the cakes from the oven, carefully lift them out of the ramekins or muffin tin, and set them on dessert plates. Serve the warm cakes with small scoops of vanilla ice cream, berries, and a dusting of confectioners' sugar.

Do Ahead The cake batter can be made a day or two in advance and refrigerated, covered. Scoop the batter into ramekins or a muffin tin misted with vegetable oil spray 1 hour before baking so the batter can come to room temperature.

Baking Chocolate Cake in a Mug

It's a rainy day, a snow day, or a long holiday weekend with the kids at home from school. How about letting everyone bake a cake in a mug? Begin with a 12-ounce coffee mug. (If you're unsure how many ounces your coffee mug holds, fill it with water, then pour the water into a measuring cup.) Add 4 tablespoons each of flour, sugar, and unsweetened cocoa and stir to mix. Crack an egg into the mug and add 3 tablespoons each of milk and vegetable oil. Stir. Add a dribble of pure vanilla extract and stir in 2 tablespoons of mini chocolate chips if you like. Stir until combined. Place the mug in a 1,000-watt microwave oven and cook the cake on high power until set, about 3 minutes. Transfer the cake to 2 bowls and top it with vanilla ice cream. Serves 2.

★ RAZZLE-DAZZLE

Toss raspberries with Grand Marnier or Cointreau (orange liqueurs) and a little granulated sugar to taste. Spoon these boozy berries on top of the cakes before serving.

Chocolate Cream Cheese Brownies

MAKES: 16 BROWNIES
PREP: 15 MINUTES
BAKE: 45 TO 48 MINUTES
COOL: 40 MINUTES

Full disclaimer—I love homemade brownies. I also love the convenience of a brownie mix in the pantry. This little dandy of a recipe has saved my day plenty of times in the past six years or as long as I have been making them. The brownies are perfect for a bake sale, either sold by the pan or by the square. I like the Ghirardelli double chocolate brownie mix, but any simple brownie mix works, too. To make a 13-by-9-inch pan for a larger crowd, buy two boxes of brownie mix and double the recipe for the cream cheese "goo." The larger pan will take about ten minutes longer to bake. A confession—I love to eat them frozen.

FOR THE BROWNIES

Vegetable oil spray, for misting the baking pan

All-purpose flour, for dusting the baking pan

1 package (about 20 ounces) chocolate brownie mix

⅓ cup vegetable oil, or melted unsalted butter

1 large egg

⅓ cup warm water

½ cup miniature semisweet chocolate chips

FOR THE CREAM CHEESE GOO

4 ounces (half an 8-ounce package) cream cheese, at room temperature

2 tablespoons (¼ stick) unsalted butter, at room temperature

¼ cup granulated sugar

1 tablespoon all-purpose flour

1 large egg

½ teaspoon pure vanilla extract

① Make the brownie batter: Place a rack in the center of the oven and preheat the oven to 325°F. Lightly mist a 9-inch-square metal baking pan with vegetable oil spray, then dust it with flour. Shake out the excess flour. Set the pan aside.

② Place the brownie mix, oil, egg, and the warm water in a large mixing bowl (or, follow the directions on the package of mix, adding what is needed). Using a wooden spoon, stir the brownie mix 40 to 50 strokes, then fold in the chocolate chips with a rubber spatula. Set the brownie batter aside.

③ Make the cream cheese "goo": Place the cream cheese, butter, sugar, flour, 1 egg, and the vanilla in a second large mixing bowl. Beat with an electric mixer on low speed until the ingredients come together and the batter is smooth, 1 to 2 minutes.

④ Transfer half of the brownie batter into the prepared baking pan and, using a rubber spatula, spread it out evenly to reach the corners. Spoon the cream cheese batter on top of the brownie batter, spreading it out with a clean rubber spatula to evenly reach the corners.

Drop the remaining brownie batter by spoonfuls onto the cream cheese layer. Using a knife, drag the batter through the cream cheese layer to create a marbled effect.

⑤ Bake the brownies until the edges are set and the center is still a little soft, 45 to 48 minutes. Transfer the pan to a wire rack and let the brownies cool for about 20 minutes. Place the pan of brownies in the refrigerator to cool for another 20 minutes before cutting the brownies into approximately 2-inch squares. For optimum slicing, freeze until nearly firm, then cut into squares.

Keep these brownies on the counter for up to 5 days. If you want to freeze them for longer storage, cover the whole pan with heavy-duty aluminum foil and place them in the freezer for up to 2 months. Or, you can cut the brownies into squares, place them on a sheet of heavy-duty foil, and cover with more foil, securing the sides. Freeze for up to 1 month. Thaw the cut or uncut brownies on the kitchen counter for 2 to 3 hours.

★ RAZZLE-DAZZLE

Add 1/3 cup dried cranberries to the brownie batter before baking the brownies. Or, add 1/2 teaspoon grated orange zest to the cream cheese mixture before baking. Brush the brownies with 2 tablespoons brewed espresso or Kahlúa right after they come out of the oven.

Little St. Simons Apricot Oatmeal Bars

MAKES: ABOUT 64 BARS
PREP: 15 TO 20 MINUTES
BAKE: 35 TO 40 MINUTES
COOL: 2 HOURS

Missy Myers used to vacation on Little St. Simons Island off the coast of Georgia when she was a child. After a long morning at the beach, she and her family were starving and looked forward to these oatmeal bars in a picnic lunch. Missy still makes the bars, and she finds that switching apricot preserves with other preserves such as peach or cherry makes this recipe even more versatile and valuable.

3 cups all-purpose flour

3 cups quick-cooking oats

2 cups packed light brown sugar

2 teaspoons baking powder

1 teaspoon salt

1½ cups (3 sticks) unsalted butter, melted

3 cups apricot or peach preserves

① Place a rack in the center of the oven and preheat the oven to 350°F.

② Place the flour, oats, brown sugar, baking powder, and salt in a large bowl and stir to combine. Pour in the melted butter and stir with a wooden spoon to make a crumbly mixture. Press 5 cups of the oat mixture into the bottom of a 18-by-12-inch jelly roll pan. Spread the apricot preserves evenly over the oat mixture and then crumble the remaining oat mixture randomly over the top of the preserves.

★

★★ ★
★ RAZZLE-DAZZLE

Use raspberry preserves instead of the apricot and add ½ teaspoon of pure almond extract to the oat mixture for a linzer torte version of the bars.

③ Bake the bars until they are bubbly around the edges and lightly browned, 35 to 40 minutes. Transfer the jelly roll pan to a wire rack for the bars to cool completely, at least 2 hours. Slice the bars and serve.

Do Ahead

For easiest slicing, bake the bars, let them come to room temperature, then refrigerate them for an hour before slicing. The bars keep, covered, at room temperature for up to 4 days or in the refrigerator for 1 week.

TAILGATE TRADITIONS • BAKE SALE SUCCESS!

Easiest Bar Cookie in the World

MAKES: 2 TO 2½ DOZEN BARS OR SQUARES
PREP: 10 MINUTES
BAKE: 25 TO 30 MINUTES
COOL: 1 HOUR

Sameera Lowe is a busy mother of three boys, and she relies on this recipe when they need a quick snack. It is similar to the "magic bars" or seven layer bars I enjoyed as a child, but Sameera is a wise mom and has omitted the coconut and nuts, which kids don't really like anyway. That makes these bars less expensive and quicker to assemble, too. I like either peanut butter chips or butterscotch chips in this recipe. You choose.

8 tablespoons (1 stick) unsalted butter

13 graham crackers, crushed to make crumbs (2 heaping cups)

1 can (14 ounces) sweetened condensed milk

1 cup (6 ounces) semisweet chocolate chips

1 cup (6 ounces) either butterscotch or peanut butter chips

① Place a rack in the center of the oven and preheat the oven to 350°F.

② Cut the butter into tablespoons and place it in a medium-size microwave-safe bowl. Melt the butter in a microwave oven on high power, about 1 minute. Stir in the graham cracker crumbs. Press the crumb mixture into the bottom of a 13-by-9-inch glass baking dish. Pour the condensed milk evenly over the crumb mixture. Scatter the chocolate chips and then the butterscotch or peanut butter chips over the top.

③ Bake the bars until crisp around the edges and on top, 25 to 30 minutes. Place the baking dish on a wire rack and let the bars cool completely, about 1 hour. For two dozen bars, slice the short side of the pan into 4 rows and the longer side into 6 rows. For slightly more bars, slice the short side into 5 rows and the long side into 6 rows. Enjoy!

Do Ahead

Pulse the graham crackers in a food processor or place them in a large resealable plastic bag and roll a rolling pin over them to crush them into crumbs. The bars keep, tightly covered, at room temperature for 3 days. Covered in the fridge, they keep for 1 week.

Crispy Cinnamon Shortbread

MAKES: ABOUT 24 PIECES
PREP: 25 MINUTES
BAKE: 20 TO 25 MINUTES
COOL: 1 HOUR

When I used to hear about what other children were offered in their lunch boxes, I'd swoon. My mother, as much as she was a wonderful cook, did not relish packing lunch boxes. I got a peanut butter sandwich, chips, and an apple. Or, on a good day, I got a turkey sandwich from the freezer that my mom had made ahead and frozen. Let's just say my sisters and I preferred cafeteria food. But my friend Martha's mom made these cinnamon shortbread wafers for her children as a treat and lunch box stuffer. If you are looking to put a little pizzazz in lunch boxes, bake sales, or just the little things you bake at home, this recipe is a keeper.

Vegetable oil spray, for misting the jelly roll pan

1 cup sugar

1 tablespoon ground cinnamon

2 cups all-purpose flour

½ teaspoon salt

1 large egg, separated

1 cup (2 sticks) unsalted butter, at room temperature

1 teaspoon pure vanilla extract

⅔ cup finely sliced almonds or chopped pecans (optional)

1. Place a rack in the center of the oven and preheat the oven to 350°F. Lightly mist an 18-by-12-inch jelly roll pan with vegetable oil spray and line the pan with parchment paper. Set the pan aside.

② Place the sugar and cinnamon in a small bowl and stir to combine. Set the cinnamon sugar aside.

③ Place the flour and salt in a large mixing bowl. Stir to combine. Add the egg yolk, butter, vanilla, and half of the reserved cinnamon sugar. Using an electric mixer, beat on low speed until well combined, about 1 minute. Transfer the shortbread dough to the parchment-lined pan. Using a spatula, press the dough to the edges of the pan.

④ Beat the egg white with a fork until it is frothy, about 1 minute. Using a pastry brush or the back of a large spoon, spread the egg white over the dough. Sprinkle the pecans or almonds, if using, over the egg white and top with the remaining cinnamon sugar.

⑤ Bake the shortbread until it is golden brown, 20 to 25 minutes. Transfer the pan to a wire rack and let the shortbread cool completely, about 1 hour. Break up the shortbread into 24 or so pieces with your hands. The shortbread will keep, tightly covered, at room temperature for up to 5 days.

MONEY SAVER: This shortbread is a low-cost alternative to expensive cookies and snacks. To save money, buy butter when it's on sale and freeze it for up to 6 months. Always freeze nuts of all kinds until you need to use them because nuts go rancid at room temperature. Freezing preserves their flavor and conserves your money.

How to Make Puppy Chow—Don't Feed It to the Dogs!

I learned early on that the most popular item at a school bake sale is puppy chow. Not the dog food but the snack food you make at home and place in small plastic sandwich bags to sell. Begin by placing 1 cup of chocolate chips, 1½ cups of creamy peanut butter, and 1 stick of butter or margarine in a large microwave-safe bowl. Microwave this on high power until everything has melted, about 1 minute. Stir in 1 teaspoon of pure vanilla extract and 8 to 9 cups of rice or corn Chex cereal. Place the cereal mix in a 2-gallon resealable plastic bag and add 1½ cups of confectioners' sugar. Seal the bag and shake it until the cereal is well coated. Spread the cereal mix out onto waxed paper to cool, then place it in sandwich bags or store it in an airtight container. (You can tweak this recipe by adding more peanut butter and less butter but keep the chocolate and cereal amounts the same.)

For a fabulous almond variation of the shortbread,
reduce the vanilla extract to ½ teaspoon and add
½ teaspoon of pure almond extract. Use sliced almonds
instead of pecans on top.

Jazz up the blondie for a child's birthday cookie cake. Omit the pecans and bake the blondie in a skillet and turn it out onto a serving platter or cake stand. Insert candles, light them, sing "Happy Birthday," slice the cake, scoop vanilla ice cream on top, and eat.

Big Skillet Chocolate Chip Blondie

MAKES: ONE 10-INCH COOKIE CAKE
PREP: 10 MINUTES
BAKE: 22 TO 26 MINUTES
COOL: 1 HOUR (optional)

When your mother is the Cake Mix Doctor there is cake all the time. So, by the time it gets to your birthday, you will want to branch out and express your individualism and not have cake . . . again. My son has never been big on the fancy layer cakes. Give him a doughnut cake or a cookie cake and he is just fine. So one year, in a pinch, I tried to duplicate those giant store-bought cookie cakes that mothers dash with to school parties when it's their child's birthday. And you know, the result was pretty darned good. I think I could be a convert to cookie cakes like this one. Especially since you can mix, bake, and serve it from the same pan.

12 tablespoons (¾ cup; 1½ sticks) unsalted butter

1½ cups lightly packed light brown sugar

2 cups all-purpose flour

2 teaspoons baking powder

½ teaspoon salt

2 large eggs, beaten

1 teaspoon pure vanilla extract

1 cup semisweet chocolate chips

½ cup chopped pecans (optional)

Vanilla ice cream (optional), for serving

1. Place a rack in the center of the oven and preheat the oven to 350°F.

2. Place the butter in a 10-inch cast-iron skillet over low heat. Stir the butter until it melts, then stir the brown sugar into the butter until well combined. Remove the skillet from the heat.

3. Place the flour, baking powder, and salt in a small bowl and stir to mix. Spoon the flour mixture into the skillet with the butter and brown sugar and make a well in the center. Add the eggs and vanilla to the well and stir the flour mixture up and into the eggs until the mixture is smooth, 1 to 2 minutes. Fold in the chocolate chips. Scatter the pecans over the top, if desired.

4. Bake the cookie cake until the edge is lightly brown and the center is still a little soft to the touch, 22 to 26 minutes. Remove the skillet from the oven. Scoop the warm cookie cake into bowls and serve it with vanilla ice cream, if desired. Or let the cookie cake cool for about 1 hour, then cut it into slices and serve on plates.

Do Ahead To take the cookie cake to a potluck or book club, carry it right in the skillet. Cover the skillet with aluminum foil or plastic wrap for transit. And if you are really thinking ahead, you can bake the cake several weeks before the event, remove it from the skillet, then freeze it well wrapped in aluminum foil and tucked in a resealable plastic bag. Thaw on the kitchen counter for 2 to 3 hours.

Sylvia's Peanut Butter Cookies

MAKES: 4 DOZEN COOKIES
PREP: 5 TO 7 MINUTES
BAKE: 11 TO 13 MINUTES PER BATCH

Years ago Sylvia Carter, a columnist for *Newsday*, met me for a cup of coffee in New York City. We were talking food, of course, and Sylvia shared her amazing peanut butter cookie recipe with me. We marveled that it doesn't have any flour. The recipe was written using Skippy peanut butter but I have tested it with other brands, and they work, too. Who knows why this cookie works, but it does. It is a helpful recipe to have on hand if you want to bake gluten free or you want to bake but there is no flour in the house. Plus it is a snap to prepare in less than ten minutes!

2 cups creamy or crunchy peanut butter

2 large eggs

2 cups sugar

2 teaspoons baking soda

① Place a rack in the center of the oven and preheat the oven to 350°F.

② Place the peanut butter, eggs, sugar, and baking soda in a large bowl. Using a wooden spoon, mix until well combined, 1 to 2 minutes. Working in batches, drop heaping teaspoons of the cookie dough onto an ungreased baking sheet, spacing them 1½ to 2 inches apart (see Note).

③ Bake the cookies until they are golden brown and crisp, 11 to 13 minutes. Transfer the baking sheet to a wire rack and let the cookies cool on it for about 2 minutes. Then using a spatula, transfer the cookies to the rack to cool. Repeat with the remaining cookie dough.

For the traditional crosshatch design on the top of the peanut butter cookies, roll the dough into balls that are about 1-inch wide. Place the balls of cookie dough on the baking sheet and, using a dinner fork, press gently on each once and then again at a 90-degree angle to make the crosshatch indentations with the tines of the fork.

Do Ahead You can freeze the peanut butter cookies in resealable plastic freezer bags for up to 1 month. Thaw on the kitchen counter for 30 minutes.

★ RAZZLE-DAZZLE

Add 1/2 cup of miniature semisweet chocolate chips to the batter before baking.

Kathleen's Sugar Cookies

MAKES: ABOUT 5 DOZEN COOKIES
PREP: 10 MINUTES FOR THE DOUGH,
PLUS 1 HOUR FOR DECORATING THE COOKIES
CHILL: AT LEAST 1 HOUR
BAKE: 10 TO 12 MINUTES PER BATCH

My children have made these cookies for Christmas, Valentine's Day, Easter, and Halloween for as long as we can remember, and this recipe is named for my older daughter. Our system was that I made the dough, cut it into shapes, and placed the trees, wreathes, Santas, pumpkins, hearts, bells—whatever was in season—on baking sheets for each of my children. They slathered the cookies with egg white and sprinkled on colored sugars to decorate. It was a wonderful, messy sugar fest with often more sprinkles on the floor than on the cookies. I learned to drape the kitchen floor with an old sheet before my kids began and then carry the sheet outside and shake it all out. The other trick is to chill the cookie dough well before rolling it out. Make the dough the night before everyone decorates the cookies and your day will be saved.

FOR THE COOKIE DOUGH

1 cup (2 sticks) unsalted butter, at room temperature

1 cup granulated sugar

2 large eggs

2 teaspoons pure vanilla extract

3 cups all-purpose flour

FOR DECORATING THE COOKIES

1 large egg white, lightly beaten with a fork

Colored sugars of your choice

① Make the cookie dough: Place the butter and granulated sugar in a large bowl and, using an electric mixer on medium speed, beat until light and fluffy, 1 to 2

For the Young Artist

Little ones love sugar cookies, and often the easiest way to include children in the baking process is to let them design the toppings. It's easy to set out a bowl of sprinkles for kids to dust over the top before the cookies go into the oven. But if you'd like to change things up a bit, try these two fun alternatives. The edible egg yolk paint is great for last-minute cookies, whereas the confectioners' sugar glaze is best when you have time to let the cookies rest so the glaze can harden.

FOR EDIBLE PAINT (ALIAS PAINTBRUSH COOKIES): Mix 2 egg yolks and ½ teaspoon of water in a small bowl. Divide the egg yolk mixture among several small cups. Tint each cup with a few drops of a different liquid food coloring. Using small, clean, new paintbrushes, paint the unbaked cookies. If the egg yolk paint becomes too thick, add a little water. Then, bake the cookies.

FOR CONFECTIONERS' SUGAR GLAZE: Combine 1 cup of sifted confectioners' sugar and 1 to 2 tablespoons of warm low-fat milk, until you achieve the desired consistency. Tint the frosting, if desired, with a few drops of food coloring. You can also add a dash of almond flavoring. If the frosting gets too runny, add more confectioners' sugar.

minutes. Add the eggs and vanilla and beat well. Beat in the flour on low speed until just combined. Cover the bowl and refrigerate the cookie dough at least 1 hour, preferably overnight.

2. Place a rack in the center of the oven and preheat the oven to 350°F. Line a cookie sheet with parchment paper or leave ungreased.

3. Working with a little of the dough at a time, roll it out on a floured surface to about a ⅛-inch thickness. Keep the remaining dough refrigerated. Cut with cookie cutters and transfer the cookies carefully to the baking sheet, spacing them about 1 inch apart. If you like, and there is enough room in your refrigerator, chill the cookies on the baking sheets for about 5 minutes before baking. This helps cookies retain their shape if you've overworked the dough or the kitchen is hot.

4. Decorate the cookies: If you are using colored sugars, brush the cookies with a little egg white before sprinkling on the colored sugar. If you would like to add an edible paint (see box), do so now. If you are going to frost the cookies with a powdered sugar glaze (see box), bake the cookies first.

5. Bake the cookies until they are golden brown, 10 to 12 minutes. Transfer the

baking sheets to wire racks and let the cookies cool on them for about 1 minute. Then, using a spatula, transfer the cookies to the wire racks to cool. Repeat with the remaining cookie dough.

Do Ahead For best results, freeze the unbaked cookie dough, then let it thaw in the refrigerator overnight before rolling it out and cutting.

The cookies can be kept in a tightly covered container at room temperature for up to 2 weeks, or store the cookies in a tightly covered container in the freezer for up to 6 months. Thaw on the kitchen counter for 30 minutes.

Mindy's Butterscotch Cookies

MAKES: 4 DOZEN COOKIES
PREP: 15 MINUTES
BAKE: 10 TO 12 MINUTES PER BATCH
COOL: ABOUT 15 MINUTES

When my friend Mindy sets her mind on a recipe she will test and tweak it endlessly until she gets it just right. About six years ago she got on a butterscotch cookie jag. She thought about the cookies, obsessed about them really, and set about perfecting the old Schrafft's butterscotch cookie that she loved. Schrafft's was a Boston candy company that expanded into the restaurant business in Boston and New York City in the first half of the twentieth century. The restaurants were known for their white tablecloths, dishes perfect for ladies lunching, ice cream, and these cookies. After tasting the original version and then tasting Mindy's I can tell you that Mindy's is better. Bake these cookies for no reason at all, and they will vanish. Bake them for a bake sale, and they will vanish. Bake them ahead of time and freeze them so only you know they are hidden in the freezer, and they will not vanish quite so quickly.

1 cup (2 sticks) unsalted butter, at room temperature

1½ cups packed dark brown sugar

1 large egg

2 tablespoons dry milk powder

1 tablespoon pure vanilla extract

2 cups all-purpose flour

½ teaspoon baking soda

½ teaspoon salt

1 cup finely chopped pecans (optional)

1. Place a rack in the center of the oven and preheat the oven to 375°F.

2. Place the butter and brown sugar in a large bowl and beat with an electric mixer on medium speed until creamy, 1 to 2 minutes. Add the egg, dry milk powder, and vanilla and beat just to combine the egg.

3. Place the flour, baking soda, and salt in a small bowl and stir to mix. Fold the dry ingredients into the butter and brown sugar mixture with a rubber spatula until well combined. Fold in the pecans, if using (see Razzle-Dazzle). Working in batches, roll the cookie dough into 1-inch balls. Place the cookie balls on an ungreased baking sheet, spacing them about 2 inches apart.

4. Bake the cookies until they are flat and crisp, 10 to 12 minutes. Transfer the baking sheet to a wire rack and let the cookies cool on it for about 1 minute. Then, using a metal spatula, transfer the cookies to the wire rack to cool, about 15 minutes. Repeat with the remaining cookie dough.

Do Ahead

The butterscotch cookies can be frozen in resealable plastic freezer bags for up to 3 months. Thaw on the kitchen counter for 1 hour.

★
 ★ ★
★ RAZZLE-DAZZLE

Rather than adding the pecans to the cookie dough you can roll the balls of dough in them. The pecans crisp while the cookies bake and wind up looking a little dressier.

Our Crescent Cookies

MAKES: 4 DOZEN COOKIES
PREP: 20 TO 25 MINUTES
BAKE: 18 TO 22 MINUTES

I have never met an adult or child who did not adore these cookies. They are my Christmas go-tos, and when I was a little girl they were my mother's go-tos, too. If by chance we have eaten all of them by the time my sister and her family arrive at our house for the holidays, I am always hoping she's brought reinforcements. What makes this recipe so doable is that the dough has few ingredients and can be made a day ahead. Form it into crescent shapes and then, once baked, dust the cookies with confectioners' sugar while they are still a little warm, so the sugar will stick. Store the cookies in metal tins—not plastic—to keep the cookies crisp.

1 cup (2 sticks) lightly salted butter, at room temperature

2 teaspoons pure vanilla extract

½ cup confectioners' sugar, plus 2 cups confectioners' sugar, for dusting the cookies

2 cups all-purpose flour (see Note)

1 cup finely chopped pecans

① Place a rack in the center of the oven and preheat the oven to 325°F.

② Place the butter and vanilla in a large mixing bowl and, using an electric mixer, beat on low speed until creamy in texture, about 1 minute. Add the ½ cup of confectioners' sugar and mix just to combine. Add the flour and pecans and mix just until combined, about 30 seconds. The dough will be stiff.

3. Pinch off ½-inch pieces of dough and shape them into crescents roughly ½ inch long. Place these on ungreased baking sheets, spacing them about 2 inches apart. Bake the cookies until they turn light brown, about 20 minutes. Transfer the baking sheets to wire racks and let the cookies cool on them for about 2 minutes. Then, using a metal spatula, transfer the cookies to the racks to cool partially, 3 to 4 minutes.

4. Place the 2 cups of confectioners' sugar in a shallow bowl or baking dish and carefully press the warm cookies into the sugar, dusting off the excess. Place the cookies on the racks to cool completely. Repeat with the remaining cookie dough and confectioners' sugar.

 I always use White Lily flour in this recipe because it is lower in gluten and protein than other all-purpose flours like Gold Medal or King Arthur. That contributes to a softer and more tender cookie. If you use a flour other than White Lily, reduce the amount in this recipe to 1¾ cups.

 You can make the cookie dough a day in advance and refrigerate it, covered. The cookies can be stored in metal tins for 1 week.

★ ★ ★ ★ RAZZLE-DAZZLE

For festive occasions, forgo the powdered sugar and dredge the warm crescent cookies in colored sugar sprinkles: red, pink, and white for Valentine's Day; pastels for Easter; red, white, and blue for July 4; orange and black for Halloween; red and green for Christmas; or blue and silver for Hanukkah.

Ella's Easy Peach Pie

MAKES: ONE 9-INCH PIE
PREP: 15 TO 20 MINUTES
BAKE: 50 TO 55 MINUTES
COOL: 15 MINUTES (optional)

Our friend Ella is a gifted cook, and her simple method of baking a fruit pie has been a favorite for the past ten years. What I love about this method is that you can use any fruit in season—peaches, plums, blueberries, apples, and so on. The rest of the ingredients should be in your kitchen, as long as you keep some frozen pie crusts handy. The pie bakes in less than an hour, but it will slice more evenly if you let it rest at least fifteen minutes. So have patience. If you can't wait, spoon the pie into bowls like a cobbler and pass the vanilla ice cream.

2 frozen store-bought or homemade pie crusts (9-inches each)

¾ cup plus 1 tablespoon sugar

1½ tablespoons all-purpose flour (see Note)

7 medium-size firm-ripe peaches, peeled, pitted, and sliced (3 cups)

½ lemon (for 1 tablespoon juice)

2 tablespoons (¼ stick) butter

2 tablespoons milk

1. Place a rack in the center of the oven and preheat the oven to 350°F. Transfer 1 pie crust to a glass pie pan if you wish or leave it in its aluminum foil pan.

2. Place the pie crust in its pan on a baking sheet. Stir together ½ cup sugar and the flour and spoon it onto the bottom of the crust. Scatter the sliced peaches and their juices on top of the sugar and flour mixture. Sprinkle ¼ cup of the sugar over the peaches, then squeeze the lemon juice over the peaches. Cut the butter into small pieces and scatter these on top.

the side by pressing them into the crust. Brush the top of the crust with the milk and sprinkle the remaining tablespoon of sugar over it.

④ Place the pie on top of the baking sheet in the oven and bake it until the crust is golden brown and the juices bubble up from under the crust, 50 to 55 minutes. (Those bubbly juices will land on your baking sheet, not all over the oven.) Let the pie cool for about 15 minutes before slicing.

SAVE THE DAY NOTE Ripe summer peaches are deliciously juicy, and it's important for the pie filling to absorb some of the juice they give off in baking by adding a little flour. I stress "little" because if you add too much, you lose the real fruit flavor of those gorgeous peaches. So add the 1½ tablespoons, but no more. The filling will be juicy, but oh so wonderful.

③ Remove the remaining pie crust from its pan and cut it into ½-inch strips. Layer these over the top of the peaches in a lattice pattern, making sure to secure the ends of the strips to the bottom crust at

★
★ ★
★ RAZZLE-DAZZLE

Use 2 cups of sliced peaches and 1 cup of fresh raspberries for a peach melba taste combination.

Mary's Pumpkin Praline Pie

MAKES: ONE 9- OR 10-INCH PIE
PREP: 20 TO 25 MINUTES
BAKE: 52 MINUTES TO 1 HOUR
COOL: 2 HOURS

Judy Wright remembers her mother, Mary Kane, making this pumpkin pie every year for Thanksgiving in Rhode Island. Mary's parents were from Sicily, so the food heritage runs deep in their family. Whether the ingredients are Italian- or American-based, they were sure to come together in a wonderful dish. With its praline topping of pecans and brown sugar, this is a pumpkin pie with attitude and sustenance. Enjoy it warm on Thanksgiving or better yet, cold the next day.

FOR THE PUMPKIN PIE

3 large eggs

½ cup granulated sugar

½ cup packed light brown sugar

1 tablespoon all-purpose flour

1 teaspoon ground cinnamon

½ teaspoon salt

½ teaspoon ground nutmeg

½ teaspoon ground allspice

1 can (15 ounces) pumpkin

1 can (12 ounces, 1½ cups) evaporated whole milk

1 store-bought 9- or 10-inch deep-dish pie crust, thawed for about 10 minutes if frozen (see Note)

FOR TOPPING AND SERVING

¾ cup chopped pecans

2 tablespoons (¼ stick) lightly salted butter, melted

1 tablespoon light brown sugar

Sweetened whipped cream, for serving

1. Place a rack in the center of the oven and preheat the oven to 450°F. Transfer 1 pie crust to a glass or stainless steel pie pan if you wish or leave it in its aluminum foil pan.

2. Make the pumpkin pie: Place the eggs, granulated sugar, ½ cup of brown sugar, flour, cinnamon, salt, nutmeg, allspice, pumpkin, and evaporated milk in a large bowl and, using an electric mixer, beat on medium-high speed until well combined, about 2 minutes. Pour the pumpkin filling into the pie crust.

3. Bake the pie until the crust begins to brown, about 10 minutes, then reduce the temperature to 350°F and bake the pie until the filling begins to set, 30 to 35 minutes longer.

4. Meanwhile, make the praline topping: Place the pecans, butter, and 1 tablespoon of brown sugar in a small bowl and stir to combine.

5. Remove the pie from the oven and sprinkle the praline topping around the edge, pressing it slightly into the filling. Leave the center of the pie free of topping. Return the pie to the oven and bake it until the filling has browned and is almost completely set but still a little jiggly in the center, 12 to 15 minutes.

6. Transfer the pie to a wire rack to cool for about 2 hours. Serve slices of the pie at room temperature with dollops of whipped cream.

 If you cannot find a deep-dish pie crust, bake the pie in a regular pie crust. Pour the leftover filling into 2 small custard cups and set these aside to bake at 350°F for 20 to 25 minutes for incredibly delicious pumpkin custards.

 Bake the pumpkin pie a day in advance and keep it lightly covered with aluminum foil in the refrigerator. Reheat in a 350°F oven, covered with foil, until heated through, about 20 minutes. The pie will keep in the refrigerator for up to 5 days.

Ole Miss Fudge Pie

MAKES: ONE 9-INCH PIE
PREP: 10 MINUTES
BAKE: 25 TO 30 MINUTES

Ann Buchanan is a great cook who has the gift of pulling off the simplest of recipes with flair. She has an artistic eye, and she cares about food. It seems like everyone I know from Mississippi has this same deep love of good simple cooking. Think ripe tomatoes atop Bibb lettuce with crumbled blue cheese, or freshly made chicken salad, or this amazing fudge pie. When Ann was a student at the University of Mississippi in Oxford, she picked up this recipe, which is a favorite throughout the Mississippi Delta region and is often called chocolate chess pie. It needs the ingredients you most likely have on hand—cocoa, evaporated milk, eggs, and vanilla—so it is always ready to save your day.

4 tablespoons (½ stick) lightly salted butter

3 tablespoons unsweetened cocoa

1¼ cups sugar (see Note)

½ cup evaporated milk (from a 5-ounce can)

2 large eggs, beaten

1 teaspoon pure vanilla extract

1 store-bought 9-inch pie crust, thawed if frozen (not a deep-dish crust)

Unsweetened whipped cream or vanilla ice cream, for serving

① Place a rack in the center of the oven and preheat the oven to 325°F. Transfer the crust to a glass pie pan if you wish or leave it in its aluminum foil pan.

② Place the butter in a medium-size saucepan over medium heat. Stir until melted, then stir in the cocoa, sugar,

★
★ ★
★ RAZZLE-DAZZLE

As if this pie didn't have enough pizazz, you can
add even more by topping the whipped cream or
ice cream with dark chocolate shavings
(see Razzle-Dazzle, page 347).

and evaporated milk. Cook, stirring, until the sugar dissolves and the mixture comes together, 3 to 4 minutes. Remove the pan from the heat and let cool slightly.

③ When the chocolate mixture is cool to the touch, vigorously stir in the eggs and vanilla, stirring quickly so that the eggs do not curdle if the mixture is too hot. Pour the filling into the pie crust.

④ Bake the pie until the crust has lightly browned and the filling is still a little jiggly in the center, 25 to 30 minutes. Transfer the pie to a wire rack to cool for 15 minutes before slicing.

⑤ Serve slices of the pie with unsweetened whipped cream or vanilla ice cream.

 If you want to make the fudge pie slightly less sweet, then decrease the sugar to 1 cup.

Disguising a Premade Pie Crust

I love the ease of a frozen pie crust, but like to make it less obvious that I'm using one. So, I thaw the crust slightly and place it on a cutting board. I roll the edges until they are flattened, losing the grooves and creases that give away the fact it was once in a foil baking pan. Then I place the rolled crust into my pie pan and crimp the edges into scallops with my fingers, or simply roll the edge of the crust under and press down on it with a fork to neatly seal the crust to the pie pan.

 Bake the fudge pie in the morning and let it sit on the counter until it's time to serve. Drape waxed paper over the top of the pie to cover it. The pie keeps for 1 day at room temperature and up to 5 days in the refrigerator.

Cindy's Chocolate Meringue Pie

MAKES: ONE 9-INCH PIE
PREP: 30 MINUTES
COOK: 12 TO 15 MINUTES
BAKE: 18 TO 20 MINUTES
COOL: 3 HOURS

Cindy McCarville, who lives in Thompson Station, Tennessee, sent me this recipe years ago. She said the recipe was perfected by her mother in Nebraska. And while some families look forward to pumpkin pie on Thanksgiving, Cindy went on to say that it wouldn't be Thanksgiving in Nebraska without a chocolate pie. Cindy serves it with whipped cream, but I added a basic meringue because it's a light topping and also economical since you have the egg whites left over from the filling.

FOR THE CHOCOLATE PIE

1 frozen store-bought 9-inch deep-dish pie crust

3 large eggs, at room temperature

1¼ cups granulated sugar

⅓ cup all-purpose flour

¼ cup unsweetened cocoa powder

½ teaspoon salt

1¾ cups whole milk

2 tablespoons (¼ stick) unsalted butter, at room temperature

1 teaspoon pure vanilla extract

FOR THE MERINGUE

¼ teaspoon cream of tartar

¼ cup granulated sugar

1. Make the chocolate pie: Bake the pie crust following the directions on the package. Let the crust cool on a wire rack while you make the pie filling.

2. Separate the eggs, placing the yolks in a small bowl and the whites in a medium-size stainless steel or glass bowl. Set the egg whites aside for the meringue.

3. Place the 1¼ cups of sugar and the flour, cocoa powder, and salt in a heavy medium-size saucepan and whisk to combine well. Set the pan aside.

4. Pour the milk into a large microwave-safe measuring cup. Heat the milk in a microwave oven on high power until very hot, about 2 minutes. Slowly pour the hot milk into the saucepan with the cocoa mixture, whisking to combine.

5. Place the saucepan over medium-high heat and heat the cocoa mixture, whisking constantly, until it just begins to boil, 4 to 5 minutes. Remove the saucepan from the heat and keep whisking the cocoa mixture for about 30 seconds. Add a couple of tablespoons of the hot cocoa mixture to the egg yolks, whisking the yolks, then add the egg yolk mixture to the saucepan, whisking constantly. Place the saucepan over low heat, add the butter and vanilla, and whisk until well incorporated, 1 to 2 minutes. Pour the chocolate pie filling evenly into the cooled pie crust.

6. Make the meringue: Using an electric mixer, beat the egg whites on high speed until frothy, 1 to 2 minutes. Add the cream of tartar and continue beating on high speed. Gradually add the ¼ cup of sugar. Beat the egg whites until they are stiff and glossy and the sugar is dissolved, 4 to 5 minutes.

7. Pile the meringue by spoonfuls on top of the hot chocolate filling. Using a spatula, push the meringue to the edge of the crust to seal in the filling. Smooth the top of the pie.

8. Bake the pie until the meringue is just lightly browned, 8 to 10 minutes. Transfer the pie to a wire rack to cool to room temperature, about 3 hours before serving.

Kentucky Brown Sugar Pie

MAKES: ONE 9-INCH PIE
PREP: 20 MINUTES
BAKE: 18 TO 20 MINUTES
COOL: ABOUT 3 HOURS

A week before this cookbook deadline rolled around, my friend Beth invited me to her house for dinner. I had been typing a wonderful butterscotch pie recipe that took a lot of steps to make and, although it was a delicious pie, I was worried the recipe was too labor-intensive for most folks. At the dinner party Beth left the table to go to the kitchen, and she returned with slices of this brown sugar pie, piled high with meringue. Aha! My time-consuming pie, I thought. Taking a bite only confirmed it. This had to be my wonderful butterscotch pie. But, it wasn't, Beth modestly said. It was simply brown sugar pie, an old Kentucky family recipe given to her by her sister Jackie Drake, who lives in Bloomfield, Kentucky. The pie takes about twenty minutes to pull together, and Beth shared the recipe.

FOR THE BROWN SUGAR PIE

1 store-bought 9-inch pie crust, thawed if frozen

1 cup packed dark brown sugar

⅓ cup all-purpose flour

¼ teaspoon salt

2 cups whole milk

3 large eggs, at room temperature

1 tablespoon salted or unsalted butter

1 teaspoon pure vanilla extract

FOR THE MERINGUE

¼ teaspoon cream of tartar

4 tablespoons granulated sugar

1. Transfer the pie crust to a glass pie pan if you wish or leave it in its aluminum foil pie pan. If it's not a preformed pie crust, fit it into a glass pie plate.

2. Make the brown sugar pie: Bake the pie crust following the directions on the package until it is light brown. Let the crust cool on a wire rack while you make the pie filling. Leave the oven on, adjusting the temperature if necessary, to 400°F.

3. Place the brown sugar, flour, and salt in a medium-size saucepan and stir to combine. Slowly whisk in the milk. Place the pan over medium heat and cook, stirring constantly, until the filling begins to thicken and is bubbly, 4 to 5 minutes. Reduce the heat to low and continue to cook the filling until it has completely thickened, 2 minutes longer. Remove the pan from the heat.

4. Separate the eggs, placing the yolks in a small bowl and the whites in a medium-size stainless steel or glass bowl. Set the egg whites aside for the meringue. Beat the egg yolks with a fork to combine. Add 3 tablespoons of the hot filling to the egg yolks and stir well to combine. Then whisk the egg mixture into the saucepan of filling. Place the pan over low heat and cook, whisking, until the yolks are well combined and the filling is thick, creamy, and smooth, about 2 minutes. Remove the pan from the heat and stir in the butter and vanilla. Pour the filling into the baked crust.

5. Make the meringue: Using an electric mixer, beat the egg whites on high speed until frothy, 1 to 2 minutes. Add the cream of tartar and continue beating on high speed. Gradually add the granulated sugar. Beat the egg whites until they are stiff and glossy and the sugar is dissolved, 4 to 5 minutes.

6. Pile spoonfuls of the meringue on top of the pie filling. Using a spatula, push the meringue to the edge of the crust to seal in the filling. Smooth the top of the pie.

7. Bake the pie until the meringue is just lightly browned, 8 to 10 minutes. Transfer the pie to a wire rack to cool to room temperature, about 3 hours before serving.

Do Ahead Let the eggs come to room temperature, taking them out of the refrigerator half an hour before you plan to make the pie.

John's Little Fried Apple Pies

MAKES: 16 TO 20 PIES
PREP: 1 HOUR
COOL: 1 HOUR
COOK: 2 MINUTES PER BATCH

When my son, John, was in the Boy Scouts and the annual cooking contest rolled around, you had better believe there was a little stress at our house selecting the right recipe to enter. It needed to be a campfire recipe, something that could be prepared over a wood fire or a propane grill. John wanted to make fried pies, and at first I winced at the thought because that sounded like a lot of trouble for a boy of ten. But then I thought about crescent roll dough and making the pies with dried fruit—apples or peaches—that you could cook down with water, sugar, and cinnamon until soft. It might just be possible to fry up these pies on a camping trip and sprinkle them with confectioners' sugar for a real down-home treat. So John practiced the recipe at home and then took it to the cook-off, where he came in second. The winner? Chocolate doughnuts—they were pretty good, too.

1 cup dried apples or peaches

About 2 cups water, or to cover the fruit

½ cup granulated sugar

¼ teaspoon ground cinnamon, or more to taste

2 packages (8 ounces each) refrigerated crescent roll dough

About 2 cups vegetable oil, for frying

¼ cup confectioners' sugar, for dusting

1. Place the dried fruit in a saucepan and add water to cover. Add the granulated sugar and cinnamon and cook over medium-low heat, stirring, until the fruit cooks down and is soft and the water has evaporated, about 30 minutes. Set the fruit filling aside to cool for at least 1 hour.

2. Unwrap the crescent roll dough and place it on a flat surface. Using the rim of a clean soup can or a round cookie cutter, cut the dough into 2- to 3-inch circles. You will get 8 to 10 circles per can of crescent dough, depending on the size. Spoon a teaspoon of the fruit filling into the center of each circle, fold the dough over to form a half-moon shape, and, using a fork, press the cut edges of the dough together to seal them.

3. Pour enough oil into a heavy skillet to fill it to a depth of 1 to 2 inches. Place the skillet over medium-high heat and watch it carefully. The oil needs to be hot before adding the first pie. To test the oil, you can pinch off a piece of the crescent dough and place it in the skillet. When the dough sizzles and browns, you are ready to cook the pies.

4. Carefully slide 4 to 6 pies at a time into the hot oil and let them brown on one side, about 1 minute. Then, using a slotted spoon, turn the pies over to brown them on the second side, about 1 minute. When the pies have browned, transfer them on top of a paper bag or paper towels to drain. Repeat with the remaining pies.

5. Sprinkle the pies with confectioners' sugar and serve warm.

 Do Ahead Make the fruit filling the day ahead and refrigerate it until you are ready to fry the pies.

Lemon Icebox Pie

MAKES: ONE 8- OR 9-INCH SQUARE PIE
PREP: 20 TO 25 MINUTES
FREEZE: AT LEAST 4 HOURS

The day my friend Martha's daughter had her wisdom teeth removed I was testing this recipe. Talk about good timing. You've heard that ice cream soothes the pain after wisdom teeth surgery? Try smooth, cold lemon icebox pie. Even if you have no plans for oral surgery, try this pie. It's a great do-ahead and is loved by all ages.

2 medium-size lemons

½ cup graham cracker crumbs

3 large pasteurized eggs (see Note), at room temperature

½ cup granulated sugar

1 cup heavy (whipping) cream

1 cup fresh blueberries, raspberries, or blackberries (optional), for serving

① Rinse and pat the lemons dry. Grate 1½ to 2 tablespoons of zest from the lemons and set it aside. Cut the lemons in half and squeeze ⅓ cup juice from them. Set the juice aside.

② Measure 2 tablespoons of the graham cracker crumbs and set them aside for the topping. Place the remaining crumbs in the bottom of an 8- or 9-inch square metal baking pan. Set the pan aside.

③ Separate the eggs, placing the whites in a large bowl and the yolks in a small bowl. Using an electric mixer, beat the whites on high speed until they are stiff and glossy, 4 to 5 minutes, gradually adding the sugar. Set the beaten egg whites aside.

④ Using the same beaters, beat the yolks on medium speed until they are thick and lemon colored, about 1 minute. Set the beaten yolks aside.

⑤ Place the cream in a cold medium-size bowl and, using clean beaters, beat on high speed until peaks form, about 4 minutes. Fold in the lemon zest and juice with a rubber spatula. Beat just to combine. Fold the beaten cream and the egg yolks into the beaten egg whites until just incorporated. Spoon this mixture over the graham cracker crumbs in the pan, spreading it evenly to the edges of the pan with the back of a large spoon or spatula. Sprinkle the reserved graham cracker crumbs on top. Cover the pan with plastic wrap and place it in the freezer until well frozen, at least 4 hours.

6 Slice the pie into squares and serve it on plates with the blueberries, raspberries, or blackberries, if desired.

SAVE THE DAY NOTE Be sure to buy pasteurized eggs because the eggs in this recipe are not cooked.

Do Ahead This recipe must be made ahead of time because it takes 4 hours for the pie to freeze solid enough to cut into servings. It will keep, covered, in the freezer for up to 2 weeks.

FREEZE IT • SUPER BOWL PARTY • SERVE TO YOUR BOOK CLUB

Bebe's Ice Cream Pie

MAKES: ONE 9-INCH PIE
PREP: 20 TO 25 MINUTES
BAKE: 8 TO 10 MINUTES
COOL: ABOUT 30 MINUTES
FREEZE: 1 HOUR

In my childhood home there was a massive white vault of a chest freezer in the basement that my father dutifully defrosted once a year. Everyone had respect for that freezer because it held valuable cargo—ice cream pies, frozen fruit salads, pecan-dredged angel food rum balls, chocolate sheet cake with poured fudge frosting—you get the idea. Our mother was one of five girls, and she was used to cooking for a crowd. So she often cooked too much, or liked to be prepared, so the leftovers went into the freezer. On most days there was an ice cream pie, so basic to her repertoire that she varied it with the season, using vanilla in the summer, butter pecan in the fall, peppermint in the winter. It was her save-the-day recipe because it came together quickly and it was always ready to slice and serve.

FOR THE PIE

> 1 package (8 to 9 ounces) thin chocolate wafers (see Note)
>
> 8 tablespoons (1 stick) unsalted butter, melted
>
> 2 pints top-quality ice cream of your choice, vanilla, caramel, strawberry, peppermint, or coffee

FOR THE SAUCE

> 4 tablespoons (½ stick) unsalted butter
>
> 2 ounces unsweetened chocolate
>
> ¾ cup plus 2 tablespoons granulated sugar
>
> Pinch of salt
>
> 1 small can (5 ounces) evaporated milk
>
> 1 teaspoon pure vanilla extract

① Place a rack in the center of the oven and preheat the oven to 350°F.

② Make the pie: Place the chocolate wafers in a food processor and pulse until crumbs form, 10 to 12 pulses. Pour in the melted butter and process again to combine well. Press the chocolate crumb mixture into the bottom and up the side of a 9-inch metal or glass pie pan. Cover the crumb mixture with aluminum foil, pressing down gently on the mixture. Place the pan in the oven. Let the crust bake until it is crisp and set, 8 to 10 minutes. Remove the crust from the oven and place it on a wire rack to cool completely, about 30 minutes.

③ Remove the ice cream from the freezer and let it soften for 10 to 15 minutes. When the crust has cooled, spoon the soft ice cream into the crust, smoothing the top. Place the pie in the freezer for the ice cream to set, about 1 hour.

④ Meanwhile, make the warm fudge sauce: Place the 4 tablespoons of butter and the chocolate in a small heavy saucepan over low heat and cook, stirring, until the chocolate melts, 3 to 4 minutes. Turn off the heat. Stir in the sugar, salt, and evaporated milk. Place the pan back over low heat and cook, stirring, until the fudge sauce begins to simmer and is thick enough to coat a spoon, 12 to 15 minutes. Remove the pan from the heat and stir in the vanilla.

⑤ To serve, remove the pie from the freezer. Slice it into serving pieces and spoon the warm fudge sauce on top.

Look for the chocolate wafers near the ice cream and toppings aisle in the supermarket. If you cannot find the wafers, you can use 8 ounces of Oreo wafers, with the filling removed.

Make this pie up to 2 weeks in advance, keeping it covered with aluminum foil in the freezer. Make the sauce a couple of days in advance, keep it in the fridge, and warm it over low heat before serving the pie.

★ RAZZLE-DAZZLE

Use two flavors of ice cream for the pie, alternating spoonfuls of them. Use 2 cups of one flavor and 2 cups of the other. Combos I like are pistachio and chocolate, vanilla and coffee, strawberry and vanilla, and caramel and chocolate.

Fresh Blueberry and Lemon Tart

MAKES: ONE 9-INCH TART
PREP: 15 MINUTES
BAKE: 40 TO 45 MINUTES
COOL: AT LEAST 20 MINUTES

In my *What Can I Bring? Cookbook* there is a cranberry tart recipe that everyone adores. But through the years that recipe has been tweaked, much to my delight because the sign of a great recipe is that people are actually using it and adapting it to ingredients they have on hand. Many readers have told me they make the tart with blueberries when they come into season. Add a little lemon zest and this tart is a whole new recipe. It is light and fresh and spur-of-the-moment, ready when you are to tote to spring and summer gatherings or make ahead for a dinner party. And it is especially beloved at birthday parties of pie lovers, too!

12 tablespoons (1½ sticks) lightly salted butter, melted, plus melted butter, for brushing the pie pan

2 cups fresh blueberries, rinsed and well drained

1½ cups granulated sugar

1 cup all-purpose flour

2 large eggs, beaten

1 lemon

Vanilla ice cream, for serving

① Place a rack in the center of the oven and preheat the oven to 350°F. Lightly brush a 9-inch glass or ceramic pie pan with melted butter.

② Scatter the blueberries in an even layer in the bottom of the pie pan. Sprinkle ½ cup of the sugar over them. Set the pie pan aside.

③ Place the butter, flour, eggs, and the remaining 1 cup of sugar in a large mixing bowl and stir with a wooden spoon to combine well. Grate the zest of the

lemon over the mixing bowl. Cut the lemon in half, remove the seeds, and squeeze the juice into the bowl; you will have about 1 teaspoon of lemon zest and 2 tablespoons of lemon juice (the measurements don't have to be exact). Stir to combine the lemon zest and juice in the batter. Pour the batter over the blueberry mixture.

④ Bake the tart until it is lightly browned and the center has nearly set, 40 to 45 minutes. Transfer the tart to a wire rack to cool for about 20 minutes, then slice it and serve warm with vanilla ice cream. Or let the tart cool completely, about 1 hour, before serving.

Do Ahead Make the blueberry tart a day ahead and keep it lightly covered with plastic wrap or waxed paper at room temperature.

No-Brainer One-Pan Cobbler

My mother made a homemade pie two or three times a week. My grandmother is said to have baked one daily. What about you? If you'd rather go for something quicker, here is an easy method for making fruit cobbler. My family loves blackberries, but you can also do this with blueberries, or a mixture of blueberries and peaches.

Preheat the oven to 375°F. Place 4 cups of fresh berries in an 8-inch square baking pan that has been lightly greased with butter. Squeeze the juice of ½ lemon over the berries. Stir together 1 egg, 1 cup of sugar, and 1 cup of flour until the mixture looks like coarse meal. Spoon this over the fruit. Melt 6 tablespoons of butter and drizzle this over the topping. Bake the cobbler until it is bubbly and browned, about 35 minutes. Let the cobbler rest for 10 to 15 minutes and serve it warm spooned into bowls and topped with vanilla ice cream.

★
★ ★
★ RAZZLE-DAZZLE
Use 1 cup of blueberries and 1 cup of raspberries.

Fall Harvest Fruit Crisp

MAKES: ONE 9-INCH CRISP
PREP: 20 MINUTES
BAKE: 1 HOUR AND 10 TO 15 MINUTES

When you want to cook with fresh apples and pears in the fall but you can't always get your hands on a great pie recipe, or when you are hungry for pie but don't have the time to make a crust, make a crisp. Here is a basic blueprint for a recipe you can make with apples or pears, or both. Crisps can be made ahead and baked at the last minute. They're favorites of all ages. They can be dished up right from the pan, baked in individual ramekins, or plated on your grandmother's china. One recipe but so many possibilities.

THE FRUIT

6 medium-size apples and/or pears, peeled, cored, and thinly sliced (6 cups)

3 tablespoons granulated sugar

1 tablespoon all-purpose flour

¼ teaspoon ground cinnamon

FOR THE TOPPING

1 cup all-purpose flour

5 tablespoons light brown sugar

2 tablespoons granulated sugar

½ cup finely chopped pecans or almonds (optional)

8 tablespoons (1 stick) lightly salted butter, chilled and cut into ½-inch pieces

Ice cream, for serving

1. Place a rack in the center of the oven and preheat the oven to 350°F.

2. Prepare the fruit: Place the apples and/or pears in a 9-inch deep-dish pie pan and toss them with the 3 tablespoons of granulated sugar, 1 tablespoon of flour, and the cinnamon. Set the fruit aside.

3. Make the topping: Toss the 1 cup of flour with the 5 tablespoons of brown sugar, 2 tablespoons of granulated sugar, and the nuts, if using, in a small bowl. Add the butter, and, using 2 knives, cut it into the flour mixture until the pieces are the size of peas.

4. Sprinkle the topping over the fruit. Place the pie pan on a baking sheet and place the baking sheet in the oven. Bake the crisp until the fruit bubbles up and the topping is golden brown, 1 hour and 10 to 15 minutes. Serve the crisp warm with ice cream.

Do Ahead The crisp can be assembled up to 4 hours before placing it in the oven. Cover the pie pan with waxed paper and keep it on the counter until it is time to bake.

★
★ ★
★ RAZZLE-DAZZLE

Add ¼ cup raisins that have been soaked in 2 tablespoons warm brandy or rum.

Lemon Snow Pudding

SERVES: 6 TO 8
PREP: 30 TO 35 MINUTES
CHILL: 65 TO 70 MINUTES PLUS 4 HOURS TO SET

Shirley Hutson was a home economics teacher in Massachusetts before moving with her husband to Tennessee and raising their children. She has always cooked honestly, simply, and deliciously—check out the impressive roast lamb on page 183 and this simple soft meringue dessert. The recipe is adapted from a 1954 Betty Crocker cookbook, but the dessert itself dates back much further and is similar to the French dessert *oeufs à la neige*. It saves the day because it can be made two days in advance to fit into your busy schedule.

¾ cup sugar

1 envelope unflavored gelatin

1¼ cups boiling water

1 tablespoon grated lemon zest

¼ cup fresh lemon juice
(from 2 large lemons)

Ice

2 large egg whites from pasteurized eggs

Custard Sauce (recipe follows),
for serving

1 cup fresh raspberries (optional),
for serving

① Place the sugar and gelatin in a medium-size saucepan and stir to mix. Add the boiling water to the sugar mixture. Place the pan over medium-high heat and cook, stirring occasionally, until the gelatin mixture just comes to a boil, 3 to 4 minutes.

② Remove the pan from the heat and stir in the lemon zest and juice. Pour the gelatin mixture into a medium-size bowl and nestle it in a larger bowl or sink filled with ice. Cool the mixture in the ice bath for about 10 minutes. Then, stir the gelatin mixture and place the bowl in the refrigerator to cool until the mixture mounds when dropped from a spoon, about 45 minutes.

③ Using a electric mixer, beat the egg whites until stiff, 5 to 6 minutes. Slowly blend the gelatin mixture into the beaten whites until just blended, using the same beaters and with the mixer on the lowest speed, 10 to 15 seconds. Place the bowl back in the refrigerator for 8 to 10 minutes to keep the mixture from separating into gelatin on the bottom and egg whites on the top.

④ Remove the pudding from the refrigerator and fold it with a spatula until well blended. Pour the pudding into a glass or ceramic serving dish and refrigerate it, covered, until thoroughly set, about 4 hours.

⑤ Scoop the pudding into small serving bowls. Pour the chilled Custard Sauce on top and serve it with fresh raspberries, if desired.

Do Ahead The lemon pudding can be made up to 2 days in advance and refrigerated, covered.

MONEY SAVER: In this recipe, a little goes a long way.

Custard Sauce

MAKES: ABOUT 1½ TO 2 CUPS

The custard sauce for the Lemon Snow Pudding is also delicious served warm over gingerbread poached apples or pears, Roasted Peaches with Brown Sugar and Spices (page 343), chocolate cake, plum puddings and fruitcakes, most any dessert that you wish to enrobe in custardy goodness.

1½ cups whole milk

2 large eggs, at room temperature

¼ cup sugar

¼ teaspoon salt

1 teaspoon pure vanilla extract

① Pour the milk into a heavy medium-size saucepan and warm it over medium heat without stirring until small bubbles form around the edge of the pan and the milk steams a bit, about 5 minutes. Do not let it come to a boil.

2. Meanwhile, place the eggs, sugar, and salt in a medium-size metal or glass bowl. Using an electric mixer, beat on medium speed until well combined, about 1 minute. Set the egg mixture aside.

3. Remove the milk from the heat. Slowly add about ¼ cup of the hot milk to the egg mixture, whisking vigorously. Place the saucepan with the remaining milk over medium-low heat. Slowly pour the warm egg mixture into the hot milk, whisking as you pour. Continue to whisk (or stir with a spatula) while the mixture thickens, 10 to 15 minutes. Do not heat the custard too quickly or the eggs will curdle. The custard is done when it thinly coats a metal spoon.

4. Remove the pan from the heat and add the vanilla, stirring to combine. Pour the custard into a glass bowl and cover it. Refrigerate the custard until ready to serve. It will keep up to 3 days.

Roasted Peaches with Brown Sugar and Spices

SERVES: 4
PREP: 15 MINUTES
BAKE: 15 MINUTES
COOL: 20 TO 25 MINUTES

I have made this do-ahead dessert every summer when peaches are plentiful and my family can't get enough ice cream. While simple sliced ripe peaches are pretty darned wonderful over vanilla ice cream, you can take that idea a step further and roast the peaches with brown sugar, cinnamon, cloves, and nutmeg and arrive at a dessert that is much, much more. Select ripe peaches that are still a little firm so they hold together well while roasting.

2 tablespoons (¼ stick) unsalted butter

½ cup packed light brown sugar

1 cinnamon stick (3 inches)

5 whole cloves

Pinch of ground nutmeg

3 tablespoons water

1 teaspoon pure vanilla extract

4 large peaches, cut in half and pitted

Vanilla ice cream, for serving

① Place a rack in the center of the oven and preheat the oven to 300°F.

② Place the butter, brown sugar, cinnamon stick, cloves, nutmeg, and water in a 13-by-9-inch glass baking dish. Place the baking dish in the oven until the sugar dissolves, 5 to 7 minutes. Remove the baking dish from the oven and stir the butter mixture. Stir in the vanilla.

Bake a mixture of peaches and apricots, and serve up a little of both over ice cream. For adults, instead of the vanilla add a tablespoon or two of bourbon or dark rum.

How to Store Fresh Peaches

If peaches are firm when you bring them home, place them in a fruit bowl or on the kitchen windowsill for a day or two. Once they soften, they are ready to eat or will need to be refrigerated. But don't refrigerate ripe peaches for longer than a few days as refrigeration causes peaches to shrivel.

(3) Place the peaches, cut side down, in the baking dish and spoon some of the butter mixture over them.

(4) Bake the peaches until they are tender, about 15 minutes. Remove the baking dish from the oven and let the peaches cool in the juices until cool enough to handle, 20 to 25 minutes. Peel off the peach skins. Spoon vanilla ice cream into bowls and slice the peaches on top of the ice cream. Spoon the cooking juices on top of the peaches, discarding the cinnamon stick and cloves.

Do Ahead You can bake these peaches a few hours in advance and leave them covered at room temperature. Place them in a preheated 350°F oven for a few minutes to reheat the cooking juices before serving the peaches over ice cream.

Brandy Alexanders (Easiest Dessert in the World)

SERVES: 10 TO 12
PREP: 10 TO 15 MINUTES

My friend David Patterson is probably the best cook on the planet. He does not labor over cooking—it just comes naturally. Well traveled, David eats in the best restaurants and works to duplicate the recipes. When we are invited to dinner at Libby and David's house, we are always in for a treat. One night the dessert was simply an ice cream brandy alexander. Wow. An adult milkshake—what a treat and incredibly easy.

1 container (1½ quarts) good vanilla ice cream

2 ounces brandy

5 ounces crème de cacao

2 teaspoons unsweetened cocoa, for dusting

① Remove the ice cream from the freezer and let it soften on the kitchen counter for 15 to 20 minutes, depending on the temperature of your kitchen.

② Place the ice cream in a large bowl and stir in the brandy and crème de cacao. Blend with a wooden spoon until it is as smooth as you can get it. Spoon the ice cream mixture quickly into 10 to 12 wine glasses and dust each with a little of the cocoa before serving.

Top the servings with chocolate shavings instead of cocoa. To make chocolate shavings easily, take a 4-ounce bar of bittersweet chocolate and run a vegetable peeler across the flat side of the bar, toward you, to create curls. The warmer the chocolate, the longer the curl will be. If the chocolate is cold you will make short gratings of chocolate, but this is fine and they look great piled on top of the dessert.

Watermelon Granita

SERVES: 4
PREP: 5 MINUTES
FREEZE: 40 TO 45 MINUTES

When it's hot outside, so hot you don't want to cook and can't imagine eating dessert, well, you can make a quick meal-ender that will quench your thirst and satisfy your sweet tooth. Granitas—or grainy and coarse sorbets—are so easy to make using fresh melon. Here is the blueprint, the formula. You plug in the fruit.

2 cups coarsely chopped watermelon

¼ cup sugar, or more to taste

1 tablespoon fresh lime juice or lemon juice

1 cup ice cubes

① Place the watermelon, sugar, lime juice, and ice cubes in a blender and puree until smooth. Pour the melon mixture into a 13-by-9-inch metal baking pan and place it in the freezer. Freeze the granita until it is slushy but firm, 40 to 45 minutes.

② To serve, using a big spoon, scrape the granita into short glasses or tall goblets. Serve at once.

★ RAZZLE-DAZZLE

Make a cantaloupe granita, using lemon instead of lime juice. Or to really blow people away, make both watermelon and cantaloupe granitas, and serve them side by side. Garnish with fresh mint leaves.

Conversion Tables

Please note that all conversions are approximate but close enough to be useful when converting from one system to another.

Approximate Equivalents

1 STICK BUTTER = 8 tbs = 4 oz = ½ cup = 115 g

1 CUP ALL-PURPOSE PRESIFTED FLOUR = 4.7 oz

1 CUP GRANULATED SUGAR = 8 oz = 220 g

1 CUP (firmly packed) BROWN SUGAR = 6 oz = 220 g to 230 g

1 CUP CONFECTIONERS' SUGAR = 4½ oz = 115 g

1 CUP HONEY OR SYRUP = 12 oz

1 CUP GRATED CHEESE = 4 oz

1 CUP DRIED BEANS = 6 oz

1 LARGE EGG = about 2 oz or about 3 tbs

1 EGG YOLK = about 1 tbs

1 EGG WHITE = about 2 tbs

Weight Conversions

U.S./U.K.	METRIC	U.S./U.K.	METRIC
½ oz	15 g	7 oz	200 g
1 oz	30 g	8 oz	250 g
1½ oz	45 g	9 oz	275 g
2 oz	60 g	10 oz	300 g
2½ oz	75 g	11 oz	325 g
3 oz	90 g	12 oz	350 g
3½ oz	100 g	13 oz	375 g
4 oz	125 g	14 oz	400 g
5 oz	150 g	15 oz	450 g
6 oz	175 g	1 lb	500 g

Liquid Conversions

U.S.	IMPERIAL	METRIC
2 tbs	1 fl oz	30 ml
3 tbs	1½ fl oz	45 ml
¼ cup	2 fl oz	60 ml
⅓ cup	2½ fl oz	75 ml
⅓ cup + 1 tbs	3 fl oz	90 ml
⅓ cup + 2 tbs	3½ fl oz	100 ml
½ cup	4 fl oz	125 ml
⅔ cup	5 fl oz	150 ml
¾ cup	6 fl oz	175 ml
¾ cup + 2 tbs	7 fl oz	200 ml
1 cup	8 fl oz	250 ml
1 cup + 2 tbs	9 fl oz	275 ml
1¼ cups	10 fl oz	300 ml
1⅓ cups	11 fl oz	325 ml
1½ cups	12 fl oz	350 ml
1⅔ cups	13 fl oz	375 ml
1¾ cups	14 fl oz	400 ml
1¾ cups + 2 tbs	15 fl oz	450 ml
2 cups (1 pint)	16 fl oz	500 ml
2½ cups	20 fl oz (1 pint)	600 ml
3¾ cups	1½ pints	900 ml
4 cups	1¾ pints	1 liter

Oven Temperatures

°F	GAS MARK	°C	°F	GAS MARK	°C
250	½	120	400	6	200
275	1	140	425	7	220
300	2	150	450	8	230
325	3	160	475	9	240
350	4	180	500	10	260
375	5	190			

Note: Reduce the temperature by 20°C (68°F) for fan-assisted ovens.

Index

Note: Page references in *italics* indicate photographs.

A

Adam's linguine with asparagus pesto, 135–37

Almond(s):
  apple, and a tart cherry vinaigrette, spinach salad with, 111–12
  and bacon spread, crunchy, 28–29
  Joy's kale and brussels sprouts salad, 99–101, *100*
  Susie's Catalina chicken salad, 83–84

Ann's fresh tomato pie, 127–29, *128*

Ann's tomato salad with roasted garlic dressing, 113–14, *115*

Appetizers:
  Cara's cocktail shrimp, 42–44, *43*
  Jana's cheese olivettes, 36–38, *37*
  Kathy's New Year's caviar, *20*, 21–22
  quick stuffed mushrooms from the hors d'oeuvre queen, 41
  slow-cooked caramelized onion pizza, 45–47, *46*

  stuffed jalapeño peppers Witowski, 39–40
  see also Dips; Spreads

Apple(s):
  almonds, and a tart cherry vinaigrette, spinach salad with, 111–12
  Beth's autumn salad with maple vinaigrette, 104–6, *105*
  and butternut squash soup, curried, 65–66, *67*
  cheddar baked, G's, 239–40
  fall harvest fruit crisp, 337–39, *338*
  pies, John's little fried, 328–29
  Virginia's cranberry relish, 122–23

Apricot(s):
  oatmeal bars, Little St. Simons, 295–97, *296*
  and onions, braised pork tenderloin with, 175–76, *177*

Artichoke(s):
  chicken ambassador, 150–51
  dip, Pat's, 18, *19*

Arugula:
  the easiest salad in the world, 114
  watermelon, and cucumber salad with lime vinaigrette, *116*, 117–18

Asparagus:
  pesto, Adam's linguine with, 135–37
  soup, fast (easiest soup in the world), 64–65

Aunt Cathleen's blueberry snack cake, 271–72, *273*

Avocado(s):
  big fat Greek salad, 90–92
  and pink grapefruit salad, Libby's, 119–22, *121*
  succotash salad with cilantro lime vinaigrette, 107–10, *108*

B

Bacon:
  and almond spread, crunchy, 28–29
  and cheddar torte with pepper jelly, 30–31
  Shellie's spaghetti carbonara, 132–34, *133*

Banana:
  bread, Hawaiian, 246–47
  muffins, fresh, 243–45, *244*

Barb's one-pound pork chops, 173–74

Bars:
  apricot oatmeal, Little St. Simons, 295–97, *296*
  big skillet chocolate chip